Therapeutic Modalities for Athletic Injuries

ATHLETIC TRAINING EDUCATION SERIES

CRAIG R. DENEGAR, PhD, ATC, PT
PENN STATE UNIVERSITY

DAVID H. PERRIN, PhD, ATC
SERIES EDITOR
UNIVERSITY OF VIRGINIA, CHARLOTTESVILLE

HUMAN KINETICS

Library of Congress Cataloging-in-Publication Data

Denegar, Craig R.
    Therapeutic modalities for athletic injuries / Craig R. Denegar.
        p. cm. -- (Athletic training education series)
    Includes bibliographical references and index.
    ISBN 0-88011-838-5
        1. Sports injuries--Treatment. 2. Sports physical therapy. I. Title. II. Series.

RD97 .D46 2000
617.1'027--dc21

99-057433

ISBN: 0-88011-838-5

Permission notices for material reprinted in this book from other sources can be found on pages xiv–xv.

Acquisitions Editor: Loarn D. Robertson, PhD; **Series Editor and Developmental Editor:** Kristine Enderle; **Managing Editor:** Amy Flaig; **Assistant Editors:** Derek Campbell and Susan C. Hagan; **Copyeditor:** Julie Anderson; **Proofreader:** Sue Fetters; **Indexer:** Sharon Duffy; **Permission Manager:** Heather Munson; **Graphic Designer:** Stuart Cartwright; **Graphic Artist:** Brian McElwain; **Photo Editor:** Clark Brooks; **Cover Designer:** Stuart Cartwright; **Photographer (interior):** Tom Roberts, except where otherwise noted; **Illustrators:** Argosy and Brian McElwain; **Printer:** United Graphics; **Binder:** Dekker & Sons

Printed in the United States of America   10   9   8   7   6   5   4   3   2   1

Human Kinetics
Web site: **http://www.humankinetics.com/**

United States: Human Kinetics, P.O. Box 5076, Champaign, IL 61825-5076
1-800-747-4457
e-mail: humank@hkusa.com

Canada: Human Kinetics, 475 Devonshire Road Unit 100, Windsor, ON N8Y 2L5
1-800-465-7301 (in Canada only)
e-mail: humank@hkcanada.com

Europe: Human Kinetics, P.O. Box IW14, Leeds LS16 6TR, United Kingdom
+44 (0)113-278 1708
e-mail: humank@hkeurope.com

Australia: Human Kinetics, 57A Price Avenue, Lower Mitcham, South Australia 5062
(08) 82771555
e-mail: liahka@senet.com.au

New Zealand: Human Kinetics, P.O. Box 105-231, Auckland Central
09-523-3462
e-mail: humank@hknewz.com

To my wife, Sue,
for her love, support,
and sacrifices made so I can
work, write, and play.

And to our sons,
Charlie and Cody,
who bring joy to our lives
and provide a daily reminder
of what is really important.

CONTENTS

INTRODUCTION TO THE ATHLETIC TRAINING EDUCATION SERIES

The five textbooks of the Athletic Training Education Series—*Introduction to Athletic Training, Assessment of Athletic Injuries, Therapeutic Exercise for Athletic Injuries, Therapeutic Modalities for Athletic Injuries,* and *Management Strategies in Athletic Training,* second edition—were written for student athletic trainers and as a reference for practicing certified athletic trainers. Many textbooks have been written that in one way or another address the competencies in athletic training. However, absent from these books has been a coordinated approach to the competencies that serves to optimally prepare student athletic trainers for the National Athletic Trainers' Association (NATA) certification examination. If you are a student athletic trainer, you must master the material included in each of the content areas delineated in the NATA publication *Competencies in Athletic Training.* The philosophy of the Athletic Training Education Series is to address these competencies in a comprehensive and sequential manner, while avoiding unnecessary duplication.

The series covers the educational content areas developed by the Education Council of the National Athletic Trainers' Association for accredited curriculum development. These content areas and the text (or in some cases, texts) of the series that primarily addresses each content area are as follows:

- Risk management and injury prevention (*Introduction* and *Management Strategies)*
- Pathology of injury and illnesses (*Introduction, Therapeutic Exercise, Therapeutic Modalities,* and *Assessment)*
- Assessment and evaluation (*Assessment* and *Therapeutic Exercise)*
- Acute care of injury and illness (*Introduction* and *Management Strategies)*
- Pharmacology (*Introduction* and *Therapeutic Modalities)*
- Therapeutic modalities (*Therapeutic Modalities)*
- Therapeutic exercise (*Therapeutic Exercise)*
- General medical conditions and disabilities (*Introduction* and *Assessment)*
- Nutritional aspects of injury and illness (*Introduction)*
- Psychosocial intervention and referral (*Introduction, Therapeutic Modalities,* and *Therapeutic Exercise)*
- Health care administration (*Management Strategies)*
- Professional development and responsibilities (*Introduction* and *Management Strategies)*

The authors for this series—Craig Denegar, Susan Hillman, Peggy Houglum, Richard Ray, Sandy Shultz, and I—are six certified athletic trainers with well over a century of collective experience as clinicians, educators, and leaders in the athletic training profession. The clinical experience of the authors spans virtually every setting in which athletic trainers practice, including the high school, sports medicine clinic, college, professional sport, hospital, and industrial settings. The professional positions of the authors include undergraduate and graduate curriculum director, head athletic trainer, professor, clinic director, and researcher. The authors have chaired or served on the NATA's most important committees, including the Professional Education Committee, the Education Task Force, Education Council, Research Committee of the Research and Education Foundation, Journal Committee, Appropriate Medical Coverage for Intercollegiate Athletics Task Force, Continuing Education Committee, and many others. The six authors of the series have created the most comprehensive and progressive collection of texts and related instructional materials presently available to athletic training students and educators. These materials, designed to accompany an accredited athletic training curriculum, will also serve to optimally prepare you for successful completion of the certification examination.

You will find several elements common to all the books in the series. These include

- chapter objectives and summaries tied to one another so that students can know and achieve their learning goals,
- chapter opening scenarios that illustrate the importance and relevance of the chapter content,
- cross-referencing among texts for a complete education on the subject, and
- thorough reference lists for further reading and research.

To enhance instruction, the series also includes Microsoft® PowerPoint presentations and instructor guides that comprise features such as course syllabuses, lecture and chapter outlines, case studies, and test banks. Where most appropriate, laboratory manuals accompany texts. Other features vary from book to book, depending on the requirements of the subject matter, but all include various aids for assimilation and review of information, extensive illustrations, and material to help the student apply the facts in the text.

Beyond the introductory text by Hillman, the order in which the books should be used is determined by the philosophy of your curriculum director. In any case, each book can stand alone so that an entire curriculum doesn't need to be revamped to use one or more parts of the series.

When I entered the profession of athletic training nearly 25 years ago, one text—*Prevention and Care of Athletic Injuries* by Klafs and Arnheim—covered nearly all the subject matter necessary to pass the NATA Board of Certification examination and practice as an entry-level athletic trainer. Since that time we have witnessed an amazing expansion of the subject matter necessary to practice athletic training and an equally impressive growth of practice settings in which athletic trainers work. I trust you will find the Athletic Training Education Series an invaluable resource as you prepare for a successful career as a certified athletic trainer and a most useful reference in your professional practice.

David H. Perrin, PhD, ATC
Series Editor

PREFACE

Therapeutic modalities are used by certified athletic trainers, physical therapists, and other health care professionals to treat physically active and nonactive individuals who have musculoskeletal injuries. Appropriately applied, therapeutic modalities can relieve pain and, in some cases, shorten recovery time. Although therapeutic modalities have been used for centuries, many questions remain about how therapeutic modalities affect the body and which modalities are most effective in a particular situation.

For more than a decade, I have taught undergraduate and graduate courses to athletic training and physical therapy students on the theory and application of these modalities. As the body of knowledge has grown, I have refined my clinical practice, which in turn has influenced my classroom presentation. Teaching has also helped me appreciate how difficult it is for health care professionals in training to understand the *hows* and *whys* of modality application in the clinical setting.

This text, as well as the rest of this series from Human Kinetics, was written for the entry-level athletic training student. Early in their education, student athletic trainers observe the evaluation, treatment, and rehabilitation of injured physically active individuals and then practice newly acquired skills under the supervision of the sports medicine team. During this time, student athletic trainers must grow from simply asking how something is done to asking why it is done. Understanding the reasons behind the various aspects of clinical practice is one of the greatest challenges of becoming a certified athletic trainer.

Success as a certified athletic trainer demands the integration of knowledge. Anatomy, physiology, biomechanics, and the basic sciences form the foundation for successful practice. Studying injury prevention, injury evaluation, treatment, and rehabilitation prepares certified athletic trainers for the unique responsibilities of caring for physically active people. In writing this text I have attempted to be sensitive to the needs of the primary audience. Undergraduate student athletic trainers are often developing their knowledge in the basic sciences and are asking how more than why. Thus, I have worked to present the essential contributions from the basic sciences as they apply to therapeutic modalities as clearly and concisely as possible.

However, I have not lost sight of the student's goal of practicing as a certified athletic trainer. Like all health care providers, certified athletic trainers must have a sound rationale for the plans of treatment they develop. Many of the concepts and theories presented in this text are inherently complex. Unfortunately, I know of no shortcuts for learning about the use of therapeutic modalities. Therefore, the material is presented in sufficient depth to help you fully understand the implications and limitations of contemporary science. I hope this text will provide a resource throughout your development as an athletic trainer.

The human body is well adapted to recover from musculoskeletal injury. In the normal, relatively healthy, physically active population, there is very little evidence that therapeutic modalities used by certified athletic trainers speed the repair of damaged tissue. However, we commonly interpret a return of function as evidence of tissue repair. In fact, return of function often precedes the completion of tissue maturation by weeks and even months. Chapter 11 addresses the impact of therapeutic modalities on wound healing, especially in relation to slow-to-heal wounds. There is ample evidence that several modalities can speed healing in slow-to-heal wounds such as decubitus ulcers. Exciting work continues in the area of nonunion fractures.

But at present, we do not have evidence that the modalities used in treating the vast majority of injuries sustained by physically active individuals speed tissue healing.

If therapeutic modalities used by certified athletic trainers do not speed tissue repair, why are these treatments done? You should ask this question as you read this text and throughout your clinical practice. Therapeutic modalities have been used by athletic trainers and other health care professionals for many years. Some of the rationales used in the past for modality application are no longer valid in light of new knowledge. Conversely, advances in physiology and neuroscience have provided new explanations for the response to modality application. Throughout this text I return to issues of physiological response and treatment efficacy. Often modalities are applied without a thorough understanding of the physiological response, and evidence of treatment efficacy is sparse throughout physical medicine. Our knowledge base is incomplete.

The "holes" in our knowledge base are frustrating to the student and practicing clinician. The certified athletic trainer, faced with treating an injured individual, may find success in applying therapeutic modalities that cannot be explained fully. Many students and clinicians are uncomfortable using therapeutic modalities because of uncertainties concerning physiological response and clinical efficacy.

This text was written to provide entry-level athletic training students with an understanding of the clinical application of therapeutic modalities. The first part of the text introduces the rehabilitation process. The second part is devoted to understanding the physiological response to tissue injury and the phenomenon of pain. The four chapters in the third part focus on the physical principles of superficial heat and cold, electrotherapy, ultrasound, and mechanical energy. Each chapter also discusses the physiological responses to modality application. The final part of the book addresses the application of therapeutic modalities as part of a comprehensive plan of care designed to help the injured person recover. The chapters on management of acute musculoskeletal injuries, restoration of neuromuscular control, and management of persistent pain were written to help you integrate your understanding of tissue healing and pain with the physics and physiological responses to the modalities discussed in the third part of the text.

Case studies are presented to help you develop a sound rationale for modality application and to reinforce safe application practices. These case studies also illustrate the use of therapeutic modalities as a part of rehabilitation rather than as the definitive treatment. The rationales for modality application are based on the available research and contemporary theory. However, I have not hesitated to point out the "holes" in our knowledge. I apply therapeutic modalities every day in my clinical practice. First, I assure that my treatments are administered safely, then I strive to develop a sound rationale for each application in the context of a comprehensive plan of care. Experience, however, has led me to apply modalities in some situations because of previous clinical observations rather than because of a well-founded, research-based rationale.

Athletic training is a combination of science and art. This book will help you become a better athletic trainer by providing a contemporary scientific basis balanced with the realities of day-to-day clinical practice. All health care providers should stay abreast of our expanding knowledge base. Your career as a certified athletic trainer will be an ongoing process of learning and professional growth. This book and the series from Human Kinetics provide an outstanding foundation on which to build a career in athletic training. I wish you well in that journey.

ACKNOWLEDGMENTS

This book would not have been possible without the work, help, and understanding of many people. A big thank-you to the athletic training students, faculty, and sports medicine staff at Penn State University for inspiration and support throughout this project. Special thanks to Dr. Jay Hertel for his review of early drafts; Mr. Todd Evans for his work on final revisions; Ms. Tammy Hughes for taking care of all of the details; and Dr. Bill Buckley, Mr. John Miller, Jay, and Tammy for their help in getting all of the work done while I was busy writing. Finally, special thanks to my friend and mentor, series editor Dr. Dave Perrin.

CREDITS

Chapter 1 (list on p. 6) Adapted, with permission, from R.W. Scott, 1998, *Professional ethics: A guide for rehabilitation professionals* (St. Louis: Mosby), 53–55.

Figure 1.3 Adapted, by permission, from J.H. Gieck and E.N. Saliba, 1988, The athletic trainer and rehabilitation. In *The Injured Athlete*, 2nd ed. (Philadelphia: Lippincott), 230.

Figure 1.5 Adapted, by permission, from J.H. Gieck and E.N. Saliba, 1988, The athletic trainer and rehabilitation. In *The Injured Athlete*, 2nd ed. (Philadelphia: Lippincott), 230.

Figure 1.6 Reprinted, by permission, from R.R. Ray, Jr., 1994, *Management strategies in athletic training* (Champaign, IL: Human Kinetics), 147.

Figure 3.6 Adapted by permission of The McGraw-Hill Companies, Inc., from L. Langley, 1974, *Dynamic anatomy and physiology*, 4th ed. (New York: McGraw-Hill), 389–391.

Figure 4.1 Reprinted, by permission, from C.R. Denegar and O.H. Perrin, 1992, "Effect of transcutaneous electrical nerve stimulation, cold and a combined treatment on pain, decreased range of motor and strength loss associated with delayed onset muscle soreness," *Journal of Athletic Training* 27 (3): 202.

Figure 4.2 Reprinted, by permission, from M.S. Margolis, 1983, Spatial properties of pain. In *Pain Measurement and Assessment*, edited by R. Melzack (New York: Raven), 216.

Figures 4.4 and 4.5 Adapted, by permission, from J.H. Wilmore and D.L. Costill, 1999, *Physiology of sport and exercise*, 2nd ed. (Champaign, IL: Human Kinetics), 72.

Table 4.3 Reprinted, by permission, from C.R. Denegar and E.F.H. Bowman, 1996, "Electrotherapy in the treatment of athletic injuries," *Athletic Training Sports Health Care Perspectives* 2 (2): 108–115.

Figure 5.2 Adapted, by permission, from C.R. Denegar and A. Peppard, 1997, "Evaluation and treatment of persistent pain and myofascial pain syndrome," *Athletic Therapy Today* 2 (4): 40.

Figures 5.3 and 5.4 Reprinted, by permission, from C.R. Denegar and A. Peppard, 1997, "Evaluation and treatment of persistent pain and myofascial pain syndrome," *Athletic Therapy Today* 2 (4): 42.

Figures 6.2 and 6.3 Reprinted, by permission, from J. Hertel and C.R. Denegar, 1998, "A rehabilitation paradigm for restoring neuromuscular control following athletic injury," *Athletic Therapy Today* 3 (5): 13–14.

Figure 6.4 Reprinted, by permission, from Human Kinetics, 2000, *Progressive Rehabilitation of Lower Extremity Sport Injury Pass Course* (Champaign, IL: Human Kinetics), 52.

Figure 8.2 Reprinted, by permission, from J.H. Wilmore and D.L. Costill, 1999, *Physiology of sport and exercise*, 2nd ed. (Champaign, IL: Human Kinetics), 71.

Figure 9.6 Reprinted, courtesy of Chris Castel. © International Academy of Physio Therapeutics, Inc.

Figure 9.9 Reprinted, by permission of Butterworth Heinemann Publishers, a division of Reed Educational & Professional Publishing Ltd., from J. Low and A. Reed, 1994, *Electrotherapy explained: Principles and practice*, 2nd ed. (Oxford, UK: Butterworth Heinemann), 230.

Figure 10.2 Adapted, by permission, from J.H. Wilmore and D.L. Costill, 1999, *Physiology of sport and exercise*, 2nd ed. (Champaign, IL: Human Kinetics), 74.

Figures 10.10 and 10.11 Reprinted, by permission, from C.D. Clemente, 1981, *Anatomy—A regional atlas of the human body* (Baltimore: Urban and Schwarzenberg), 465 and 471.

Figure 10.12 Reprinted from W.H. Hollinshead and C. Rosse, 1985, *Textbook of anatomy*, 4th ed. (Philadelphia: Harper & Row), 928.

Figure 13.2 Reprinted, by permission, from C.R. Denegar and A. Peppard, 1997, "Evaluation and treatment of persistent pain and myofascial pain syndrome," *Athletic Therapy Today* 2 (4): 40.

CHAPTER ONE

Therapeutic Modalities: Contemporary Use and Current Issues

OBJECTIVES

After reading this chapter, the student will be able to

1. discuss how state regulation of athletic training may influence the use of therapeutic modalities in the care of physically active individuals,

2. identify the hierarchy of components in a progressive rehabilitation plan, and

3. discuss guidelines for progressing an athlete through a comprehensive plan of care.

It is your first day working as a certified athletic trainer for a sports medicine clinic. Your position primarily involves service to a local high school but also involves a few hours in the clinic each morning. A varsity football player for the local high school sprained his ankle on the first day of practice yesterday. The team physician has evaluated the injury and referred the athlete to the clinic for treatment.

Questions arise, and the answers lead to more questions. What will be the plan of care for this injured athlete (i.e., short- and long-term treatment goals)? Can therapeutic modalities be used to achieve any of these goals? You identify pain control, restoration of range of motion, and return to full weight bearing as goals to be achieved within 7 to 10 days, and you choose therapeutic modalities including cold and transcutaneous electrical nerve stimulation. Can you, as a certified athletic trainer, administer these modalities to this athlete in the sports medicine clinic? Who has the answers?

Chapter 1 introduces a progressive rehabilitation paradigm from which treatment goals can be developed. In addition, the chapter discusses medical–legal issues affecting modality application, including regulation of practice and negligence. These issues are basic to the practice of athletic training and the use of therapeutic modalities.

The use of therapeutic modalities or physical agents in treating human ailments is not new. Massage, "cupping" (applying heated shells over painful areas), and the use of electric eels are mentioned in archives dating back to early Greek and Roman cultures. However, there was little scientific evidence to support the treatments administered by early practitioners. Today, therapeutic modalities are primarily applied by providers whose professional origins date back less than 100 years. Although several medical and allied medical care providers, including physicians, chiropractors, podiatrists, and dentists, may administer or apply therapeutic modalities, this practice is undertaken primarily by physical therapists and certified athletic trainers. Athletic trainers have applied therapeutic modalities since the beginnings of the profession (figure 1.1) and have contributed to the collective knowledge of therapeutic modalities through writing and research.

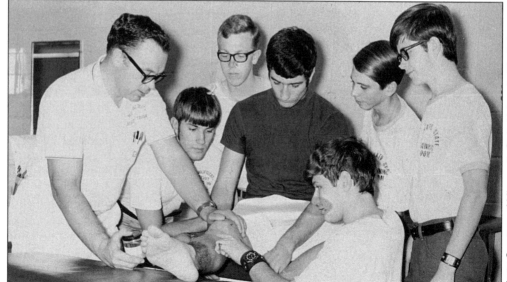

Figure 1.1 An early athletic training room.

Photo Courtesy of Minnesota State University Mankato.

Therapeutic modality literally means a device or apparatus having curative powers. Heat, cold, massage, ultrasound, and diathermy have been used by athletic trainers since the profession's early days. These treatments may be better classified as *physical agents*, treatments that cause some change to the body. The scientific basis for the use of these therapeutic modalities has grown, providing a greater understanding of how modality applications may help athletic trainers achieve treatment goals and return injured athletes to sports.

Athletic trainers' educational preparation to use these modalities, however, has been challenged. As athletic trainers have sought recognition through state credentialing and establishment of practice acts, the use of therapeutic modalities has been an issue. Because internships are no longer the route to athletic training certification, all athletic trainers will receive formal preparation in the safe use of therapeutic modalities based on the best available science.

To effectively use therapeutic modalities to treat physically active individuals and other patients, we must cooperate and share knowledge. Our collective understanding of the physics of therapeutic modalities, physiological responses to therapeutic modalities, and clinical benefits of these modalities is evolving. Over the last 70 years, therapeutic ultrasound, diathermy, and the therapeutic use of electricity have been developed. Researchers are exploring how to best use these and other therapeutic modalities. As we learn more, our practices change, which is critical to our profession. The health care system is changing, and all providers are under increasing scrutiny to demonstrate improved patient outcomes and cost-effectiveness.

More athletic trainers than ever are working outside the traditional setting of the professional, college, and high school athletic training room. The profession is seeking greater recognition of the certified athletic trainer as a care provider to physically active individuals. Thus, although many athletic trainers practice in traditional settings, sheltered from some of the changes in health care, such as capitated services, these issues touch all in the profession.

Much has been learned about how therapeutic modalities affect the body, and we have developed a theoretical basis for the application of therapeutic modalities following musculoskeletal injuries. The bulk of this text relies on "logical argument" to establish a rationale for the use of therapeutic modalities. Evidence that application of a therapeutic modality improves treatment outcomes or hastens the return to athletic competition, however, is often lacking. Until more is discovered through research, certified athletic trainers and other health care providers must rely on the existing knowledge and clinical observations to guide the use of therapeutic modalities in clinical practice.

LEGAL ASPECTS OF THERAPEUTIC MODALITY APPLICATION: PRACTICE ACTS AND NEGLIGENT TREATMENT

Athletic training has been recognized as a distinct allied medical profession in many states through the development of practice acts and state credentialing. Recognition of the profession and higher educational standards influence the practice of athletic training. The certified athletic trainer must comply with regulations set forth by the state in which he or she practices, including regulations that affect the therapeutic modalities an athletic trainer may apply, to whom the athletic trainer may administer treatment, and the setting in which the athletic trainer may render treatment. The agency responsible for regulating athletic training practice can provide you with copies of the relevant practice act; these materials are also often available through state athletic trainers' associations or societies.

Changes in athletic training regulation and the education of athletic trainers have also elevated the standard of care expected from certified athletic trainers. Before the days of certification by the National Athletic Trainers' Association (NATA), there was no standard by which to judge athletic trainers' actions. Today, certification by the NATA Board of Certification (NATA–BOC), recognition of athletic training as a profession by individual states through licensure or certification, and higher educational standards have defined the standards of athletic training and elevated levels of practice. Failure to practice according to these standards, including causing injury by therapeutic modality application, may constitute negligence.

STATE REGULATION OF ATHLETIC TRAINING

Athletic trainer certification by NATA–BOC is determined by an examination that tests the applicant's knowledge and skills in preventing, recognizing, treating, and rehabilitating athletic injuries as well as performing administrative aspects of athletic training. A standard of preparation has been established through the examination and a competency list established to define the breadth of knowledge required for athletic trainer certification.

Therapeutic modalities are addressed in a subsection of *Athletic Training Educational Competencies for Health Care of the Physically Active* (NATA, 1999). Through education and supervised clinical experience, the athletic trainer learns how and when to apply therapeutic modalities and then demonstrates the associated knowledge and skills during the certification examination. The certified athletic trainer has met established standards to practice athletic training and to use therapeutic modalities. One might then assume that a certified athletic trainer's practice is governed by the National Athletic Trainers' Association's *Code of Ethics* (NATA 1993), the *Role Delineation Study* (NATA 1995), and the *Athletic Training Educational Competencies* (NATA 1999).

Such an assumption should never be made. Although NATA has established educational criteria for certification, administers the examination through NATA–BOC, requires evidence of continuing education to maintain certification, and has developed the NATA *Code of Ethics*, the *Role Delineation Study*, and the *Athletic Training Educational Competencies*, the practice of athletic training may be governed by the state in which the athletic trainer practices. Athletic training is governed by state statutes in over half of the United States. Thus, although a certified athletic trainer may feel qualified to use a specific therapeutic modality or administer a particular treatment, state laws specify what the athletic trainer may legally do. The certified athletic trainer must understand and practice within the boundaries of the state's practice act. Failure to do so may lead to revocation of a state license or certification and loss of practice privileges.

It is not possible to review the regulations of all states that have recognized athletic training as a health care profession by establishing practice acts. In addition, these regulations change often. This text and the instruction you receive are intended to develop your knowledge and skills related to the clinical competencies established by the profession. It is your responsibility to learn how the laws of your state affect what you can do and whom you can treat.

CONSENT TO TREAT AND TORT

Other medical and legal considerations relate to athletic training in general and the use of therapeutic modalities. This text is not intended to cover the legal and administrative aspects of athletic training and sports medicine in detail. However, two issues closely related to the application of therapeutic modalities are covered: informed consent and liability in tort.

Informed Consent

Informed consent refers to the right of physically active individuals to receive information about their diagnosis and treatment options and consent to treatment. Informed consent has received little attention from certified athletic trainers. Schools and community youth athletic programs receive parental consent to provide immediate treatment of injuries. However, few athletic training rooms have policies regarding obtaining consent for modality application or participation in therapeutic exercises. Furthermore, although individuals entering sports medicine clinics sign forms giving health care providers permission to treat them, these individuals often do not provide informed consent for specific treatments.

Often a bond of trust exists between the physically active individual and the certified athletic trainer, whereby the individual believes that the athletic trainer will provide the best possible care. Additionally, the injured person may have observed treatments administered to others and may know what to expect. These two factors lead to an implied consent to receive treatment with specific modalities and participate in specific exercises.

Failure to receive consent prior to treatment does not routinely lead to litigation against a certified athletic trainer. However, you should not ignore this issue. Make it a habit to explain any proposed treatment to the injured person and provide an opportunity for questions. This facilitates communication in the sports medicine clinic, where the injured person is encountering an unfamiliar health care facility and providers. It is also good practice in the athletic training room, where explaining the rehabilitation plan and proposed treatments engages the injured individual and allows the certified athletic trainer to review his or her responsibilities in the rehabilitation plan (figure 1.2).

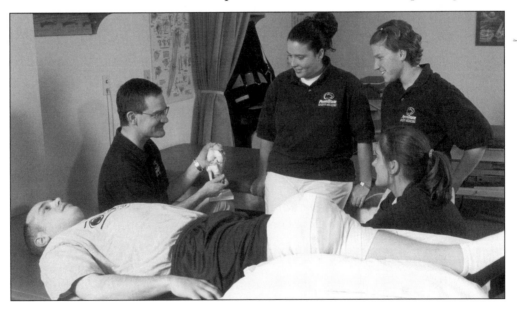

■ **Figure 1.2** Explaining the rehabilitation plan and proposed treatments allows the athletic trainer to review his or her own responsibilities as well as inform the injured individual.

The components of informed consent, as described by Scott (1998), are presented here. Clearly, components 2 through 5 are directly related to the application of therapeutic modalities. This text is intended to provide the certified athletic trainer and athletic training student with the physical and physiological principles for modality application, the mechanisms by which the therapeutic benefits of modalities are achieved, and the contraindications and precautions for modality use. With this background, the certified athletic trainer can provide physically active individuals with what they need to make informed decisions about their health care.

Liability in Tort for Negligent Treatment and Professional Negligence

A *tort* is a private, civil legal action brought by an injured party, or the party's representative, to redress an injury caused by another person. Negligence entails doing something that an ordinary person under like circumstances would not have done

Components of Informed Consent

The injured physically active person should be informed of the following:

1. The diagnosis or findings of a physical examination
2. The recommended treatment procedures and rehabilitation plan
3. The prognosis if the recommended treatment is administered or rehabilitation plan completed
4. The risks and benefits of the recommended treatment and rehabilitation plan
5. Reasonable alternatives to the proposed treatment and rehabilitation plan, with the potential risks, benefits, and prognosis
6. The prognosis if no treatment is administered or rehabilitation completed

Adapted from Scott 1998.

(a negligent act or an act of commission) or failing to do something that an ordinary, reasonable, prudent person would have done under similar circumstances. This general definition can be more clearly focused by replacing *ordinary person* with *certified athletic trainer*. The professional standards established through national certification, the NATA *Code of Ethics* and Standards of Practice, and state regulation of athletic training have created a level of expectation for athletic training.

When a certified athletic trainer fails to act appropriately or acts inappropriately in providing athletic training services and injures an individual, the certified athletic trainer may be found negligent in tort. In relation to the application of therapeutic modalities, negligence in tort is likely to involve a negligent act. The certified athletic trainer is responsible for ensuring that the equipment used to apply modalities is properly maintained and calibrated and is in good working order, and that the modalities are applied in a manner that does not harm the individual. Negligent acts include burns caused by a moist heat pack with too little toweling for insulation, cold-induced nerve injury caused by inadequate instructions for applying ice packs at home, or electrical shock caused by faulty wiring on a poorly maintained transcutaneous electrical nerve stimulator. The certified athletic trainer must recognize when the application of a modality is contraindicated, must know how to apply a modality safely, and must instruct the individual properly if he or she is to self-administer a modality. Failure to do any of these things may constitute negligence if harm occurs with use of a therapeutic modality.

THE REHABILITATION PLAN OF CARE

A team approach to treating physically active individuals is necessary, because no single health care provider has all of the skills and resources necessary to guide the athlete through rehabilitation. The rehabilitation plan of care is founded on the medical diagnosis provided by the physician and the physical examination of the injured athlete by the certified athletic trainer. The medical diagnosis is critical to determine whether surgery is necessary, to determine whether medications are indicated, and to estimate the rate of progression that the healing tissues will tolerate.

The physician and certified athletic trainer must also identify specific short-term goals for the injured athlete. A medical diagnosis may be a Grade II lateral ankle sprain. However, the rehabilitation plan of care addresses not the lateral ankle sprain but the pain; loss of motion; loss of strength; decreased neuromuscular control; and inability to fully bear weight, walk, run, jump, cut, or play basketball: in other words, the signs, symptoms, impairments, disabilities, and handicaps resulting from the injury. In addition, the physician and certified athletic trainer must identify factors that may limit adherence to rehabilitation, including the athlete's psychological–emotional response to the injury. Finally, the short-term goals that are established to address specific needs such as pain control or improved neuromuscular control must be tied to the individual's achievement of long-term goals. Thus, the medical diagnosis is only part of determining the best approach to rehabilitation.

Developing a rehabilitation plan of care may sound difficult; however some basic concepts make the process much easier. First, a basic rehabilitation model should be used as the framework for the plan of care. Second, the plan of care must address the problems identified in the physical examination; thus, a plan of care is individualized. Third, the plan of care should be progressive, with clearly identified performance or time-specified criteria for progression to more complex and challenging activities.

PROGRESSIVE REHABILITATION MODEL

Clinicians generally agree on the order of priorities in a progressive rehabilitation plan of care. The model presented in figure 1.3 is based on the work of Worrell and Reynolds (1994). The first priority in rehabilitation is to control pain and swelling and protect injured tissues. Pain is one of the worst of human experiences; it makes us miserable, affects sleep, and alters neuromuscular control and function. Once a diagnosis is established, pain has served its purpose (warning the individual that something is wrong) and should be alleviated to the greatest degree possible.

The second priority is restoring range of motion about the involved joints. Injury and inflammation result in swelling, muscle guarding, and loss of motion. Functional recovery usually requires normal amounts of joint range of motion.

The third priority is to restore neuromuscular control and muscular endurance (neuromuscular control is discussed in detail in chapters 6 and 12). Pain, swelling, and joint instability alter how the nervous system coordinates muscle contractions. Neuromuscular control and muscular endurance must be reestablished so the athlete can perform the low-resistance, high-repetition activities that are the foundation of strength and power training.

The fourth priority is to restore strength and power. *Strength* is the ability to do work, whereas *power* is a measure of the rate at which the work is done. Success in sports requires muscular strength and power. Generally, strength is addressed first with slow, controlled exercises. Power training is then added through plyometric exercises, sprinting, and other rapid movement training.

Fifth, the sport-specific needs of the athlete must be met. A basketball player who can run, jump, and cut may not be ready to return to the game because of inability to

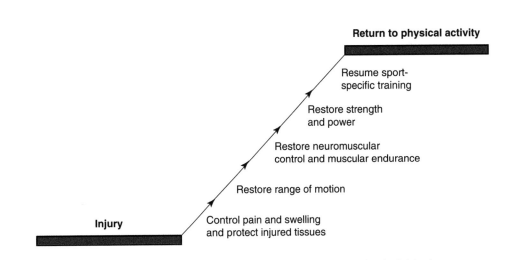

Return to physical activity

Resume sport-specific training

Restore strength and power

Restore neuromuscular control and muscular endurance

Restore range of motion

Control pain and swelling and protect injured tissues

Injury

❚ **Figure 1.3**   A progressive model for rehabilitation of physically active individuals.

Adapted from Gieck and Saliba 1988.

backpedal, or a football player may not be ready to return to the offensive line because of poor footwork. Each sport and athletic activity places a unique demand on the body. As a rehabilitation plan of care progresses, it should become more specific to the demands of the individual's sport and work activities.

Therapeutic modalities are primarily used to alleviate pain and allow individuals to initiate therapeutic exercises to improve range of motion and regain neuromuscular control. The certified athletic trainer should understand how the modality application affects the body and the rationale for each modality application. Modality application is not a treatment but a passive intervention that enables individuals to meet specific, short-term rehabilitation goals.

In addition to working toward specific goals related to the injury, the sports medicine team must also strive to maintain the individual's overall fitness level. Exercise to maintain cardiovascular fitness and strength should be incorporated into the rehabilitation plan as soon as it is safe to do so. Stationary cycling, stair climbing, aquatic exercises, and circuit training can be used to maintain fitness while protecting healing tissues and can provide some variety in the injured person's routine. Physically active individuals also experience a withdrawal phenomenon when their regular physical exercise routine is disrupted by injury. Including safe aerobic exercise and weight training in the rehabilitation plan helps individuals cope with this disruption. Figure 1.4 provides an example of an individualized plan of care.

Monitoring Progress

Progress implies change, and a team physician I once worked with was fond of saying, "If things do not stay the same they will get better or worse." There are numerous potential pitfalls in the evaluating and rehabilitating of injured individuals. Incomplete diagnoses, poor adherence, and excessive activity can prevent recovery from injury and return to competition. The sports medicine team must monitor an individual's progress during rehabilitation, discouraging excessive or inappropriate activities and adding challenging activities when appropriate.

Two factors guide progression. The first is tissue healing. In some circumstances, such as fractures and anterior cruciate ligament (ACL) reconstruction, the time the body needs to repair the tissues is relatively well established. Although pain is often a reasonable guide for exercise progression, the team physician may specify a time frame of restricted activity.

The second factor is successful completion of short-term goals related to the earlier stages of rehabilitation. If healing tissues are adequately protected, the initial short-terms goals will be based on the first three rehabilitation priorities. For example, following a lateral ankle sprain there may be a considerable amount of pain. Appropriate short-term goals may include reducing pain to a rating of 2 (on a scale of 0 = *no pain*, 10 = *worst pain imaginable*) at rest in 2 days and a rating of 2 in full weight bearing in 1 week. If range of motion is lost, restoring full ankle range of motion in 10 days is a reasonable short-term goal.

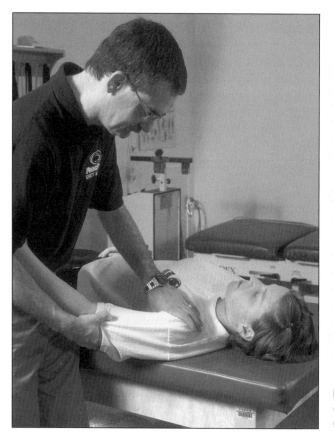

∎ **Figure 1.4**   A plan of care is individualized with clear criteria to check progress toward more complex and challenging activities and recovery.

Progression should be performance based. For example, a physically active person may ask how long she must remain on crutches after spraining her lateral ankle ligaments. These ligaments are not stressed by walking but only by extreme ankle inversion. Thus, a good guide for return to full weight bearing is a normal, pain-free walking gait. If walking is painful, the first goal of rehabilitation has not been fully achieved. Limping is an altered neuromuscular pattern to avoid pain. Thus, to this physically active person, progression is simple and performance oriented.

Communication is essential to monitoring the injured person's progress through rehabilitation. Each individual will respond differently, and feedback from the athlete is vital. Some individuals must be cautioned repeatedly about being overly aggressive, whereas others must be encouraged to do more. Much of the individual response hinges on a person's response to pain. Some individuals approach therapeutic exercise with a "no pain, no gain" mentality. The sports medicine team must help such individuals interpret their pain sensation to protect healing tissues. Other individuals will stop exercise at the first sensation of pain, even though some discomfort is expected at various stages of most rehabilitation programs. Individuals who know what to expect will be better able to interpret their pain and make progress with their rehabilitation. Figure 1.5 shows theoretical and realistic return-to-activity models.

The final stage in recovery from injury is the return to unrestricted training, practice, and competition. Clearance to return to sport activity is a team decision. The individual must feel physically and psychologically ready. The team physician and certified athletic trainer must consider whether the injured tissues can withstand the stresses of sport and whether the individual's overall level of fitness is sufficient for him or her to play effectively without undue risk of injury. Coaches can provide valuable insight into the physical capabilities and psychological motivation of physically active individuals. Most importantly, clearance to return to play must be based on performance assessment as well as physical examination. The person evaluated solely in an office or athletic training room may appear capable of returning to sport, yet field evaluation may reveal significant losses of sport-specific agility, power, or endurance. Ideally, the certified athletic trainer and coaches should evaluate the individual's functional performance and gain physician approval before giving final clearance for unrestricted activity.

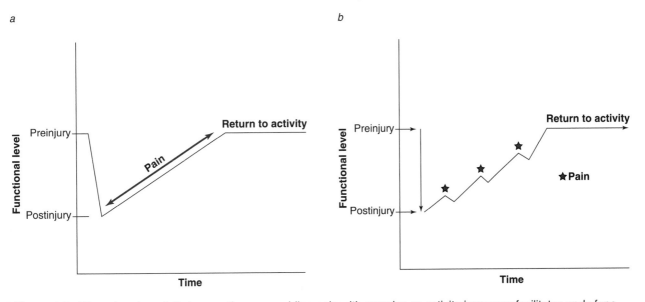

a *b*

Figure 1.5 The return to activity is a continuum; avoiding pain with exercise as activity increases facilitates early functional recovery *(a)*. Recovery of function is delayed when the threshold of healing tissue is exceeded and pain occurs *(b)*.

Adapted from Gieck and Saliba 1988.

Documenting Progress

Paperwork is the bane of health care providers. Preparing and maintaining good records is often challenging but essential work. This subject is given considerable attention in the final text in the series: *Management Strategies in Athletic Training*, second edition. However, it would be remiss not to mention documentation in this chapter.

Good records are needed to assess the benefits of treatment and rehabilitation. As mentioned early in the chapter, there is greater demand in the managed care environment for health care providers to demonstrate that what they do makes a difference in patient care. Good records also are essential in a defense against a charge of negligence. Malpractice cases often take years to reach the courtroom, and a good memory will never prevail over good documentation. Figure 1.6 provides an example of an individual injury evaluation and treatment record.

Recording also facilitates communication and identifies problems. The certified athletic trainer may see an individual daily in a traditional athletic training setting; however, encounters in a clinical setting may occur only weekly or even less frequently. Without a complete record of the case, you may not recall specific details of the individual's problem or previous treatments. Develop good record-keeping skills and make a habit of documenting the modalities and specific parameters you select in treating each individual.

Individual Injury Evaluation and Treatment Record

Name _____ Sport _____ Body part _____

Date injury occurred _____ Date injury reported _____ New ___ Old ___

Primary complaint _____ Secondary complaint _____

Subjective evaluation:

Objective evaluation:

Assessment:

Plan:

Evaluator's initials _____

Date	Treatments and progress

■ Figure 1.6 Individual injury evaluation and treatment record.

Reprinted from Ray 1994.

SUMMARY

1. *Discuss how state regulation of athletic training may influence the use of therapeutic modalities in the care of physically active individuals.*

   Athletic training is regulated in many states through state practice acts. The state practice act defines what an athletic trainer may do, whom the athletic trainer may treat, and where treatments can be administered. Although the certified athletic trainer may be educated and trained to use therapeutic modalities to treat musculoskeletal injuries, state regulations may restrict modality application depending on the setting, amateur or professional status of the individual being treated, or modality used.

2. *Identify the hierarchy of components in a progressive rehabilitation plan.*

   A progressive rehabilitation plan consists of five stages: (1) controlling pain and swelling and protecting damaged tissues, (2) restoring range of motion, (3) restoring neuromuscular control and muscular endurance, (4) restoring strength and power, and (5) resuming sport-specific training.

3. *Discuss guidelines for progressing an athlete through a comprehensive plan of care.*

   Progression through a comprehensive rehabilitation plan of care is based on protecting healing tissues and achieving short-term goals. If healing tissues are adequately protected, pain during and following activity is the primary guide to progression. Active exercise should be pain-free, and the individual should be able to do tomorrow what was done today.

CITED REFERENCES

The National Athletic Trainers' Association Board of Certification: *Role Delineation Study*, 3rd ed. Philadelphia, Davis, 1995.

National Athletic Trainers' Association: *Athletic Training Educational Competencies for the Health Care of the Physically Active*. Dallas, NATA, 1999.

National Athletic Trainers' Association: *Code of Ethics*. Dallas, NATA, 1993.

Scott RW: *Professional Ethics: A Guide for Rehabilitation Professionals*. St. Louis, Mosby, 1998.

Worrell TW, Reynolds NL: Integrating physiologic and psychological paradigms into orthopaedic rehabilitation. *Orthop Phys Ther Clin North Am* 3:269-289, 1994.

ADDITIONAL SOURCES

Canavan PK: *Rehabilitation in Sports Medicine*. Stamford, CT, Appleton & Lange, 1998.

Herbert DL: *Legal Aspects of Sports Medicine*. Canton, OH, Professional Reports Corp., 1990.

Zachazewski JE, Magee DJ, Quillen WS: *Athletic Injuries and Rehabilitation*. Philadelphia, Saunders, 1996.

CHAPTER TWO

Psychological Aspects of Rehabilitation

OBJECTIVES

After reading this chapter, the student will be able to

1. compare and contrast the contemporary stage model and biopsychosocial model of psychological response to injury,

2. discuss the impact that cognitive appraisal can have on the athlete's psychological and emotional response to injury,

3. identify influences over an individual's ability to cope with an athletic injury,

4. identify factors that improve an athlete's adherence to a rehabilitation plan,

5. identify common barriers to successful completion of rehabilitation, and

6. discuss assessment of treatment outcomes in the context of natural history, placebo, and "true" treatment effect.

A retired man who is an avid golfer enters a sports medicine clinic for treatment of his shoulder, which was injured when he tripped while carrying his golf bag. He complains of stiffness and a loss of motion in the shoulder. However, his primary concern is that the injury is preventing him from playing golf and that this disability might be permanent. Physical examination reveals an extensive contusion to the right shoulder; however, the joint appears to be stable and the rotator cuff intact. He responds well to transcutaneous electrical nerve stimulation (TENS) and moist heat, prescribed to reduce pain and spasm, and active assistance and active range of motion exercise during his initial treatment. Swinging a short iron is included in the initial therapy session. He is far less anxious on leaving the clinic than when he entered.

He complies well with his home care program and requires just four additional treatments in the clinic. He gradually progresses his golfing activities, beginning on the driving range, then playing 9 holes, and after 4 weeks of recovery, playing 18 holes.

Effective rehabilitation requires a comprehensive plan of care with specific, progressive goals. This text was written to develop your skills in applying therapeutic modalities to achieve some rehabilitation goals. Two important concepts were introduced in chapter 1: (1) A rehabilitation plan of care is based on medical diagnosis and evaluation of the injured person's needs, and (2) each individual will respond uniquely to injury, requiring you to individualize the plan of care to treat the person, not just the injury.

Perhaps the most important concept in treating individuals with musculoskeletal injuries is that the mind and body are connected. In the situation described at the beginning of this chapter, the patient's program included swinging a golf club, a sport-specific exercise that alleviated much of the individual's anxiety about playing golf again. The anatomical connection between mind and body is obvious and not a new concept. The relationships between physical injury and psychological response, and between psychological dysfunction and somatic pain, are complex. This chapter is about those relationships. Before applying a therapeutic modality, you will need to appreciate the psychological aspects of rehabilitation, just as you understand the physical aspects of injury.

This chapter is based on the clinical skill and the wisdom of mental health professionals, physicians, certified athletic trainers, and physical therapists who have shared their knowledge and experience. Certified athletic trainers work closely with individuals before and after injury, and the understanding, personal attention, and caring attitude that athletic trainers can provide significantly impact a person's psychological and physical recovery. The mind–body relationship is complex and strongly influences response to injury as well as recovery, and a single chapter is not sufficient to cover all related issues. This chapter presents several issues related to the mind–body connection, including the psychological response to injury, compliance with a treatment plan, barriers to success in rehabilitation, and placebo effects.

Each of these issues relates to an individual's response to treatment with therapeutic modalities. Furthermore, the complex interrelationships among psychological, physical, and social factors present the greatest obstacle in evaluating the efficacy of therapeutic interventions. Treatment outcomes studies will indicate which therapeutic interventions are most effective. Until more is known, the optimal treatment plan for each individual will result from a holistic approach to evaluation and treatment. Rather than present only the physical aspects of rehabilitation (treatment outcomes), this books takes a more holistic approach, which is why this chapter precedes discussion of the physiology of injury, modality application, and therapeutic exercise.

PSYCHOLOGICAL RESPONSE TO INJURY

Many athletic trainers are introduced to the concept of psychological response to injury by way of Kubler-Ross's writings about death and dying. Kubler-Ross (1969) described a five-stage psychological response to terminal illness, which included stages of denial and isolation, anger, bargaining, depression, and acceptance. Previous scholars applied this paradigm to injury, suggesting that the injured person first denies the severity of the injury and then expresses anger. A bargaining stage might include statements such as, "If the ligament isn't torn I will train in the weight room every day." Unrealistic bargaining was thought to give way to depression, followed by acceptance of the injury and the consequences. More recent work has emphasized that physically active individuals may experience some of these responses following injury, but they are not dying. Furthermore, these individuals do not progress through stages. These individuals may express anger at the time of the injury or not until they become bored with the routine and slow progression of rehabilitation. Most injured athletes do not experience depression. Thus, the paradigm described by Kubler-Ross does not adequately describe the typical psychological response of athletic injury.

This death-and-dying model of psychological response to athletic injury has been challenged and over time replaced. More recent models are predicated on the uniqueness of the individual response to an injury and the recognition that many factors influence how people cope and how well they adhere to a plan of care following injury.

BIOPSYCHOSOCIAL MODELS OF DISEASE AND INJURY

Several biopsychosocial models are used to describe psychological response to athletic injury. Nagi (1965) described a model with four components of injury and response: disease, impairment, functional limitation, and disability. If *musculoskeletal injury* replaces *disease*, this model is easily applied to injured physically active people (figure 2.1).

For example, consider a volleyball player who injured her knee. The injury was diagnosed as a Grade II tibial collateral ligament sprain. The sprain to the ligament was the musculoskeletal injury. The player experienced pain, loss of motion, and loss of strength following the injury. These impairments resulted in functional limitations, such as the inability to walk without assistance or perform physical tasks, including sport-specific activities like running and jumping. This volleyball player could not play her sport, work part-time as a waitress on the weekends, participate in physical education, or go hiking with her family. These limitations on performance in sports, school, employment, and family activities represent her disabilities.

In this model, injury is more than tissue damage; attention is focused on the individual's entire response to the injury. This model presents an enlightening concept: To understand the physically active person's psychological response to an injury, one needs to appreciate the impact of the injury on the athlete's life, not just the pathology.

Figure 2.1 Nagi model of the process of disablement in the context of musculoskeletal injury in physically active people.

COGNITIVE APPRAISAL MODELS

In response to the inadequacies of stage models such as the death-and-dying paradigm, cognitive-based appraisal models have been developed. The common feature in these models is that an individual's psychological and emotional response to injury depends on his or her appraisal or understanding of the injury and the stressors present in the context of the injury and rehabilitation. Recall the case study of the golfer presented at the beginning of the chapter. His response to injury changed dramatically after he understood the nature of his injury and the limitations it was likely to place on his life. He did not work through stages of response to injury; rather, his psychological and emotional response was altered by his cognitive appraisal of his injury, impairments, functional limitations, and disabilities.

The cognitive appraisal models are distinguished from the stage models in three important ways. The first distinction is that some or most of the labeled stages may be absent in the cognitive appraisal models. For example, most injured athletes do not become depressed (Wegener 1999). Depression can be a significant barrier to recovery and must be recognized and treated when it occurs, but its occurrence is the exception rather than the rule.

The second distinction is that the psychological and emotional response to injury does not progress in a structured order in the cognitive appraisal models (Wegener 1999; Yukelson and Heil 1998). Injured individuals may express little anger and frustration following an injury, accept their situation and cope, and then become angry and confrontational following a setback in rehabilitation. Such a response may also be associated with individuals' perceptions that their progress is slower than expected. This response seems to be associated with programs that vary little from day to day and week to week.

The third distinction is that cognitive appraisal models imply that the individual's psychological and emotional response to injury is affected by his or her understanding of the injury and the psychosocial environment (figure 2.2). Thus, whether a physically active person adapts and copes effectively following injury or demonstrates maladaptive behaviors can be influenced by members of the sports medicine team as well as the athlete's peers, friends, family, and coaches.

Remember the golfer described at the beginning of this chapter? Understanding the physically active person's perception of the injury and our natural fear of the

▌ **Figure 2.2**   One determinant of an individual's psychological–emotional response to injury is his or her understanding of the nature and severity of the injury.

unknown is crucial. Had attention been focused solely on the injured shoulder and not the person, this golfer's primary concern and goal may have been overlooked. More important, however, the certified athletic trainer would have lost the opportunity to impact the psychological response to the injury. Swinging a golf club is not standard in shoulder rehabilitation programs. However, including this activity assured the athlete that his season was not over.

Knowledge and understanding (cognition) alter the psychological–emotional response to injury (Wegener 1999). Providing the type and amount of information that injured people need takes experience and practice. Some individuals ask a lot of questions and want detailed information. For others, the information needs to be more general and less detailed. Finding the right level is important and quite subjective. Don't be overly simplistic and "talk down," but don't try to impress someone with your knowledge. If an injured person wants more information than is provided, he or she often has less confidence in the care providers and is less compliant with a plan of care. However, an individual who feels overwhelmed by information will be confused and anxious. You must listen and observe; the initial evaluation is a critical time to promote effective coping following injury.

PERSONALITY AND ENVIRONMENTAL INFLUENCES

An individual's ability to cope following injury is influenced by many factors. Some people are natural worriers, tending to overreact to life's frustrations, whereas others seem to manage the ups and downs effectively. One's ability to cope also depends upon his or her current situation and life stressors. An athlete who coped effectively with an off-season injury in high school may maladapt to a similar in-season injury in college, because the college environment, the pressure to return to competition, and decreased daily support from family, teammates, and coaches alter the individual's stressors and coping resources (Wegener 1999).

The sports medicine team cannot influence all of the factors that promote a maladaptive response. However, a holistic approach to care of the physically active individual will improve understanding of the individual's situation. An athletic training room and clinical environment that promote attention to the individual's needs are essential. Crowded, noisy facilities can leave the injured individual asking, "Does anybody care?" Such an environment also diminishes the likelihood of identifying maladaptive behaviors, intervening within the limits of one's training and ability, and making appropriate referrals (Fisher and Hoisington 1998; Fisher et al. 1993).

An injury will force the athlete to adapt. Whether that adaptation is functional or dysfunctional depends on many factors. Certainly the severity of the injury, timing of the injury, and coping resources available to the athlete strongly influence the individual's response. The psychological and emotional response does not proceed through a series of stages, and the response can differ significantly from person to person and within the same individual under different circumstances. The sports medicine team must create an atmosphere conducive to compliance with rehabilitation, must respect the unique nature of each person's response, and must identify barriers to treatment compliance and recovery.

MAXIMIZING COMPLIANCE WITH A REHABILITATION PLAN OF CARE

Perhaps the greatest influence on adherence to rehabilitation and a positive psychological and emotional adaptation following injury is the rapport established with the injured athlete's caregivers. Certified athletic trainers are often in a unique position among health care professionals in that a working relationship with the physically active individual is established before an injury occurs. Additionally, high school and college athletes are usually familiar with the athletic training room environment and have confidence in the ability of the sports medicine staff to provide a high standard of care.

One major difference between working in a high school, college, or professional setting and working in a sports medicine clinic is the nature of the initial encounter with the injured person. Because the preestablished rapport between the injured individual and the certified athletic trainer that is present in the traditional setting is absent in the clinical setting, individuals are uncertain and anxious about what they will experience. Many general orthopedic patients enter the sports medicine clinic believing that therapy and rehabilitation are unlikely to relieve their condition. Thus, there is a premium placed on the initial encounter. A caring, empathetic demeanor is essential. The certified athletic trainer must learn about the problem in terms of the injury, impairment, disability, and handicap. The injured individual should leave with an understanding of these issues, the program that will be used to address rehabilitation goals, and his or her responsibilities in resolving the problem. Conducting a successful initial evaluation in a sports medicine clinic requires practice, refined attention to verbal and nonverbal communication, and portrayal of oneself as a competent, caring health care provider.

SET GOALS

The importance of setting obtainable yet challenging short- and long-term rehabilitation goals has been noted by sport psychologists and sport rehabilitation specialists (Gieck 1990; Locke and Latham 1985; Worrell and Reynolds 1994). Often these goals seem obvious to the certified athletic trainer; however, the establishment and achievement of rehabilitation goals are novel to the injured individual. Figure 2.3 shows short- and long-term rehabilitation goals for the senior golfer with the sore shoulder described earlier.

Both the injured individual and the certified athletic trainer must agree on rehabilitation goals. Often clinicians establish treatment goals without listening to what the patient views as important. On the other hand, the athletic trainer cannot adopt unrealistic goals expressed by the injured person to guide rehabilitation. Individuals with injuries tend to look only at the ultimate goal: return to competition. Often the time frame for achieving the ultimate goal is unrealistic, and important steps in a progressive plan of care are ignored. By incorporating the individual's ultimate goal into the plan of care, you can educate clients on the need to achieve simpler, short-term goals (e.g., achieve full knee range of motion) as part of the comprehensive plan to achieve the ultimate goal (e.g., return to playing varsity soccer following ACL reconstruction).

Short-term goals

• Pain relief at rest and early motion exercises within 5 days

• Independent in-home exercise program within 5 days

• Pain-free golf swing with short irons and putting within 10 days

Long-term goals

• Pain-free golf swing with woods and long irons and putting within 3 weeks

• Return to golf within 4 weeks

∎ **Figure 2.3**   Short- and long-term goals for an injured golfer.

The injured person may not value the short-term goal until it is placed in the context of achieving the ultimate goal. Adherence to a plan of care and achievement of short-term goals are improved when the goals and values are addressed as the plan of care is formulated.

Establishing short-term goals that are integral to returning to sports has an additional positive influence, especially when the recovery period is lengthy. The person recovering from a surgery such as ACL reconstruction can become frustrated by the perception that day-to-day progress is too slow. This can be countered by the positive reinforcement provided when short-term goals are achieved. Short-term goals that can be realistically accomplished in 1 to 3 weeks yet are challenging seem to work best. The individual who is reminded of the short-term goals accomplished can better cope with the frustrations inherent in a long course of rehabilitation.

SHARE RESPONSIBILITY

Treatment and rehabilitation of the injured individual are not "done to" the individual but are "done by" the individual. Through active involvement in establishing goals, the individual learns what responsibilities he or she has if rehabilitation is to be successful (figure 2.4). You must remember that the injury is not your problem. Often new clinicians can become overly possessive of the patient and the patient's problem. The duty of the certified athletic trainer, like all other care professionals, is to provide a high standard of care, not to accept all of the responsibility for achieving goals.

Physically active individuals like supervision by a certified athletic trainer during their rehabilitation (Fisher and Hoisington 1998; Fisher et al. 1993). The presence of a certified athletic trainer during rehabilitation encourages individuals to do what is expected of them. In a busy athletic training room, however, daily supervision is not always possible. Furthermore, in the current managed care environment, most people treated in a sports medicine clinic must be willing to comply with a program of independent or home-based exercises due to limitations on the number of covered treatments sessions. Thus, you must effectively teach and convey the importance of the exercise program.

To increase adherence to a home exercise program, you can (1) have the individual perform each exercise before leaving the sports medicine clinic, (2) provide written instructions as well as illustrations, (3) provide an exercise log to record performance, and (4) have the individual demonstrate the exercise program at the beginning of the next treatment session. Proper performance of the exercise program should be positively reinforced. If an injured person is unable to complete the exercise program, he or she has not complied with the plan of care. In this situation you must first reconsider the appropriateness of the program. If some exercises increased pain or were beyond the individual's capacity, the exercise program must be modified. However, if the individual has no specific complaints about the exercise program, a nonjudgmental review of the exercise should

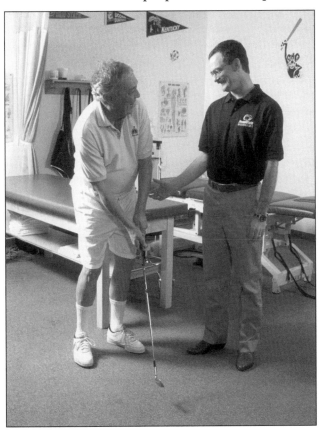

▌Figure 2.4 The injured individual should be actively involved in establishing goals if the rehabilitation plan of care is to be successful.

dominate the treatment session. Failure to successfully complete the exercise program on the next return visit is strong evidence that the person is unwilling or unable to accept responsibility for getting better. Although this type of person is frustrating to work with, remember that it is the individual's problem, not yours.

FOCUS ON TODAY

The longer a rehabilitation plan will require to complete, the more imposing the task appears. Individuals can get lost in the big picture of their rehabilitation and lose focus and motivation. Thoughts can become irrational and catastrophic in nature. "I will never be able to play again," is sometimes heard from the individual who is frustrated by the pace of recovery and anxious about the future. You can help the physically active work through these problems by focusing on what can be accomplished today. Successful rehabilitation requires a lot of small accomplishments, not a miracle cure. Focus the injured person on the short-term goals to be achieved today or this week. Be patient and empathetic. Use thought stopping and positive imagery as well as examples of successful outcomes to combat irrational thinking and assist the individual during periods of frustration and doubt. For example, following a lateral ankle sprain, a soccer player becomes frustrated by his slow return to full weight bearing. His thought, "I will never be able to play again," is "stopped" and replaced with, "Rehabilitation takes time; Bobby hurt his knee badly last year but is now playing better than ever." The soccer player is encouraged to stop negative thinking, replace negative thoughts with positive ones, and envision his return to top-level play.

MINIMIZE SUFFERING

Pain is a universal human experience and a signal that something is wrong. Pain is usually what causes people to seek medical care. Although nearly all humans experience pain, the psychological and emotional response is very individual. One of the challenges in health care is understanding each individual's response in relation to the severity of the injury or illness.

Pain control is almost always the first goal in a comprehensive rehabilitation plan. Many of the therapeutic modalities discussed in this book have analgesic (pain-relieving) effects. Through a professional and empathetic demeanor and effective initial treatment (including pain control), the certified athletic trainer can build a bond of trust with the injured individual. If the athletic trainer fails to decrease the person's pain during the first one to two treatments, adherence with the rehabilitation program may decline or the individual may seek care elsewhere.

Physically active people often have a different perspective on pain than non-active people, which has important implications for the certified athletic trainer. Physically active people view the pain experienced in training and conditioning as a challenge to be overcome. Thus, during rehabilitation, these people may have difficulty differentiating pain due to irritation of healing tissues (bad pain) from the pain of strenuous effort (good pain) and may be overly aggressive in rehabilitation. You must help physically active individuals interpret whether the pain they are experiencing during and after rehabilitation indicates further tissue injury, which will ultimately slow their recovery.

Physically active people are very attuned to their bodies. The self-inflicted pain of conditioning is expected and tolerated. However, the same is not true of the pain associated with medical procedures and rehabilitation. Byerly and colleagues (1994) reported that the more pain athletes experienced during their rehabilitation, the less they adhered to their plan of care. Athletes, however, reported that pain during therapeutic exercise was less of a deterrent to rehabilitation adherence than athletic trainers perceived it to be (Fisher and Hoisington 1998). Thus, you must monitor the rehabilitation plan closely and make modifications when self-reported pain affects compliance. Athletes and athletic trainers agree that an accurate appraisal of the pain to be experienced is important to adherence with a plan of care. Discuss issues related to pain with your clients honestly and with empathy. Individuals who feel they are suffering without need will not comply with a plan of care and will often seek treatment elsewhere.

Finally, although each individual responds differently to pain and injury and these individual differences should be respected, physically active people are generally more willing to begin and progress through a rehabilitation plan. This is important for the certified athletic trainer used to working with highly competitive athletes, who may encounter relatively less active people in a clinical environment. Physically active people like to exercise, want to exercise, and feel comfortable with exercise. The differences between physically active and sedentary individuals are great. The sedentary person often struggles to learn therapeutic exercises, views exercise as a chore rather than a means of recovery, and stops at the slightest discomfort or exertion. These patients require greater instruction and supervision as well as patience on the part of the health care provider. You must be sensitive to the lower tolerance of pain and effort as well as the greater need for positive reinforcement and encouragement in less active people.

BARRIERS TO SUCCESSFUL REHABILITATION

Injured physically active and relatively nonactive individuals present to the certified athletic trainer with personal and psychological issues that can impact their successful completion of rehabilitation. Sometimes you can help physically active individuals overcome these barriers by building a bond of trust and simply caring and listening. Sometimes you can identify someone who would benefit from psychological or psychiatric care. Unfortunately, there are some barriers to successful rehabilitation that you cannot change. It is important to remember that the patient has the problem and not to become physically and emotionally exhausted trying to change what you cannot. This section identifies some of the barriers to successful rehabilitation common to physically active as well as nonactive people.

SECONDARY GAIN

A physically active individual whose performance has not lived up to expectations may find solace in that fact he or she tried to play while hurt but could not. Another individual may avoid the wrath of coaches or the media through a slow recovery. Others may use an injury to gain freedom from a sport in which they no longer wish to participate. In some cases, the individual may perceive that there is more to be gained by not getting better.

Secondary gain relates to tangible and intangible rewards received following injury. The notion of secondary gain is more associated with automobile accident victims with pending civil litigation or injured workers receiving nearly full salary while away from a job they dislike. However, there are many forms of secondary gain. Illness and injury can alter how others interact with a person. The injured person may gain additional attention from parents and others, may be relieved of some responsibilities at home, work, or school, or may experience other "positive" responses to injury. In some situations, the rewards of being ill or injured outweigh the rewards of returning to health.

The pursuit of secondary gain may be a poorly disguised conscious effort or a more subtle behavioral pattern. There is no single solution to treating the individual who can gain from slow progress or failure. Most work their way "through the system." You must not label someone as a malingerer without thoroughly reviewing the case (see chapter 5) yet must also guard against self-doubt and a sense of failure when those with more to gain by being injured do not respond to appropriate care.

SUBSTANCE USE AND ABUSE

Alcohol and drug abuse continues to be a significant problem in our society. The media have reported on numerous athletes facing substance-abuse problems. Collegiate athletes also tend to consume more alcohol than the average nonathletic student (Nattiv and Puffer 1991; Anderson et al. 1991; Carr, Kennedy, and Dimick 1990). Substance abuse decreases adherence to rehabilitation in general and especially affects performance of self-care and home exercise programs. Substance abuse is a sensitive issue, and few certified athletic trainers receive adequate training in the recognition, not to mention treatment, of this problem. It is a problem most certified athletic trainers do not want to confront. Drug and alcohol use increases the risk of, and impairs recovery from, injury. Thus, members of the sports medicine team should be trained to identify substance abuse, and a plan for physician involvement and appropriate treatment referral should be implemented to assist those with substance abuse problems.

SOCIAL AND ENVIRONMENTAL BARRIERS

Injuries require adjustments in daily routine. Rehabilitation based in both the athletic training room and the sports medicine clinic utilizes special equipment and requires a time commitment from the physically active individual. Some individuals will find it difficult to adhere to a rehabilitation plan because of personal commitments, time demands, and lack of access to equipment and facilities. Certified athletic trainers in college and high school settings may be less affected by these barriers to successful rehabilitation than clinic-based athletic trainers, but all athletes present with unique circumstances that favor or deter successful rehabilitation.

Many physically active individuals live in rural areas without a convenient sports medicine clinic. Their local schools have very limited training facilities, and the nearest fitness club is usually many miles away. Because they have to travel considerable distances to the sports medicine clinic, they may be unable to attend formal therapy sessions as often as they and their physicians would like. Creative home exercise programs must be developed for these people to overcome the lack of equipment, facilities, and hands-on care (figure 2.5).

Similarly, individuals with family and work responsibilities may be less compliant with rehabilitation because they lack support from others who can assume some of their responsibilities. You must account for these limitations as you develop a plan of care. Sometimes you will have to modify a program to meet the individual's needs and accept that the rate of progress may be slower. The injured individual must believe that she or he will be able to complete the rehabilitation program. If the plan of care conflicts with the time and energy available, the individual probably will not adhere to the rehabilitation plan.

In the traditional setting, injury often also results in separation from a team and the loss of social support.

© iPhotoNews.com

■ Figure 2.5   Some physically active individuals will find it difficult to adhere to a rehabilitation plan of care. Creative plans must be developed to fit the individual's needs.

The certified athletic trainer and the injured athlete's coach should explore ways to keep the athlete involved with the team, which will maximize support from peers and minimize disruption of the athlete's daily routine.

DEPRESSION, ANXIETY, AND SLEEP DISTURBANCES

People who suffer serious injuries may develop concomitant problems related to depression and anxiety. These problems and persistent pain alter sleep patterns, which further depletes the individual's energy and coping resources.

Depression affects many people at some time in their lives. It is estimated that 5% to 7% of the general population is suffering clinical depression at any one time. This rate is increased in injured persons and in patients following spinal cord injury, stroke, and heart attack. Depression is not a normal stage in the psychological response to injury but can be a significant barrier to successful rehabilitation (Wegener 1999).

Signs and symptoms of depression are discussed in more detail in chapter 5 in relation to persistent pain and somatization. The certified athletic trainer usually interacts with the injured individual more than do other members of the sports medicine team and is, therefore, in a position to recognize these signs. Depression is a treatable psychological illness that deserves medical attention. However, there is a stigma in our society regarding psychological conditions. When depression affects an individual's rehabilitation efforts, the sports medicine team must strive to provide the psychological care needed. Failure to recognize and treat depression will delay or prevent successful recovery from injury and a return to sports participation.

Anxiety disorders are characterized by excessive worry. The incidence of anxiety disorders is believed to be less than that of depression, and the effect of injury on the incidence of anxiety disorders is unknown. It is normal for an injured person to be anxious about the impact of the injury on her or his ability to participate, advancement on a team, or potential for scholarship or professional opportunities. However, extreme and unfounded worry can lead to sleep disturbances and adversely affect rehabilitation adherence. Informal counseling and relaxation techniques can be very effective in controlling anxiety. However, if someone continues to struggle, referral for psychological care is essential.

Depression, anxiety, and pain affect sleep. Anxiety is most associated with sleep onset problems, pain with midsleep awakening, and depression with early awakening (Wegener 1999). Regardless of the cause, a sleep disturbance affects a person's mood and general vitality.

Case Study

A physically active man in his mid-50s was diagnosed with shoulder impingement syndrome and sought care at a sports medicine center. He was always attentive and complied with his rehabilitation plan of care but often seemed impatient and easily agitated. His primary complaint upon initial evaluation was that his shoulder pain awakened him several times each night. In fact, the effect of the pain on his sleeping over the previous 2 months had caused him to seek care from an orthopedic surgeon. The rehabilitation plan of care did not relieve the shoulder pain. A magnetic resonance image (MRI) revealed a tear of the rotator cuff. Surgery performed to repair the damaged rotator cuff resulted in near complete relief of pain within a week. He was pleased because he could now get a full night's sleep. The difference in his mood was dramatic. He was far more pleasant and easygoing, and his wife commented that he was "his old self." This physically active man was not, in the opinion of the medical staff, depressed or overly anxious. However, the sleep disturbance resulting from the persistent shoulder pain was a significant issue. Sleep disturbances due to persistent pain can increase the risk for clinical depression. You should inquire about the impact of injury and persistent pain on sleep and recognize long-term sleep disturbance as a barrier to successful rehabilitation as well as a risk factor for depression.

CLINICAL OUTCOMES AND EFFICACY OF THERAPEUTIC MODALITIES

Very few clinical outcomes data are available to substantiate the efficacy of therapeutic modalities and other interventions used in athletic training or physical therapy. Historically, athletic trainers have used treatment strategies that "appear to work." As athletic trainers have shared their experiences with one another, new approaches to injury management have evolved. The treatments used by athletic trainers have received little scrutiny from health care providers outside of athletic training or from athletic trainers themselves. There can be four reasons for this phenomenon.

The first is simply cost and complexity. Good outcomes studies are difficult to conduct, largely due to the difficulties of controlling for the psychosocial issues discussed previously.

Second is the natural history of most musculoskeletal injuries. The vast majority of musculoskeletal injuries sustained by physically active individuals will resolve over time without treatment. Intervention by the sports medicine team provides the individual with information about the nature of the injury, symptomatic relief, and guidance regarding activity restriction. Additionally, the sports medicine team can often safely return the physically active person to sport while tissues heal. The sports medicine team cannot, however, speed tissue repair and maturation.

The third reason for the lack of study of therapeutic interventions is that the treatments administered by certified athletic trainers are administered safely. Greater investigation into the use of therapeutic modalities by certified athletic trainers has not been triggered, because there are few reports of injury during treatment by certified athletic trainers. The education of certified athletic trainers has resulted in well-prepared health care providers who practice safe treatment techniques.

The fourth reason for the lack of inquiry into the treatments administered by athletic trainers is that in traditional settings, care is free to the athlete. Thus, there is no scrutiny from third-party payers asking for evidence of effective treatment.

This situation is changing. Because we better understand the pathophysiology of musculoskeletal injury and the physiology of tissue repair, some long-held beliefs about the ability of modalities to facilitate healing have been challenged. Judgments about the efficacy of individual modality applications, therapeutic exercises, or rehabilitation plans of care are increasingly being based on studies that control for no treatment or studies that control for crossover effects of other treatments or modalities. Questions are being raised about the use of some therapeutic modalities (Denegar et al. 1992; Penderghest, Kimura, and Gulick 1998) and the need for extensive, supervised rehabilitation (Cherkin et al. 1998; Decarlo and Sell 1997). Researchers are studying which modalities promote the achievement of therapeutic goals, for which conditions treatments are most effective, and when and how frequently treatments should be applied. These investigations are complex; it is difficult to find a necessary number of similar patients to test treatment efficacy, and it is difficult to separate the effects of various components of a treatment plan. However, evidence is emerging that some modalities do not have the effects that they were once believed to have.

Because of these efforts, certified athletic trainers will be able to use their time and resources more effectively to provide optimal care in terms of cost and benefit. These efforts may also relieve some of the stress experienced by overworked athletic training staffs in overcrowded athletic training facilities. However, much of the research has focused on return to activities of daily living or work. The demands of sports are different from those of daily life, and athletes are motivated by the desire to compete. To examine the impact of athletic training services on return to sport, certified athletic trainers must assess outcomes. If we fail to do so, research involving the return of nonactive individuals to daily activities and work will be generalized to treatment of the physically active and will decrease the effectiveness of sports medicine care for this population.

A WORD ABOUT PLACEBO

The vast majority of people treated by certified athletic trainers and physical therapists believe that treatments with therapeutic modalities and other interventions enhanced their recovery from injury. This observation can be explained by the natural history of most musculoskeletal injuries and the known benefits of treatment with therapeutic modalities and exercise. There is, however, another influence the certified athletic trainer can use to help the injured athlete: placebo. *Placebo*, derived from the Latin "I will please" (Miller-Keane 1992), is a powerful influence on therapeutic interventions but is difficult to measure. Placebo is often thought of as a positive response to an inactive intervention such as providing a sugar pill in lieu of a real medication. However, bona fide interventions have a placebo effect. Believing that a medication or treatment will help can benefit the individual.

Placebo is not a treatment effect on gullible or unstable patients. It is a very real, positive mind–body response. The certified athletic trainer who can alleviate the injured person's anxiety by accurately assessing the nature and severity of an injury and establishing a plan for recovery builds a bond of trust. When the certified athletic trainer and the individual believe in the chosen treatment course, there is a high probability of success. How much of an individual's response is due to treatment and how much to placebo? We do not know and can only say that a placebo effect is surely at work to some degree. Is a placebo effect bad? Absolutely not; the placebo effect helps people feel better and recover. In fact, today's managed care system, with its lack of personal touch and empathy, suffers from the loss of placebo.

Certainly, certified athletic trainers should continue to study the effects of treatments and rehabilitation programs. However, we should also remember the power of placebo and view it as a positive influence on recovery.

SUMMARY

1. *Compare and contrast the contemporary stage model and biopsychosocial model of psychological response to injury.*

   The psychological response to injury has been described as occurring in stages, based on Kubler-Ross's work on death and dying. More recent literature suggests that the psychological response to injury is highly individual. Individuals do not experience all of the psychological responses described by Kubler-Ross, and the characteristics of the psychological response do not progress in ordered stages.

2. *Discuss the impact that cognitive appraisal can have upon the athlete's psychological and emotional response to injury.*

   The biopsychosocial model of psychological response to injury holds that an individual's understanding of the nature of the injury, its severity, and the prognosis, as well as other factors, alters the psychological response. Thus, cognition, or knowing about and understanding the injury, modifies the psychological response following that injury.

3. *Identify influences over an individual's ability to cope with an athletic injury.*

   Multiple factors influence an individual's ability to cope with an athletic injury. Some, such as the tendency to worry and overreact, are intrinsic. Others, such as stresses from school, family, and athletic responsibilities and support from friends, family, teammates, and caregivers, are extrinsic. The sports medicine team cannot control all of these influences but can help individuals cope more effectively by identifying those who are struggling and the factors contributing to their stress.

4. *Identify factors that improve an athlete's adherence to a rehabilitation plan.*

Adherence to a rehabilitation plan can be enhanced by building rapport with the injured person, setting appropriate short- and long-term goals, establishing the injured person's responsibility to the rehabilitation program, focusing on the task at hand rather than the long haul, and minimizing the individual's suffering.

5. *Identify common barriers to successful completion of a rehabilitation plan.*

Multiple factors are barriers to successful rehabilitation. Secondary gain, in terms of money or avoidance of situations or responsibilities, affects the rehabilitation process. Substance abuse, depression, anxiety, and sleep disturbances also impede rehabilitation. Family and work responsibilities and inconvenience of location or timing of appointments deter the progress of many individuals, especially those outside of high school and university settings.

6. *Discuss assessment of treatment outcomes in the context of natural history, placebo, and "true" treatment effect.*

It is very difficult to determine the true effects of treatments with therapeutic modalities. Most musculoskeletal injuries sustained by physically active people heal with time, allowing return to full athletic participation. In addition, a placebo response is common following treatment by medical and allied medical professionals. Extensive investigation is needed to identify which therapeutic modalities facilitate achievement of treatment goals and speed the rehabilitation process.

CITED REFERENCES

Anderson WA, Albrecht RR, McKeag DB, Hough DO, McGrew CA: A national survey of alcohol and drug use by college athletes. *Physician Sportsmed* 19:91-104, 1991.

Byerly PN, Worrell T, Gahimer J, Domholdt E: Rehabilitation compliance in an athletic training environment. *J Athl Train* 29:352-355, 1994.

Carr CN, Kennedy SR, Dimick KM: Alcohol use among high school athlete: A comparison of alcohol use and intoxication in male and female athletes and non-athletes. *J Alcohol Drug Educ* 36:39-43, 1990.

Cherkin DC, Deyo RA, Battie M, Street J, Barlow W: A comparison of physical therapy, chiropractic manipulation and provision of an educational booklet for treatment of patients with low back pain. *New Engl J Med* 339:1021-1029, 1998.

DeCarlo MS, Sell KE: The effects of number and frequency of physical therapy treatments on selected outcomes of treatment in patients with anterior cruciate ligament reconstruction. *J Orthop Sports Phys Ther* 26:332-339, 1997.

Denegar CR, Yoho AP, Borowicz AJ, Bifulco N: The effects of low-volt microamperage stimulation of delayed onset muscle soreness. *J Sport Rehabil* 1:95-102, 1992.

Fisher AC, Hoisington LL: Injured athletes' attitudes and judgments toward rehabilitation adherence. *J Athl Train* 28:43-47, 1998.

Fisher AC, Scriber KC, Matheny ML, Alderman MH, Bitting LA: Enhancing athletic injury rehabilitation adherence. *J Athl Train* 28:312-318, 1993.

Gieck J: Psychological considerations in rehabilitation. In Prentice WE (Ed), *Rehabilitation Techniques in Sports Medicine*. St. Louis, Mosby, 1990, 107-121.

Kubler-Ross E: *On Death and Dying*. New York, Macmillan, 1969.

Locke E, Latham GP: The application of goal setting in sports. *J Sport Psychol* 7:205-211, 1985.

Miller-Keane Encyclopedia & Dictionary of Medicine, Nursing and Allied Health, 5th ed. Philadelphia, Saunders, 1992.

Nagi SZ: Some conceptual issues in disability and rehabilitation. In Sussman MB (Ed), *Sociology and Rehabilitation*. Washington, DC, American Sociological Association, 1965, 100-113.

Nattiv A, Puffer JC: Lifestyles and health risks of collegiate athletes. *J Fam Pract* 33:585-594, 1991.

Penderghest CE, Kimura IF, Gulick DT: Double-blind clinical efficacy study of pulsed phonophoresis on perceived pain associated with traumatic tendinitis. *J Sport Rehabil* 7:9-19, 1998.

Wegener ST: *Current Concepts and Clinical Approaches in Psychology of Rehabilitation.* Paper presented at the National Athletic Trainers' Association 49th Annual Meeting and Clinical Symposia, Baltimore, MD, June 17, 1998, and the 50th Eastern Athletic Trainers' Association Annual Meeting, January 11, 1999.

Worrell TW, Reynolds NL: Integrating physiologic and psychological paradigms into orthopaedic rehabilitation. *Orthop Phys Ther Clin North Am* 3:269-289, 1994.

Yukelson D, Heil J: Psychological considerations in working with injured athletes. In Canavan PK (Ed), *Rehabilitation in Sports Medicine.* Stamford, CT, Appleton & Lange, 1998, 61-70.

ADDITIONAL SOURCES

Davis CM: *Patient Practitioner Interaction.* Thorofare, NJ, Slack, 1989.

Heil J: *Psychology of Sport Injury.* Champaign, IL, Human Kinetics, 1996.

Porter K, Foster J: *The Mental Athlete.* New York, Ballantine Books, 1986.

Purtillo R: *Health Professional and Patient Interaction*, 4th ed. Philadelphia, Saunders, 1990.

CHAPTER THREE

Tissue Injury, Inflammation, and Repair

OBJECTIVES

After reading this chapter, the student will be able to

1. describe the role of the inflammatory response in tissue healing;

2. identify key events in the acute inflammatory, repair, and remodeling phases of tissue healing;

3. identify the causes of chronic inflammation;

4. describe the events and controlling chemical mediators of the acute inflammatory response;

5. discuss the relationship between the signs and symptoms and the physiological events characteristic of the acute inflammatory response; and

6. discuss the physiological events responsible for swelling associated with tissue injury and treatment strategies for swelling.

A soccer player is assisted into the athletic training room. You and the team physician examine the player, finding that she has a Grade II sprain of the tibial collateral ligament. The physician believes that the athlete can return to soccer participation in about 6 weeks. Initially the athlete is placed in a knee immobilizer and instructed to partially bear weight using crutches. She is advised to use ice several times each day to control pain. After a few days the knee is much less painful, and gentle active range-of-motion exercises and quadriceps setting with straight leg raises are initiated. Biofeedback with electromyography (EMG) is used to improve neuromuscular control of the quadriceps. Once active, pain-free range of motion is restored, open and closed chain resistance exercises are added to the program. After 4+ weeks the athlete has full motion and strength, and stress testing of the injured ligament reveals no pain or laxity. The athlete is cleared to begin an aggressive, sport-specific program of exercises in preparation for return to top competition. What physiological events will take place over these 6 weeks as the injury is repaired? Can treatment interventions speed tissue healing? When does the tensile strength of the injured ligament return to normal?

As illustrated in the soccer player's case, understanding the physiology of inflammation and applying therapeutic modalities accordingly will best meet the needs of physically active individuals and facilitate their return to activity. Tissue injury triggers an elaborate response by the body to remove injured tissue and repair the damage. Inappropriate treatment can delay or even halt repair. This chapter provides an overview of events from the time of tissue damage until tissue repair and maturation are completed.

HEALING TISSUES AND INFLAMMATION: AN OVERVIEW

Damage to the body's tissues initiates a series of events that remove damaged tissue, provide the necessary materials for repair, and result in the maturation of new tissue. This process can take days, weeks, or many months. The specific tissue damaged, the severity of the damage, and the overall health of the individual determine the length of time required for healing. Regardless of the time frame, the events that result in tissue healing occur in order and are mediated by the same controlling factors.

Inflammation is the body's mechanism to remove damaged tissue, which is essential for tissue healing. Pain, loss of function, heat, redness, and swelling are the cardinal signs of inflammation, indicating that an injury has occurred and the body has begun healing.

Inflammation occurs in vascularized tissue in response to tissue injury; avascular or poorly vascularized tissue will not heal. Injury to the inner margins of the menisci is a good example. These tissues will not heal and must be resected from the knee if joint dysfunction occurs. The inflammatory response is nonspecific to cause, tissue type, or location; the same events occur under the influence of the same mediators during inflammation. This is in contrast to the body's immune response, which is highly specialized. Inflammatory and immune responses work together to defend the body against diseases and promote recovery after injury, although the inflammatory response to musculoskeletal injury is better understood than the immune system response. The inflammatory response is also responsible for the symptoms that cause the athlete to seek medical attention and thus protect the injured tissues.

The inflammatory response described in this chapter is based on a model of musculoskeletal injury. Inflammation occurs in response to other conditions, including infections, autoimmune diseases, illnesses, and exposure to chemical and particulate irritants. Some of these causes are discussed later in the chapter under Chronic Inflammation.

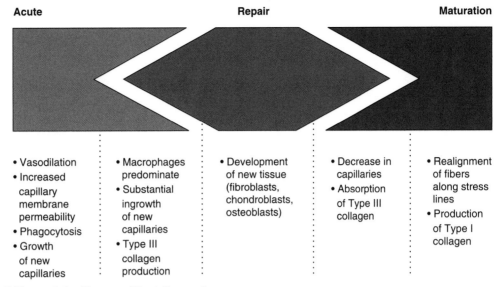

Acute   Repair   Maturation

- Vasodilation
- Increased capillary membrane permeability
- Phagocytosis
- Growth of new capillaries

- Macrophages predominate
- Substantial ingrowth of new capillaries
- Type III collagen production

- Development of new tissue (fibroblasts, chondroblasts, osteoblasts)

- Decrease in capillaries
- Absorption of Type III collagen

- Realignment of fibers along stress lines
- Production of Type I collagen

■ **Figure 3.1**   Phases of the inflammatory response.

The healing process (or inflammatory response) can be divided into three phases: acute, repair, and maturation. The three phases are not distinct, separate processes but are overlapping events. Figure 3.1 illustrates the overlap of events occurring at each phase of the inflammatory response. Because the phases have different regulatory mechanisms and purposes, we will explore each phase individually.

ACUTE PHASE OF THE INFLAMMATORY RESPONSE

Immediately following injury, the body mounts an acute inflammatory response to remove debris and allow growth of new capillaries that will transport the materials needed for tissue repair. The acute inflammatory response begins within seconds of the injury and may last up to several days depending on the severity of tissue damage.

The acute inflammatory response is initiated and controlled by chemicals released from cells or activated plasma proteins. Some of the chemical mediators of the acute inflammatory response stimulate free nerve endings and cause pain, which results in muscle spasm and triggers the body's protective mechanisms. Muscle spasm can cause more pain, resulting in a cycle of pain and spasm and a loss of function, which affects the individual's ability to be physically active. Modalities are generally applied during the acute response to injury or in the treatment of persistent pain. If healing tissues can be protected, the certified athletic trainer can speed the individual's recovery by interrupting the pain–spasm cycle and restoring functional ability.

Other chemical mediators cause an opening of the capillary beds called vasodilation. The increase in blood flow to the area results in redness and warmth over the inflamed tissue. Along with vasodilation, the walls of the capillary become more permeable, allowing plasma proteins to leak out. These proteins, along with proteins from the walls of the cells damaged in the injury, attract water. Thus, there is more water in the space between the cells, which causes swelling.

When injury occurs, small-diameter vascular structures (capillaries, arterioles, and venules) are damaged. Larger vascular structures (arteries and veins) may also be injured, which results in a loss of blood volume and can be life threatening. Fortunately, most athletic injuries do not damage the large vessels.

The acute inflammatory response lasts until the damaged tissue has been removed and a new capillary network has been formed to support tissue repair. The acute response overlaps with the repair phase but must resolve before the symptoms associated with injury and inflammation fully resolve.

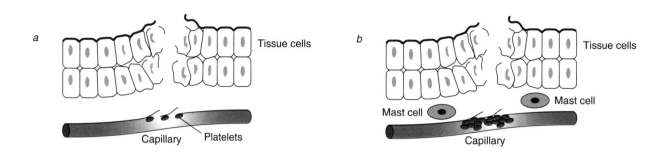

Figure 3.2   Early response to tissue damage. Tissue injury and damage to capillaries and tissue cells *(a)*. Platelet and fibrin repair of capillary damage *(b)*.

EARLY RESPONSES

Within seconds after injury to soft tissues (ligaments, tendons, muscle) or bone (figure 3.2a), platelets adhere to the site of damage in the small blood vessels and pile up. When blood contacts damaged tissues, a complex series of events converts plasma protein fibrinogen to fibrin. Fibrin forms a meshlike network of a clot, which prevents the further loss of red blood cells into the space between cells (interstitium). Epinephrine and substances released from platelets, especially thromboxane A2, result in vasoconstriction. Thus, immediately following tissue damage, the body's defense mechanisms are at work to repair damage to blood vessels and prevent further blood loss (figure 3.2b).

When large blood vessels are injured and the athlete is bleeding externally, the athletic trainer must control bleeding. Compression and elevation can help control external bleeding provided these actions do not cause further injury. If large vessels are damaged and the bleeding is internal, the injured athlete will go into hypovolemic shock. The certified athletic trainer must recognize the signs of shock and immediately stabilize the individual and activate an emergency response plan.

Signs of Shock

- Rapid, weak pulse
- Low blood pressure
- Rapid, shallow breathing
- Cool, clammy skin
- Lethargy

Most musculoskeletal injuries sustained by physically active individuals do not damage large blood vessels. Damage to the small vessels is plugged very rapidly. Athletic trainers used to be taught to immediately apply ice to an injury to control bleeding and thus prevent swelling. Although the application of cold has a place in the management of acute musculoskeletal injuries, cold has little effect on the loss of blood. The body's own mechanisms control blood loss. It is more important to carefully examine the injury than to rapidly apply cold.

The events that limit the loss of blood from small vessels begin within seconds and end in minutes. Once damage to the blood vessels has been plugged, the events of the remainder of the acute response begin. The purpose of acute inflammation is to clear away necrotic tissues and build new capillaries that will provide the nutrients needed for tissue repair. This process is controlled or mediated by a series of chemical events. The mediators of acute inflammation result in the pain, swelling, and loss of function associated with acute injury and inflammation. It is important to appreciate the essential role of these mediators in tissue healing to fully appreciate the impact of anti-inflammatory medications and therapeutic practices.

The events that occur in acute inflammation are complex and can be divided into platelet and mast cell–mediated, plasma protein–mediated, and leukocyte-mediated events. Although these mediating factors are presented separately in this text, they occur simultaneously. However, different stimuli will trigger an inflammatory response through different mediators. For example, mast cell degranulation initiates the inflammatory response following musculoskeletal injury, whereas a bacterial infection will activate the complement cascade of plasma proteins, which in turn activate mast cell degranulation.

PLATELET AND MAST CELL–MEDIATED EVENTS

Mast cells are found in the connective tissues adjacent to many of the capillaries. These cells contain large basophilic granules that contain histamine, serotonin, neutrophil chemotactic factor, and heparin. The platelets described earlier also release histamine and growth factors to help build new capillaries. Mast cells also release prostaglandins and leukotrienes. When surrounding tissues are damaged, the body mounts an immune response, or the mast cells are exposed to toxins or chemical stimulants. The mast cells release the contents of the granules and synthesize prostaglandins and leukotrienes. These chemicals stimulate an inflammatory response.

Histamine is a potent vasodilator and also increases the permeability of the capillary membrane. Neutrophil chemotactic factor attracts neutrophils (a type of white blood cell) to the area of tissue damage. Neutrophils are phagocytes, cells that can engulf and break down damaged tissues. Thus, these two chemical mediators increase local blood flow and bring more neutrophils to the area, allow for them to move from the circulation into the interstitium (space between the cells), and attract them to the site of tissue damage (figure 3.3). These cells then begin to clear away necrotic tissue and set the stage for tissue repair.

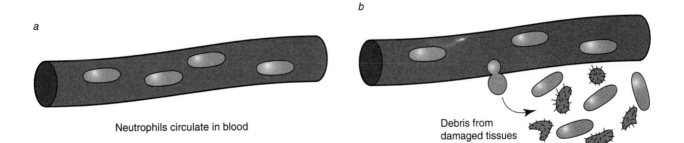

b

a

Neutrophils circulate in blood

Debris from damaged tissues

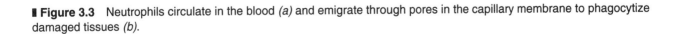

■ **Figure 3.3** Neutrophils circulate in the blood *(a)* and emigrate through pores in the capillary membrane to phagocytize damaged tissues *(b)*.

Serotonin also increases capillary membrane permeability. The increase in capillary membrane permeability is essential to the inflammatory process. Normally the pores in the capillary wall are too small to permit the passage of leukocytes (white blood cells). Thus, the increase in capillary membrane permeability permits the body to remove damaged tissues. Unfortunately, when the capillary membrane permeability increases, many plasma proteins, which are too large to slip into the interstitium under normal conditions, escape. These proteins exert an osmotic (water attracting) force. The fluid these proteins draw into the interstitium accounts for the swelling associated with tissue injury and inflammation. A more in-depth discussion of the causes and resolution of swelling is presented later in this chapter.

Heparin is a strong anticoagulant, a chemical substance that prevents clotting. It is released in small quantities under normal conditions to maintain blood flow into the capillaries. It performs the same function in an acute inflammatory response, ensuring that the neutrophils can reach the damaged tissues.

Prostaglandin E2 (PGE2) is one of many prostaglandins that regulate a variety of physiological functions. PGE2 interacts with histamine to increase capillary membrane permeability. Along with the plasma protein bradykinin, PGE2 stimulates free nerve endings, resulting in the sensation of pain. Evidence of the role PGE2 plays in the sensation of pain is found in the effects of nonsteroidal anti-inflammatory drugs (NSAIDs). All drugs in this class of medications affect the synthesis of PGE2, which is responsible for their analgesic effects.

Leukotrienes are chemicals that attract leukocytes. They are similar to neutrophil chemotactic factor, described earlier. However, leukotrienes are chemotactic to other white blood cells in addition to neutrophils. Basophils, eosinophils, lymphocytes, and macrophages are also leukocytes. Macrophages, which mature from monocytes, are very active in the latter stages of an acute inflammatory response. Basophils, eosinophils, and lymphocytes are involved with the inflammatory responses to invading organisms and toxins. These leukocytes have a more limited role following musculoskeletal injury.

Prostaglandins and leukotrienes are derived from arachidonic acid (figure 3.4). During the transformation from arachidonic acid to stable prostaglandins, free radicals are released (Kerr, Bender, and Monti 1996; Ward, Till, and Johnson 1990). These free radicals activate proteases such as collagenase, which break down adjacent cell membranes (Kerr, Bender, and Monti 1996; Ward, Till, and Johnson 1990) The purpose of the proteases is to break down the membranes of damaged cells; however,

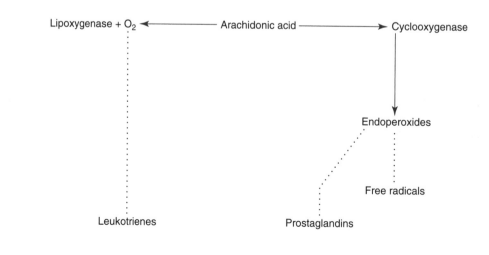

Figure 3.4   Synthesis of leukotrienes and prostaglandins from arachidonic acid.

some surrounding, healthy cells may be damaged by this process, resulting in secondary cell death or a secondary zone of injury.

The chemical mediators released from mast cells are responsible for many of the events associated with the acute inflammatory response (table 3.1). The mediators attract neutrophils and ease the movement of these cells from the blood to the area of tissue damage. The removal of the damaged tissues sets the stage for tissue repair and maturation (figure 3.5).

Table 3.1   Summary of the Mediators, Symptoms, and Purposes of the Acute Inflammatory Response

Mediator	Purpose	Relation to signs of inflammation
Mast cells		
Histamine	Vasodilation	Heat and redness
Serotonin	Increase capillary membrane permeability	Swelling
Heparin	Prevent occlusion of capillary blood flow	No direct relationship
Neutrophil chemotactic factor	Attract neutrophils to phagocytize necrotic tissue	Swelling, indirectly, because increased membrane permeability is required for neutrophil emigration
Prostaglandin E2	Increase capillary membrane permeability	Pain and swelling
Leukotrienes	Attract neutrophils to phagocytize necrotic tissue	Swelling, indirectly, because increased membrane permeability is required for neutrophil emigration
Plasma proteins		
Clotting cascade	Prevent loss of red blood cells	No direct relationship
Kinin cascade	Increase capillary membrane permeability	Pain and swelling
Complement cascade	Facilitate all aspects of acute inflammatory response	Increases all signs of inflammation
Leukocytes		
Cationic proteins	Increase capillary membrane permeability, attract monocytes, promote phagocytosis	Swelling
Neutral proteases	Facilitate all aspects of acute inflammatory response	Increases all signs of inflammation

Neutrophil

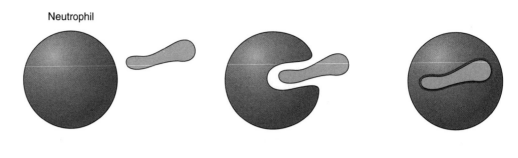

Figure 3.5   Neutrophils and macrophages remove necrotic tissue from wound areas by surrounding and engulfing the dead and damaged material.

PLASMA PROTEIN–MEDIATED EVENTS

Many proteins are found in the plasma, most in inactive states. They may be activated by antigen–antibody responses, bacteria, and chemicals released from damaged cells. The activation of some plasma proteins sets off a chain reaction that activates other plasma proteins. These chain reactions are called protein cascades.

Three protein cascades are associated with the acute inflammatory response. The clotting cascade results in a fibrous framework for tissue repair (figure 3.6). The kinin cascade results in the formation of bradykinin. The complement cascade impacts all aspects of the acute inflammatory response. These protein cascades interact and occur simultaneously with other events of the acute inflammatory response.

The clotting cascade converts the plasma protein fibrinogen to fibrin. Fibrin forms a meshlike web with platelets to temporarily repair damaged vascularized tissues. The first protein in the clotting cascade, Factor XII, or the Hagaman factor, also activates the kinin cascade (figure 3.7), first converting the plasma protein prekallikrein to kallikrein, which then activates the conversion of kininogen to bradykinin. Bradykinin increases capillary membrane permeability and interacts with prostaglandins to stimulate free nerve endings, causing pain.

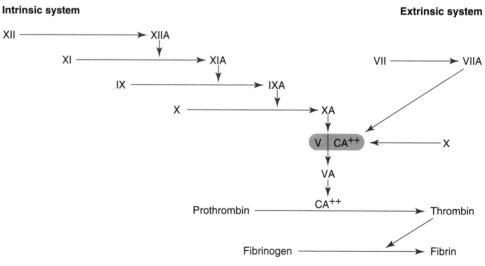

"A" indicates active form of plasm protein

Figure 3.6   Clotting cascade theory. Tissue injury initiates a cascade of events culminating with formation of fibrin.

Adapted from Langley 1974.

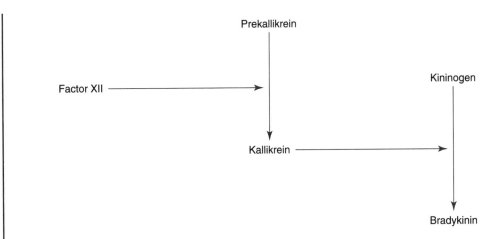

∎ Figure 3.7   Conversion of kininogen to bradykinin.

The complement cascade is a family of plasma proteins that participate in virtually every aspect of the inflammatory response, including lysis (breakdown) of membranes of dead cells, chemical attraction of leukocytes, and increased capillary membrane permeability. The complement cascade also stimulates mast cell degranulation. The complement can be activated by antigen–antibody reactions (such as those occurring in rheumatoid arthritis), proteins of the clotting cascade, and toxins released by bacteria.

The protein cascades function with the chemical mediators released from the mast cells. It should be apparent that these cascades interact. An injury or illness activates one or more cascades. If mast cell degranulation occurs first, it will trigger the plasma protein cascades. If the plasma protein system is activated first, other plasma protein systems will be activated and will stimulate mast cell degranulation. Thus, the inflammatory response is said to be nonspecific. The same events occur regardless of the precipitating stimulus.

LEUKOCYTE-MEDIATED EVENTS

The leukocytes are drawn to the area of inflammation by chemical attraction. Following a musculoskeletal injury, neutrophils are the predominant leukocytes in the area of tissue damage, and these cells begin phagocytizing necrotic tissue.

Oxygen free radicals are also produced by neutrophils (Kerr, Bender, and Monti 1996; Leadbetter 1995; Ward, Till, and Johnson 1990). As noted previously, free radicals activate proteases such as collagenase, which break down adjacent cell membranes. Healthy cells may be damaged by this process, resulting in secondary tissue death. Secondary cell death has been attributed to hypoxia (Knight 1995); however, the vasodilation and increased capillary membrane permeability occurring during the acute inflammatory response suggest adequate oxygenation of tissues. The notion of secondary injury is supported through clinical observations, and it may be better explained by free radical activity. Neutrophils are relatively short lived. When neutrophils die, chemical mediators are released from the lysosomes. Two groups of lysosomal enzymes perpetuate the inflammatory response: cationic proteins and neutral proteases.

Cationic proteins, released from the lysosomes, increase the permeability of capillary membranes and are chemotactic to monocytes. Monocytes are large leukocytes that are capable of phagocytizing much more damaged tissue than neutrophils can. Thus, when neutrophils cannot completely remove damaged tissue, the body has a mechanism to attract larger phagocytic cells. Late in the acute inflammatory response, macrophages are the predominant leukocyte in the area of tissue damage. The large leukocytes are also found in high concentrations in the inflamed joints of people with rheumatoid arthritis; these cells attack the articular cartilage of the joints, resulting in the joint dysfunction associated with this disease.

The other group of lysosomal enzymes released from neutrophils is neutral proteases. The chemical mediators stimulate the complement cascade and the kinin system. Through the lysosomal enzymes, the inflammatory response is perpetuated until the damaged tissues are removed.

REPAIR PHASE OF THE INFLAMMATORY RESPONSE

Repair implies the growth of new tissue. Once injury debris is removed and the vascular network to support tissue growth is in place, repair is well underway. The rate of repair and the type of tissue generated are influenced by several factors. The cell type of the tissue determines the course of the repair process.

Tissues are classified according to the proportion of cells in mitosis (actively dividing) normally present (Martininez-Hernandez and Amenta 1990). Tissues such as the epidermis contain cells that are continuously being replaced, classified as labile cells. Bone marrow and the cells lining the respiratory, gastrointestinal, and genitourinary tracts are also labile cells. Tissues made of labile cells have excellent regenerative capacity.

Stabile cells have less regenerative capacity. Cells that make up the tissues of the liver, pancreas, and kidneys, as well as fibroblasts, osteocytes, endothelial cells, and chondrocytes, are classified as stabile cells. Fibroblasts synthesize collagen and elastin, which are the major components of ligaments and tendon. Osteoblasts, which mature into osteocytes, form bone, and chondroblasts, which mature into chondrocytes, form cartilage. Thus bone and cartilage can regenerate but do so more slowly than tissues made up of labile cells.

Cells that have no regenerative capacity in adults are classified as permanent cells. The nerves of the central nervous system, the lenses of the eyes, and cardiac muscle have no regenerative capacity. Advances have been made in understanding why some tissues lose regenerative capacity after birth, work that has special application in the treatment of spinal cord injuries.

Skeletal muscle has limited regenerative capacity. As with other permanent tissue, large areas of muscle tissue damage are repaired by laying down scar tissue. Scar is made up primarily of collagen formed by fibroblasts. When injury is more limited, such as that associated with delayed onset muscle soreness, satellite cells mature into myofibrils, restoring functional muscle tissues.

Because excessive stress to healing tissues disrupts repair and slows recovery, you must understand how damaged tissues are repaired and the time frame over which repair occurs. In the second chapter of *Therapeutic Exercise for Athletic Injuries*, the repair of musculoskeletal tissues is covered in-depth to provide a foundation for safe, progressive programs of therapeutic exercise.

MATURATION PHASE OF THE INFLAMMATORY RESPONSE

As the repair process progresses, healing tissues are able to withstand greater stresses. As ligaments and tendons heal, Type III collagen is replaced with stronger Type I collagen (Andriacchi et al. 1988). Fiber alignment improves, and the links between fibers become stronger. In bone, new tissue matures and the mineral content increases. The rate at which tissues heal varies, and the skilled athletic trainer progresses each athlete's rehabilitation at a rate that allows healing tissue to adapt. If too much stress is applied too soon, the tissue fails and reinjury occurs. Applying too little stress does not fully prepare the tissues to withstand the demands of sports, and reinjury occurs when the individual returns to activity. In this phase, rehabilitation should progress the physically active individual through a course of functional activity and return him or her to sports participation. The rate of progress will depend on the nature and extent of the injury, the athlete's overall fitness, and the demands of the particular sport.

CHRONIC INFLAMMATION

Normally the symptoms of acute inflammatory response resolve within 3 to 10 days, indicating that repair is well underway. However, in some circumstances the symptoms of acute inflammation persist. The causes of chronic inflammation can be divided into four categories.

Sources of Chronic Inflammation

- Contamination by a foreign body or bacteria
- Invasion of microorganisms that are able to survive within large phagocytes (macrophages) such as the microorganisms responsible for tuberculosis and syphilis
- Antigen–antibody reactions such as those that occur in rheumatic diseases like rheumatoid arthritis
- Constant irritation by mechanical stress or chemical and particulate matter

It is unlikely that an athletic trainer will treat patients with tuberculosis. However, when inflammation persists, the certified athletic trainer must explore the reason. Excessive mechanical stress due to an overly aggressive treatment plan or the individual's failure to comply with instructions to rest the injured area is a common cause of chronic inflammation in athletes. Infection must also be ruled out as a cause of chronic inflammation, even when the skin has not been disrupted. In the sports medicine clinic, the certified athletic trainer may encounter clients with rheumatoid arthritis, a disabling autoimmune disease resulting in destruction of the articular cartilage.

Chronic inflammation can result in chronic pain. The causes and treatments of persistent pain are discussed in chapter 5.

Reviewing the Signs and Symptoms of Inflammation

At this point it may be helpful to review the signs (responses that you must look or test for, such as heat) and symptoms (responses that the athlete must tell you about, such as pain) of acute inflammation and identify why they occur. Heat and redness result from the vasodilation triggered by plasma proteins of the complement cascade and histamine released from mast cells. Pain results from the synthesis of PGE2 and the formation of bradykinin, which in turn stimulate free nerve endings. Other chemical mediators including substance P, which is released from free nerve endings, also cause pain. Finally, mechanical stress due to pressure and swelling contribute to pain. Loss of function is the body's natural response to pain. Muscles contract involuntarily (spasm) to splint and protect the injured area. Thus, the chemical mediators described cause the events that allow the body to clear away damaged tissues and result in the heat, redness, pain, and loss of function associated with inflammation.

SWELLING

Prevention and elimination of swelling used to be dominant themes in the education of athletic trainers. Athletic trainers would apply ice as soon as possible to slow the bleeding that would result in swelling following musculoskeletal injury. Students were also instructed in treatment strategies that supposedly would increase blood flow and reduce the swelling around injured tissues. Over the years, the validity of these treatments has been questioned.

Swelling, a key sign of inflammation, occurs following injury to the bones, ligaments, tendons, and muscles. However, in the absence of injury to large vessels, very few red blood cells are found in the fluid responsible for the increase in tissue volume or swelling. Because of the very rapid vasoconstriction around the tissue damage, the immediate attraction of platelets to the damaged area, and the formation of fibrin, little bleeding into the tissues occurs after the first moments following injury. Thus, applying ice immediately to prevent bleeding has little impact, because the body's natural reactions have bleeding well under control.

However, if the loss of whole blood does not cause swelling, what does? Earlier, the impact of increased capillary membrane permeability was introduced. When capillary membrane permeability increases, leukocytes can enter the area of damaged tissue because these cells are small enough to fit through the pores in the capillary walls. Red blood cells are too large to leak out. However, large numbers of plasma proteins leak out. Proteins exert an osmotic pressure; that is, the proteins attract water. Thus, the increase in proteins in the interstitium and the osmotic pressure the proteins exert are responsible for swelling. Osmotic pressure is caused not only by the proteins that leak from capillaries; the cells of the damaged tissues also have a protein component. When dead cells are broken down, proteins that helped form the cell walls add to the accumulation of free proteins in the interstitium and increase the osmotic pressure.

The increase in free proteins in the interstitium disrupts normal capillary filtration balance, and swelling occurs (figure 3.8). The osmotic force exerted by plasma proteins is essential to the function of the cardiovascular system. Dissolved nutrients and gases are delivered to the tissues by fluid forced into the interstitium by the pressure that plasma exerts against the capillary wall (hydrostatic pressure).

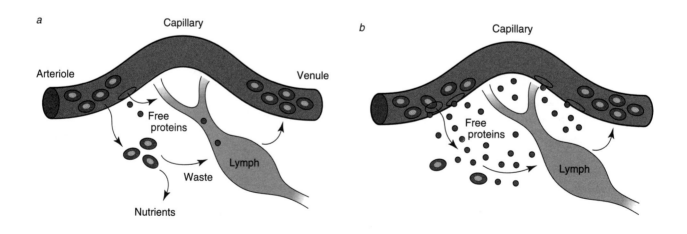

■ **Figure 3.8** Normal capillary filtration pressure balance *(a)* and an increase of free proteins following tissue injury, which disrupts normal capillary filtration pressure balance *(b)*. Free proteins attract water (osmosis), which causes swelling to occur.

However, fluid that is forced from the capillaries must be absorbed or the body would literally burst due to fluid accumulation. Because plasma proteins are large, few pass through the capillary wall. The concentration of protein increases at the venule end of the capillary. These proteins exert an osmotic pressure that pulls fluid and dissolved waste products back into the capillary. This system prevents fluid accumulation while providing a mechanism to deliver nutrients and remove waste from the tissue.

In the normal balance, plasma is forced into the interstitium under hydrostatic pressure. Nutrients are delivered to the cells and waste products removed. Plasma is reabsorbed into capillaries and venules due to osmotic pressure exerted by plasma proteins. In a disrupted process, neutrophils and plasma proteins migrate through capillary membrane pores expanded under the influence of histamine, serotonin, and other chemical mediators. The increased number of free proteins in the interstitium results in an accumulation of fluid (swelling).

A few plasma proteins do leak from the capillaries under normal conditions. These proteins cannot be absorbed into the capillary or postcapillary venule. If they were to accumulate, the osmotic pressure exerted would disrupt normal capillary filtration balance and there would be persistent swelling. However, the lymphatic system parallels the capillary system and absorbs free protein from the interstitium, thus preventing the accumulation of free proteins and chronic swelling.

How does the capillary filtration system relate to the swelling associated with inflammation? As noted previously, several chemical mediators increase the permeability of the capillary membrane. The increased size of pores in the capillary walls allows plasma proteins to leak into the interstitium in large quantities. The proteins left from the lysis of cell membranes add to the protein concentration. The osmotic force exerted by these proteins alters normal capillary filtration pressure balance and results in the retention of interstitial fluid, or swelling.

Can the certified athletic trainer influence how much swelling occurs following injury? By understanding capillary filtration pressure and the function of the lymphatic system, you can identify strategies to minimize swelling. Elevation reduces hydrostatic pressure, so less fluid is forced into the interstitium. External pressure may minimize the osmotic pressure exerted by the free proteins in the interstitium. These strategies should be incorporated into treatment following injury or surgery.

Can the application of therapeutic modalities affect the development of swelling? The effects of ice on the development of swelling have not been fully investigated. Although ice has been used for many years to treat musculoskeletal injuries, its impact on the development of swelling remains speculative. This question is addressed in greater depth in chapter 7. Recent studies have suggested that electrical currents may alter capillary membrane permeability, as discussed further in chapter 8.

Despite efforts to minimize swelling, some fluid will accumulate in the tissues. To eliminate the fluid, the free proteins that are attracting the fluid must be removed. As noted previously, these free proteins are not absorbed back into the capillary or postcapillary venule but must be absorbed by the lymphatic system. Lymph is pumped through lymphatic vessels by the contraction of surrounding muscles. Thus, movement is the best means of pumping lymph from the area surrounding the damaged tissue and stimulating the absorption of free proteins and fluid. However, the activity used to increase lymphatic drainage must not perpetuate the inflammatory process, or more protein will leak from the capillaries.

Do modalities help resolve swelling? Muscle contraction facilitates lymphatic drainage, but muscle spasm limits lymph flow. Thus, modality applications that decrease muscle spasm will promote lymphatic drainage (figure 3.9). However, modalities to increase local blood flow do little to resolve swelling, because the lymphatic, rather than vascular, capillaries absorb the free proteins. Thus, an understanding of capillary

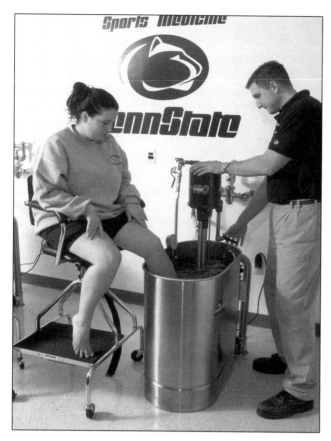

Figure 3.9 Modality applications that decrease pain and muscle spasm and promote active range of motion promote lymphatic drainage and reduce swelling.

filtration pressure tells you why swelling is associated with inflammation, how to speed the resolution of swelling, and what limits prevention strategies.

JOINT EFFUSION

The model described in the previous section explains why swelling occurs following tissue damage. However, sometimes a fluid increase within a joint capsule is unrelated to alterations in capillary filtration pressure balance. The synovial joints are lined by synovial membrane, which produces fluid that lubricates and nourishes joint surfaces. When the synovium is irritated by a loose body or torn meniscus, an excessive amount of fluid is produced. The accumulation of excessive synovial fluid results in joint effusion and impairs the function and normal mechanics of a joint.

If the irritant can be controlled or eliminated, the effusion will resolve more rapidly than swelling due to tissue damage because the synovial fluid contains fewer free proteins. Thus, the vascular system can assist the lymphatic system in absorbing the excess fluid.

SWELLING IN THE LOWER EXTREMITY DUE TO VENOUS INSUFFICIENCY

Some individuals may experience chronic swelling in their feet and ankles but no history of recent trauma. This fluid accumulation is caused by failure of the valves in the leg veins. With age, the one-way valves in the veins fail. Thus, blood in the veins that is normally pumped toward the heart backwashes. This blood exerts a hydrostatic pressure at the postcapillary venule that opposes the absorption of fluid from the interstitium. Thus, fluid accumulates in the tissues and swelling is observed. Because the concentration of free proteins in the interstitium does not increase, this swelling is more easily resolved. Elevating the feet allows gravity to pull venous blood toward the heart, decreases hydrostatic

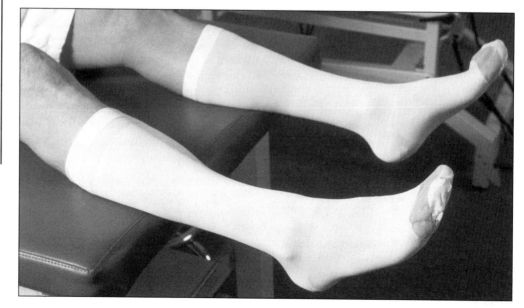

Figure 3.10 The accumulation of fluid in some individuals is caused by failure of the valves in the leg veins. Compression garments can effectively control this type of swelling.

pressure at the venule, and promotes interstitial drainage. The use of a compressive stocking increases the interstitial resistance to fluid loss and can help control edema in the feet and ankles (figure 3.10).

SUMMARY

1. *Describe the role of the inflammatory response in tissue healing.*

   Inflammation is the process by which the body removes damaged tissues and establishes a blood supply to support repair. Once damaged tissues have been removed by the phagocytic cells, damaged tissues regenerate or are repaired with scar tissues.

2. *Identify key events in the acute inflammatory, repair, and remodeling phases of tissue healing.*

   The acute inflammatory response begins with vasoconstriction and clotting. Vasoconstriction results from the actions of epinephrine and thromboxane. The clotting cascade is activated to minimize hemorrhage. This is a rapid and relatively short process. Once further blood loss is prevented, vasodilation and increased capillary membrane permeability allow for the invasion of neutrophils and later macrophages. The cells phagocytize damaged tissue. As phagocytosis occurs, a new network of capillaries is formed to support the repair phase. During repair new tissue is formed by fibroblasts, osteoblasts, or chondroblasts depending on which tissues have been damaged. Over time, stress to new tissues increases tensile strength as remodeling occurs.

3. *Identify the causes of chronic inflammation.*

   Sometimes inflammation does not proceed to repair and maturation, and the body remains in a chronic inflammatory state. There are four general causes of chronic inflammation: contamination by a foreign body or bacteria, invasion of microorganisms, antigen–antibody reactions, and constant irritation by mechanical stress or chemical and particulate matter.

4. *Describe the events and controlling chemical mediators of the acute inflammatory response.*

   The acute inflammatory response can be divided into mast cell–mediated events, plasma protein–mediated events, and leukocyte-mediated events. Chemicals released from the mast cells, including histamine, serotonin, neutrophil chemotaxic factor, and prostaglandins, collectively promote vasodilation and capillary endothelial permeability and cause pain. Plasma proteins from the clotting, kinen, and complement cascades participate in all aspects of the inflammatory response. Cationic proteins and neutral proteases attract macrophages to the area and perpetuate the inflammatory response.

5. *Discuss the relationship between the signs and symptoms and the physiological events characteristic of the acute inflammatory response.*

   The signs and symptoms of acute inflammation include heat, redness, pain, loss of function, and swelling. Heat and redness occur with vasodilation, which is caused by histamine and complement cascade proteins. Pain is caused by irritation of free nerve endings by PGE2, bradykinin, and pressure created by swelling. Loss of function stems from pain. Swelling results from the attraction of water to free proteins accumulating in the interstitium. Normally, very few plasma proteins pass through the capillary membrane. However, several chemical mediators of inflammation increase the permeability of the capillary membrane, allowing plasma protein to escape. In addition, the breakdown of the cell membranes of damaged tissue contributes to the pool of free protein in the interstitium. In short, injury and acute inflammation disrupt normal capillary filtration pressure balance. Interstitial fluid will accumulate until a new pressure balance is reached. Swelling will resolve when free proteins are removed from the interstitium by lymphatic drainage.

6. *Discuss the physiological events responsible for swelling associated with tissue injury and treatment strategies for swelling.*

Swelling results from a disruption of normal capillary filtration pressure balance. Swelling can be minimized through elevation, which decreases capillary hydrostatic pressure, and external compression, which introduces a counterforce to increased interstitial osmotic pressure. Cold application may also limit swelling through vasoconstriction but should be used in combination with compression and elevation for maximum benefit.

CITED REFERENCES

Andriacchi T, Sabiston P, DeHaven K, Dahners L, Woo S, Frank C, Oakes B, Brankd R, Lewis J: Ligament: Injury and healing. In Woo S, Buckwalter JA (Eds), *Injury and Repair of the Musculoskeletal Soft Tissues*. Park Ridge, IL, American Academy of Orthopaedic Surgeons, 1988, 103-128.

Kerr MA, Bender CM, Monti EJ: An introduction to oxygen free radicals. *Heart Lung* 25:200-209, 1996.

Knight KL: *Cryotherapy in Sports Injury Management*. Champaign, IL, Human Kinetics, 1995.

Leadbetter WB: Anti-inflammatory therapy in sports injury. *Clin Sports Med* 14: 353-410, 1995.

Martinez-Hernandez A, Amenta PS: Basic concepts in wound healing. In Leadbetter WB, Buckwalter JA, Gorden SL (Eds), *Sports Induced Inflammation*. Park Ridge, IL, American Academy of Orthopaedic Surgeons, 1990, 25-54.

Ward PA, Till GO, Johnson KJ: Oxygen-derived free radicals and inflammation. In Leadbetter WB, Buckwalter JA, Gorden SL (Eds), *Sports Induced Inflammation*. Park Ridge, IL, American Academy of Orthopaedic Surgeons, 1990, 315-324.

ADDITIONAL SOURCES

Berne R, Levy M: *Physiology*. St. Louis, Mosby, 1988.

Leadbetter WB, Buckwalter JA, Gorden SL: *Sports-Induced Inflammation*. Park Ridge, IL, American Academy of Orthopaedic Surgeons, 1990.

Woo, SLY, Buckwalter JA. *Injury and Repair of Musculoskeletal Soft Tissues*. Park Ridge, IL, American Academy of Orthopaedic Surgeons, 1988.

CHAPTER FOUR

Pain and
Pain Relief

OBJECTIVES

After reading this chapter, the student will be able to

1. describe the multidimensional nature of pain,

2. explain the role of pain in preserving health and well-being,

3. discuss how the pain response can assist in evaluating an injured athlete,

4. describe how pain is sensed and how the "pain message" is transmitted to the central nervous system, and

5. discuss contemporary theories on modulating the pain message in the central nervous system.

A tennis player presents to the athletic training room complaining of severe, well-localized back pain. What questions should you ask to determine the nature of the injury? What are the possibilities?

After evaluating this tennis player, you conclude that the pain and muscle spasm are resulting from hypomobility at one or more lumbar facets. In a subsequent evaluation, a team physician agrees with this assessment. How does the dysfunction at the facet result in pain? The tennis player is angry because the physician tells her that her back will take a few days to respond to treatment and she is unlikely to play in a match this weekend. Is there an emotional response to injury, pain, and dysfunction?

You treat this athlete with TENS and hot packs before performing joint mobilization. How will treatment with these modalities affect the body? The tennis player reports much less pain after treatment with TENS and superficial heat. What mechanisms would explain such a response?

Pain is critical to human survival. Pain causes the injured person to seek medical attention. However, pain is misery, and it limits function. The certified athletic trainer must thoroughly understand pain and the psychological response to pain and loss of function. In this case study, the tennis player's pain brings attention to her injury. Clinical experience and findings of the physical examination guide the physician's prognosis concerning return to competition. Your knowledge of injury, pain, and associated muscle spasm allows for appropriate treatments to minimize suffering and, in this case, speed return to sports.

In the previous chapter, pain was identified as one of the cardinal signs of inflammation. However, pain is far more complex than a symptom caused by the chemical stimulation of free nerve endings. As discussed in the case study, pain is a warning sign that limits function and affects an individual psychologically and emotionally. This chapter addresses the questions that arose from the case study and provides an in-depth review of the anatomy and physiology of pain and the body's pain-relieving mechanisms. The chapter addresses the function, multidimensionality, and physiology of pain and identifies nervous system structures that carry and receive sensory input. Finally, contemporary theories of pain control are described.

WHAT IS PAIN?

Pain is defined by the International Association for the Study of Pain (IASP) as "an unpleasant physical and emotional experience which signifies tissue damage or the potential for such damage" (IASP 1979, p. 249). This definition points to the complexities of the pain experience. Pain is not simply a physical experience. Pain affects the entire organism, altering physical and psychological processes. The certified athletic trainer must appreciate the impact of injury and pain on the athlete and treat from a holistic perspective. Failure to understand the emotional component of pain can affect the relationship between the health care providers and the injured individual and can slow recovery.

Much of the early intervention following injury involves relieving pain. However, despite the unpleasantness associated with pain, it is essential for human survival. Pain can protect the body by warning of impending injury. Pain also signifies that something is wrong. Most people who seek the services of a certified athletic trainer do so because of pain. Inflammation, pain, and loss of function are interrelated. Using therapeutic modalities to decrease pain will facilitate the return of normal movement and function.

The skillful athletic trainer will incorporate questions regarding pain into the interview portion of the physical exam. The answers provided by the athlete narrow the diagnostic possibilities and focus the remainder of the physical exam. Thus, although pain relief is usually the first priority of treatment, the pain experience motivates the injured athlete to seek care and helps the sports medicine team make a diagnosis.

PAIN AND THE PHYSICAL EXAM

Although the physical examination process is discussed in great detail in *Assessment of Athletic Injuries*, the interpretation of pain warrants review in this chapter. When evaluating an injured person, you should ask numerous questions to narrow the diagnostic possibilities. The interview should result in a working diagnosis that is then confirmed or refuted by the physical exam. Questions regarding when and how the injury occurred are obvious. However, you may need to ask follow-up questions to fully interpret the answers and develop a clinical diagnosis.

P-Q-R-S-T

One approach for asking questions about pain follows a *P-Q-R-S-T* format. This is easy to remember, because *P, Q, R, S,* and *T* are the waves of an electrocardiogram.

P is for provocation. Ask how the injury occurred and what activities increase or decrease the pain.

Q is for quality, or characteristics of pain. For example, does the individual experience aching shoulder pain, suggesting impingement syndrome; burning pain, suggesting nerve irritation; or sharp pains, suggesting acute injury?

R is for referral or radiation. Referred pain occurs at a site distant to damaged tissue that does not follow the course of a peripheral nerve. Radiating or radicular pain follows the course of a peripheral nerve. Pain in the jaw and left shoulder is a common referral pattern during a heart attack. Pressure on a nerve due to a herniated intervertebral disc will result in radiating pain.

S is for severity. Judging the severity of pain is subjective, but sometimes one knows that the problem is serious just from the severity of pain.

T is for timing. When does pain occur? Night pain may indicate cancer. Pain in the sole of the foot with the first steps in the morning suggests plantar fasciitis.

Certainly an acute injury with a well-described mechanism of injury will point to a working diagnosis. Trauma leads to fractures, strains, and sprains. The injured physically active person can often describe the instant and mechanism of these injuries. When the athlete cannot identify the moment of injury or a specific mechanism, the response is often dismissed by the athletic trainer.

For example, a baseball pitcher complains of shoulder pain but is unable to identify a specific injury or onset of pain. Further questioning reveals that this athlete's shoulder pain started following a tournament where he pitched three times in 4 days. Injuries with an insidious onset and a poorly defined mechanism narrow the diagnostic possibilities and should not be ignored. This baseball pitcher developed impingement syndrome due to overuse of the throwing muscles. Repetitive microtrauma can injure tendons, cause stress fractures, and lead to conditions such as plantar fasciitis, medial tibial stress syndrome, patellar femoral pain, and, as in this case, glenohumeral impingement syndrome. Thus, understanding the onset of symptoms focuses the injury evaluation and the physical exam.

Other aspects of the pain experience will also help establish the diagnosis. The quality of pain can be difficult to assess, but with experience you will appreciate the difference between the sharp, well-localized pain of a fracture and the diffuse pain associated with myofascial pain syndrome. Pain that radiates within a dermatome indicates pressure on a nerve, and is often caused by injury to an intervertebral disc or a vertebral fracture. Referred pain can be mysterious yet has predictable patterns.

You must be aware of the pattern of referred pain following injury to internal organs or indicating a heart attack. Table 4.1 identifies several medical problems with well-established patterns of referred pain.

Table 4.1   Common Referred Pain Patterns

Problem	Location of pain
Myocardial infarction	Neck, jaw, and left shoulder
Spleen injury	Left shoulder
Appendicitis	Lower abdomen and right groin
Pancreatic injury or pancreatitis	Left shoulder, low back, and middle left abdomen
Cholecystitis (gallbladder)	Right shoulder and midscapular region
Renal (kidney) disorder	Low back and left shoulder
Stomach and upper small intestine (duodenum) disorder	Left shoulder

The severity of pain indicates severity of the problem. If you have a close working relationship with the athlete, it is easier to interpret his or her reaction to pain and injury.

Finally, the timing of the pain can yield clues about the problem. Pain with specific movements or at certain times of the day may be significant. For example, a person suffering from iliotibial band friction syndrome usually complains of pain while climbing stairs or running up and down hills. Plantar fasciitis is almost always very painful upon arising in the morning and weight bearing on the injured foot. Questioning the individual about these issues usually provides a working diagnosis, allowing you to focus and organize the physical exam rather than randomly conduct a series of tests.

SENSORY AND AFFECTIVE–MOTIVATIONAL DIMENSIONS OF PAIN

Melzack (1983) described pain as having a sensory dimension and an affective–motivational dimension. The sensory component relates to what the individual feels. To assess the intensity of pain, you can use simple pain scales, such as asking the individual to rate the pain from 0 = *no pain* to 10 = *worst pain ever*, or a visual analog scale (figure 4.1). More complex assessments involve pain charts (figure 4.2) or a comprehensive questionnaire such as the Pain Disability Index (figure 4.3) to assess the impact of pain on function (Pollard 1984). The more simple scales can be used to quickly assess recovery from injury. The more comprehensive evaluations are more time-consuming but yield valuable insight about persistent and chronic pain. These instruments can also be used to study the effects of therapeutic interventions.

The affective–motivational component of pain relates to the impact of pain on the individual. For example, following injury, pain signifies that something is wrong. However, until the individual understands the severity of an injury and the impact it will have on his or her ability to compete, pain may cause considerable anxiety. Persistent pain can lead to withdrawal and depression, responses that comprise the affective–motivational aspect of pain.

The response to pain is highly individual and can be influenced by several factors, such as previous pain experiences, family and cultural background, and the specific situation. The certified athletic trainer must learn to accept individual differences in pain response and help the injured person cope with pain.

Figure 4.1 Graphic pain rating scale. The individual is asked to describe pain by marking on the line between *no pain* and *unbearable pain.* Pain is quantified by measuring the distance (to the nearest 1/2 cm) from the extreme left to the mark that the individual makes. The length is multiplied by 2, yielding scores from 0 = *no pain* to 24 = *unbearable pain.*

Reprinted from *Journal of Athletic Training* 1992.

Dull ache — Discomfort during activity

Slight pain — Awareness of pain without distress

More than slight pain — Pain that distracts attention during physical exertion

Painful — Pain that distracts attention from routine occupations such as writing and reading

Very painful — Pain that fills the field of consciousness to the exclusion of other events

Unbearable pain — Comparable to the worst pain you can imagine

No pain ———————————————————————————— Unbearable pain

Dull ache · Slight pain · More than slight pain · Painful · Very painful

Figure 4.2 Pain chart. The injured individual uses the figures to show exactly where his or her pain is and where it radiates. As precisely and with as much detail as possible, the individual uses a blue marker to indicate painful areas, a yellow marker for numbness and tingling, a red marker for burning or hot areas, and a green marker for cramping.

Reprinted from Melzack 1983.

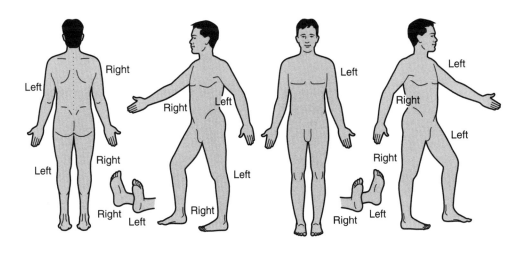

PERSISTENT PAIN

When pain persists or becomes chronic, the affective–motivational component of the pain experience becomes even more significant in evaluation and treatment. Persistent pain affects virtually every aspect of day-to-day life, from sleep patterns, to the ability to concentrate and study, to social and personal relationships. The causes and treatment of persistent pain are presented in depth in chapter 5.

This chapter focuses on the neuroanatomy and physiology of pain, which are relevant to the treatment of persistent pain. However, because of the complexities of the affective–motivational aspects of pain and an incomplete understanding of persistent pain, managing acute and persistent pain can require varied approaches.

PERCEPTION AND SENSATION

The most common use of therapeutic modalities in athletic training is to relieve pain. These modalities alter the neural input transmitted to brain centers where pain

1 *Family/home responsibilities.* This category includes chores and duties performed around the house (e.g., yard work) and errands or favors for other family members (e.g., driving the children to school).

0	1	2	3	4	5	6	7	8	9	10

No disability .... Total disability

2 *Recreation.* This category includes hobbies, sports, and other leisure activities.

0	1	2	3	4	5	6	7	8	9	10

No disability .... Total disability

3 *Social activity.* This category refers to activities involving friends and acquaintances other than family members. It includes parties, theater, concerts, dining out, and other social functions.

0	1	2	3	4	5	6	7	8	9	10

No disability .... Total disability

4 *Occupation.* This category refers to job-related activities, including nonpaying jobs, such as housework or volunteer work.

0	1	2	3	4	5	6	7	8	9	10

No disability .... Total disability

5 *Sexual behavior.* This category refers to the frequency and quality of sex.

0	1	2	3	4	5	6	7	8	9	10

No disability .... Total disability

6 *Self-care.* This category includes activities of personal maintenance and independent daily living (e.g., taking a shower, driving, getting dressed, etc.).

0	1	2	3	4	5	6	7	8	9	10

No disability .... Total disability

7 *Life-support activity.* This category refers to basic life-supporting behaviors, such as eating, sleeping, and breathing.

0	1	2	3	4	5	6	7	8	9	10

No disability .... Total disability

▮ Figure 4.3 Pain disability index. For each category, the injured individual circles the number on the scale that describes the level of disability she or he typically experiences. A score of 0 means no disability at all, and a score of 10 signifies that all of the person's normal activities have been totally disrupted or prevented by pain.

Table 4.2 **Peripheral Sensory Receptors**

Receptor	Classification	Function
Superficial Mechanoreceptors	Meissner's corpuscles Pacinian corpuscles	Pressure and touch
	Merkle cells Ruffini endings	Skin stretch and pressure
Thermoreceptors	Cold receptors Heat receptors	Temperature and temperature change
Nociceptors	Free nerve endings	Pain
Deep Proprioceptors	Golgi tendon organs	Changes in muscle length and muscle spindle tension
	Pacinian corpuscles	Change in joint position Vibration
	Ruffini endings	Joint end range, possibly heat
Nociceptors	Free nerve endings	Pain

perception and response occur. To understand how modalities can alter a pain experience, you must understand the pathways for transmission of painful (noxious) and nonnoxious sensory information.

All information related to our environment and the relationship of our bodies to the environment is transmitted to higher brain centers from peripheral receptors. Sensory receptors can be classified as special, visceral, superficial, or deep. Special receptors provide the senses of sight, taste, smell, and hearing and contribute significantly to balance. Visceral receptors perceive hunger, nausea, distention, and visceral pain. These two groups of sensory receptors have little impact on the perception and response to the pain of musculoskeletal injury.

The superficial receptors (table 4.2) transmit sensations such as warmth, cold, touch, pressure, vibration, tickle, itch, and pain from the skin (Berne and Levy 1993). The deep receptors transmit information regarding position, kinesthesia, deep pressure, and pain from the muscles, tendons, fascia, joint capsules, and ligaments (Berne and Levy 1993). The superficial and deep receptors transmit the impulses that result in the perception of pain following injury. Therapeutic modalities can stimulate some of these receptors to transmit impulses that modify the perception of pain. Thus, the superficial and deep receptors are important to our understanding of pain and pain relief.

SUPERFICIAL RECEPTORS

The superficial receptors, also called cutaneous receptors, can be subdivided into three categories based on the type of stimuli to which they respond: mechanoreceptors, thermoreceptors, and nociceptors. Mechanoreceptors respond to stroking, touch, and pressure. Some of these receptors adapt rapidly and perceive changes in stimulation. The hair follicle receptors, Meissner's corpuscles, and Pacinian corpuscles respond to changes in pressure and touch. In contrast, Merkle cell endings and Ruffini endings, which respond to pressure and skin stretch, are more slowly adapting (Berne and Levy 1993). These receptors respond to sustained stimuli.

Thermoreceptors respond to temperature and temperature change. Cold and warm receptors are slowly adapting but discharge in phasic bursts when the temperature changes rapidly. These receptors respond over a large temperature range. However, warm receptors stop discharging at temperatures that damage the skin. The pain of thermal burn results from the stimulation of free nerve endings and nociceptive afferent pathways. Cold receptors continue to discharge when tissue cooling is perceived as painful. However, cooling slows the conduction velocity of the nerves between the sensory receptor and the spinal cord (Berne and Levy 1993; Knight 1995). Thus, tissue injury due to cold (frostbite) is not particularly painful. However, when the frostbitten tissue thaws, there is considerable inflammation and pain.

Nociceptors form the third category of superficial receptor. Nociceptors, also labeled free nerve endings, are stimulated by potentially damaging mechanical, chemical, and thermal stress. These receptors are also sensitized by prostaglandin, bradykinin, substance P, and perhaps other chemical mediators of the inflammatory response as well as pressure and distention.

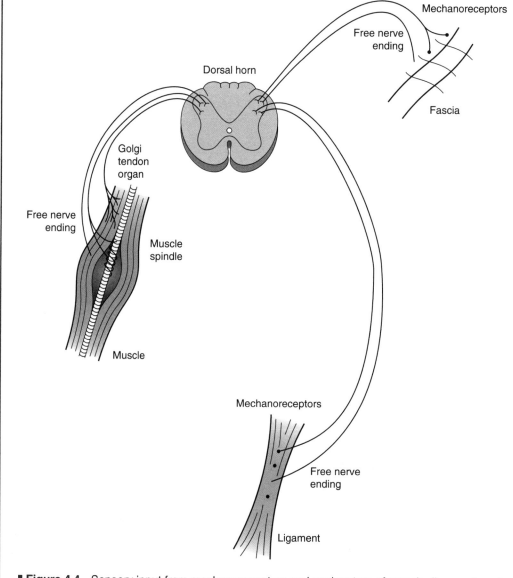

▌Figure 4.4 Sensory input from mechanoreceptors and nociceptors of muscle, ligament, and fascia.

Adapted from Wilmore and Costill 1999.

DEEP-TISSUE RECEPTORS

Ligaments and other deep tissues are supplied by mechanoreceptors (figure 4.4) and nociceptors. In muscle, specialized mechanoreceptors called Golgi tendon organs (GTO) and muscle spindles sense changes in muscle length and tension (figure 4.5). Some muscle receptors may also be sensitive to chemical stimuli.

Joint structures are supplied by rapidly and slowly adapting mechanoreceptors and nociceptors. Pacinian corpuscles adapt rapidly and respond to changes in joint position and vibration. Ruffini end organs (or Ruffini endings) are slowly adapting and are most active at the end of joint range of motion. Nociceptors or free nerve endings signify that motion has exceeded normal limits and that stabilizing structures are at risk of failing or that injury has already occurred.

The body's connective tissue or fascial network is also supplied with sensory receptors. Fascia, the "glue" that holds the body together, surrounds the muscles and organs and literally connects the body from head to toe. The innervation of these tissues has not been fully explored. However, input from mechanoreceptors and nociceptors affects the resting length and tension of muscle and is likely the

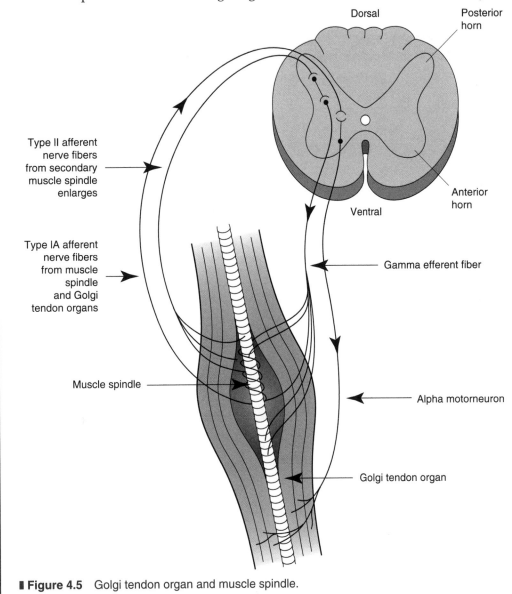

∎ Figure 4.5 Golgi tendon organ and muscle spindle.

Adapted from Wilmore and Costill 1999.

underlying cause of complex pain patterns labeled myofascial pain syndrome, discussed more extensively in chapters 5 and 13.

AFFERENT PATHWAYS

Impulses generated at the sensory receptors are transmitted to higher centers by afferent nerves. The afferent nerves are classified by location. Within some classifications, nerve fibers are subclassified based on structural and functional characteristics. This section presents the classifications and subclassifications you should know to understand pain perception and contemporary theories of modality-induced pain relief.

FIRST-ORDER AFFERENTS

Nerve fibers that transmit impulses from the sensory receptors are classified as first-order or primary afferents. The subclassifications of the first-order afferents are provided in table 4.3. These afferents are classified by type based on whether the nerve fiber is covered with myelin. Type A afferents have a myelin covering, whereas Type C afferents do not.

Table 4.3 First-Order Afferents

Type and group	Diameter (µm)	Conduction velocity (µs)	Location	Information transmitted
Myelinated				
AI	12–20	72–120	Muscle	Length and tension changes within muscle
AII	6–12	36–72	Muscle	Length and tension changes within muscle (from secondary muscle spindle endings), proprioception
A-beta	6–12	36–72	Skin	Touch, vibration
AIII	1–6	6–36	Muscle	Pressure, pain
A-delta	1–6	6–36	Skin	Touch, pressure, temperature, pain
Unmyelinated				
C	< 1	0.5–2	Muscle / Skin	Pain / Touch, pressure, temperature, pain

Reprinted from *Athletic Training Sports Health Care Perspectives* 1996.

The Type A afferents can be further categorized by group based upon fiber diameter, conduction velocity, origin, and function (Berne and Levy 1993). Type A, Group I, II, and III afferents originate from deep receptors. AI fibers are heavily myelinated, fast-conducting fibers that originate from muscle spindles and GTOs. Some AII fibers originate from muscle spindles, and others originate from Pacinian corpuscles of the joint capsules and ligaments. AII fibers are thinner and more slowly conducting than IA fibers. Type AIII afferents originate from free nerve endings and Ruffini endings in the connective tissues. These fibers are even thinner and more slowly conducting than Type AII fibers. The Type A, Group I, II, and III afferents collectively serve the senses of proprioception, kinesthesia, and pain due to deep-tissue damage.

Type A-beta and A-delta afferents originate in the skin. The A-beta fibers originate from hair follicles, Meissner's corpuscles, Pacinian corpuscles, Merkle cell endings, and Ruffini endings and are similar in diameter and conduction velocity to AII fibers. These fibers transmit sensory information regarding touch, vibration, and hair deflection. The A-delta fibers transmit information from warm and cold receptors, a few hair receptors, and free nerve endings. The free nerve endings supplied by A-delta fibers primarily respond to noxious mechanical stimulation such as pinching, pricking, and crushing.

Type C afferents are small, slowly conducting, unmyelinated fibers. Those that originate at deep receptors are primarily mechanoreceptors and nociceptors. A few Type C afferents are thermoreceptors. The C afferents from the superficial receptors also carry input from mechanoreceptors, nociceptors, and thermoreceptors. However, 50% of these fibers are from nociceptors and 30% are from heat and cold receptors.

Primary afferents synapse with second-order afferent fibers in the dorsal horn of the spinal cord or travel to the medulla in the dorsal column of the cord. Type AI and AII afferents project to the nucleus gracilis and nucleus cuneatus in the medulla. These fibers also send off collateral branches that synapse with second-order afferent fibers in the dorsal horn. Type AIII, A-beta, and A-delta, and C fibers synapse in the gray matter of the dorsal horn of the spinal cord (figure 4.6).

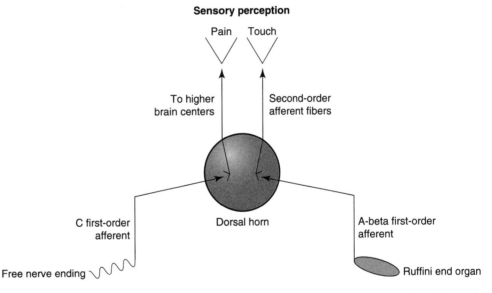

Sensory perception

▌ **Figure 4.6**   Primary afferents synapse with second-order afferent fibers in the dorsal horn of the spinal cord.

ASCENDING PATHWAYS

Multiple pathways or tracts carry sensory input to the brain. There are four pathways in the dorsal spinal cord. The most significant is the dorsal column–medial lemniscus pathway (figure 4.7) (Berne and Levy 1993). This pathway is made up of first-order afferents that ascend directly to the dorsal funiculus in the medulla. This pathway carries sensory input from Meissner's corpuscles, Merkle discs, and Ruffini endings, and it provides proprioceptive, touch-pressure, and vibration information to higher brain centers.

The other dorsal spinal pathways include the spinocervical pathway, the postsynaptic dorsal column pathway, and the dorsal spinocerebellar pathway. The spinocervical pathway carries input primarily from hair follicles. The postsynaptic dorsal column pathway provides input from mechanoreceptors and nociceptors. The dorsal spinocerebellar pathway provides input from the joint receptors of the lower extremity. The fibers in these pathways are second-order afferents.

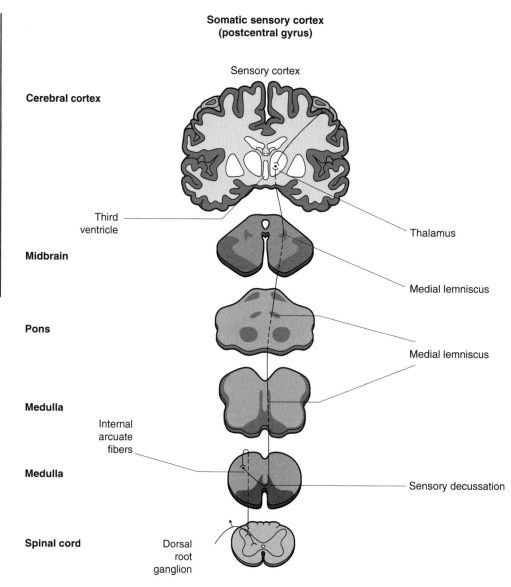

**Somatic sensory cortex
(postcentral gyrus)**

Sensory cortex

Cerebral cortex

Third
ventricle

Midbrain

Thalamus

Medial lemniscus

Pons

Medial lemniscus

Medulla

Internal
arcuate
fibers

Medulla

Sensory decussation

Spinal cord

Dorsal
root
ganglion

∎ Figure 4.7 General organization of the dorsal column–medial lemniscal system, which mediates tactile sensation and limb proprioception.

Adapted, with permission of The McGraw-Hill Companies, from J.H. Martin and T.M. Jessell, 1992, Anatomy of the somatic sensory system. In *Principles of neural science*, 3rd ed., edited by E.R. Kandel, J.H. Schwartz, and T.M. Jessell (New York: Elsevier).

There are also three sensory pathways in the ventral spinal cord (figure 4.8) (Jessel and Kelly 1991). The most significant is the spinothalamic tract, which is made up of second-order afferents that are classified as either wide dynamic range or nociceptive specific. Wide dynamic range, second-order afferents respond to a wide range of stimuli at varying intensities. They receive input from all types of first-order afferents. Nociceptive-specific second-order afferents are activated only by painful stimulation. These fibers only receive input from nociceptive first-order afferents.

In addition to the spinothalamic tract, the spinoreticular and spinomesencephalic tracts are also found in the ventral spinal cord. The second-order afferents in the spinoreticular tract respond to higher intensity stimuli, including noxious stimulation. These fibers terminate in the reticular formation. The first-order afferents to these second-order afferent fibers generally produce a large receptor field.

The spinomesencephalic tract is primarily activated by noxious stimulation. The second-order afferents in this tract terminate at the periaqueductal gray formation in the midbrain. The spinoreticular and spinomesencephalic tracts and the reticular formation and periaqueductal gray play significant roles in the body's pain modulation systems. The functions of higher brain centers in sensory perception and pain

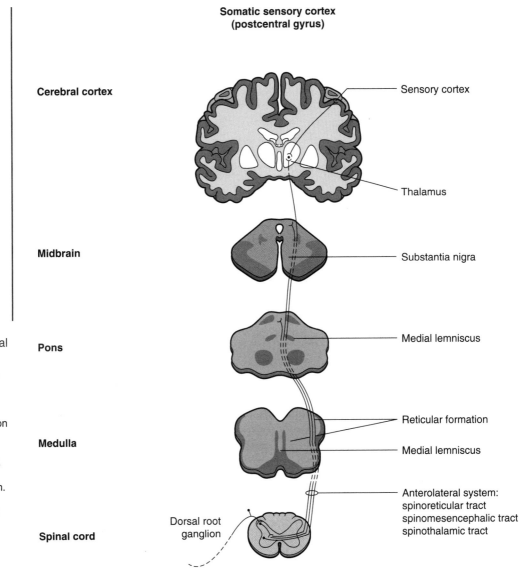

Somatic sensory cortex
(postcentral gyrus)

Cerebral cortex — Sensory cortex

— Thalamus

Midbrain — Substantia nigra

Pons — Medial lemniscus

Medulla — Reticular formation

— Medial lemniscus

— Anterolateral system:
spinoreticular tract
spinomesencephalic tract
spinothalamic tract

Dorsal root
ganglion

Spinal cord

Figure 4.8 General organization of the anterolateral system, which is part of the ventral spinal cord.

Adapted, with permission of The McGraw-Hill Companies, from J.H. Martin and T.M. Jessell, 1992, Anatomy of the somatic sensory system. In *Principles of neural science*, 3rd ed., edited by E.R. Kandel, J.H. Schwartz, and T.M. Jessell (New York: Elsevier).

modulation are discussed in subsequent sections. A greater understanding of the neuroanatomy and transmitter substances of the afferent pathways of the ventral spinal cord has advanced our knowledge of pain and the body's pain control systems. Contemporary theories on how the therapeutic modalities affect pain sensation are predicated on these advances in understanding of basic neural function.

THIRD- AND FOURTH-ORDER AFFERENTS AND INTERNEURONS

Afferent fibers that connect from second-order afferents to higher centers are classified as third-order afferent fibers. For example, third-order afferent fibers transmit input from the reticular formation to the thalamus. Fourth-order neurons transmit impulses within and between centers in the cerebral cortex. The third- and fourth-order neurons are essential to the transmission to higher centers and the perception of sensations including pain. Whether pain sensation can be modulated at these higher centers is not known.

One other subgroup of neurons bears mentioning. Interneurons are short neurons found in the spinal cord. The interneurons connect between afferent fibers and between some descending or efferent fibers and afferent nerve fibers. The interneurons modulate sensory input from the spinal cord level and are believed to play a pivotal role in modulating pain. The function of these interneurons in relation to the body's pain control mechanisms is discussed in greater detail later in this chapter.

HIGHER CENTERS

The neuronal circuitry that results in conscious awareness of sensation is very complex, but this section will discuss a few structures found in the brain stem that are important to the perception and modulation of pain (figure 4.9). Fibers in the medial lemniscus and spinothalamic tract terminate in the thalamus. The thalamus is divided into ventral posterior lateral (VPL) and ventral posterior medial (VPM) nuclei (Berne and Levy 1993). The fibers ascending from the body synapse in the VPL. Only fibers from the head and face synapse in the VPM. The thalamus is a relay center with facilitory and inhibitory circuits. The thalamus modulates input from the ascending nerves prior to transmitting it to the somatosensory cortex. Ultimately, the localization and discrimination of pain probably occur in the postcentral gyrus of the cortex of the brain.

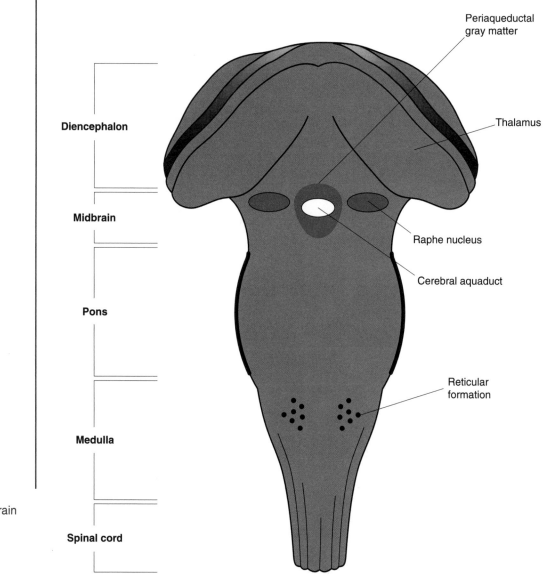

Diencephalon

Midbrain

Pons

Medulla

Spinal cord

Periaqueductal gray matter

Thalamus

Raphe nucleus

Cerebral aquaduct

Reticular formation

▌ **Figure 4.9** Brain stem structures involved in pain perception and modulation.

The thalamus also relays input to the limbic system, which regulates the emotional, autonomic, and endocrine response to pain. Thus, the thalamus relays sensory input that provides for the sensory–discriminatory and affective–motivational aspects of pain.

Fibers in the spinoreticular tract terminate in the reticular formation in the midbrain. Rather than being a distinct mass of cells, the reticular formation is a diffuse accumulation of neurons in the midbrain. The cells of the reticular formation communicate with multiple centers within the brain. The reticular formation influences the affective–motivational response to noxious stimulation and is also believed to be an important relay in one of the body's most powerful pain control mechanisms.

Another brain center that plays a significant role in pain modulation is the periaqueductal gray region of the midbrain. Fibers in the spinomesencephalic tract terminate in the periaqueductal gray. There is evidence that this brain center participates in the sensory–discriminatory and affective–motivational aspects of pain, to some extent. The periaqueductal gray is also believed to be an important relay to the raphe nucleus of the reticular formation, which is part of a descending tract responsible for modulating noxious input in the spinal cord.

SYNAPTIC TRANSMISSION AND TRANSMITTER SUBSTANCES

Communication from one nerve fiber to the next takes place at the synapse between the two nerves. Impulses from a presynaptic nerve may stimulate depolarization of the postsynaptic nerve by releasing a transmitter substance. When this occurs, the transmitter substance is facilitory. However, not all substances released from presynaptic nerves stimulate depolarization from postsynaptic nerves. Some transmitter substances are inhibitory to the depolarization of the postsynaptic nerves.

Many presynaptic nerve fibers may synapse on a postsynaptic nerve fiber (figure 4.10). Some of these facilitate transmission, whereas others inhibit transmission. Thus, depolarization of a postsynaptic nerve fiber depends on the balance between facilitory and inhibitory influences. This concept is central to contemporary theories of pain control with therapeutic modalities. Some modalities are believed to promote the release of transmitter substances that inhibit synaptic transmission in nociceptive pathways.

▋ Figure 4.10 Sensory input enters the dorsal horn of the spinal cord on large-diameter AI, AII, and A-beta fibers. Pain is transmitted from area of tissue damage or irritation by small-diameter A delta and C fibers. In the dorsal horn, large-diameter primary afferent nerves synapse with and stimulate enkephalin interneurons. The releases of enkephalin inhibit synaptic transmission of the pain message.

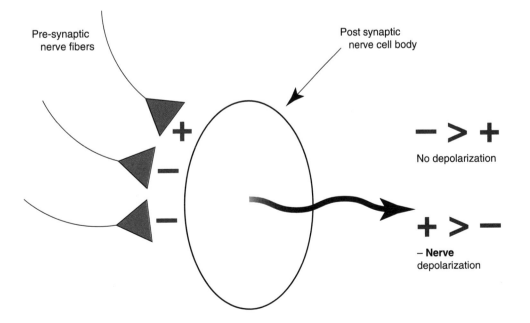

Neuroscience has significantly advanced the understanding of transmitter substances. More than 30 biogenic amine transmitters, amino acid transmitters, and neuroactive peptides have been found to influence synaptic transmission somewhere in the nervous system. Discussion of each of these neuroactive substances is beyond the scope of this text but can be found in the neuroscience texts listed in the reference section. However, a few substances, like glutamate and substance P, play a significant role in nociception and are discussed next.

Glutamate and substance P, a neuroactive peptide, are believed to facilitate synaptic transmission in the nociceptive pathways (Jessell and Kelly 1991). Beta-endorphin, dynorphin, methionine enkephalin, and leucine enkephalin are classified as opioid peptides because they bind to the same sites as the opiate drugs. These neuroactive peptides inhibit the transmission of pain impulses. Beta-endorphin is a large peptide chain found in distinct locations within the central nervous system (Jessell and Kelly 1991). Dynorphin and the enkephalins are more widespread.

It is believed that enkephalins and perhaps other opioid peptides inhibit the action of glutamate and substance P. Contemporary pain theories suggest the body has opioid pain control systems that can be stimulated through external stimuli.

PAIN CONTROL

Understanding how pain is perceived is a prerequisite to studying the body's analgesic mechanisms. The pain-relieving effects of touch, acupuncture, and other treatments have been recorded since ancient times, although how these treatments altered pain was unknown, because of inadequate knowledge regarding the human nervous system. As recently as the 1960s, pain and pain control theory revolved around the pattern theory and the specificity theory.

The pattern theory denied the existence of pain receptors and suggested that pain occurred when the rate and pattern of sensory input exceeded a threshold. The specificity theory suggested that pain was perceived when pain receptors in the periphery were stimulated and that these pain receptors were connected directly to sensory areas in the brain. Neither theory plausibly explained the pain-relieving effects of treatments long recognized as effective.

In 1965, Melzack and Wall published proposals concerning their gate control theory of pain relief. This theory plausibly explained why therapeutic modalities controlled pain, and it stimulated the development of new approaches, including transcutaneous electrical nerve stimulation. Since 1965, more has been learned about the anatomy and physiology of the nervous system, and the theoretical base has expanded. The theories presented here reflect these advances. However, as our knowledge base continues to grow, the validity of these theories will be challenged and the scientific basis for clinical application of modalities will continue to evolve.

WHY IS THEORY IMPORTANT?

The scientific basis of athletic training has advanced considerably in the past few decades; however, it remains incomplete. Although athletic trainers have always applied therapeutic modalities, the rationale behind these treatments was often based on observations handed down from athletic trainers to students. As the profession has grown, some of the assumptions made regarding therapeutic modalities have been discovered to be unfounded. Thus, the scientific and theoretical basis of athletic training has evolved.

As more has been learned about the neuroanatomy and neurophysiology of the human body, new theories have emerged and have been modified, and this information is essential in the application of therapeutic modalities. The state of the theoretical basis is the state of the art. Theory will inevitably change, but what is available today provides the foundation for much of the practice of athletic training.

The following section heavily emphasizes theory, and, where possible, presents evidence to support these theories. These concepts are not fully validated and will evolve over time. Despite such uncertainty, this theoretical basis is vital in explaining why modalities are applied and why they produce desired clinical outcomes.

THE BEGINNING OF CONTEMPORARY PAIN THEORY: GATE CONTROL

The gate control theory (figure 4.11) (Melzack and Wall 1965) provided a plausible explanation for the pain-relieving effects of modalities such as massage. This theory also led to the development of TENS, which is commonly used by athletic trainers. Thus, with a new theoretical basis, the application of therapeutic modalities in athletic training changed.

The gate control theory had a great impact, because it was the first theory to propose that pain sensation could be altered by blocking or gating impulses in the pain pathways. The theory proposes multiple mechanisms by which the body can alter noxious sensory input.

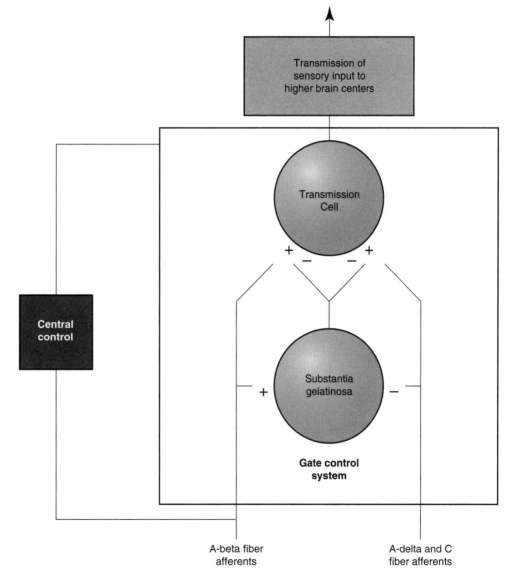

■ **Figure 4.11**   The gate control theory. Input along large-diameter (AI, AII, B) primary afferents activates inhibitory influence of substantia gelatinosa on transmission from primary to afferent nerves to a transmission cell (second-order afferent).

The gate control theory proposes that the body possesses overlapping pain control mechanisms. The theory is most recognized for proposing that input along large-diameter afferent fibers (Type IA, IIA, and A-beta) can block the transmission of noxious input at the dorsal horn of the spinal cord. Blocking impulses along nociceptive pathways in the dorsal horn prevent transmission to sensory centers in the brain and the perception of pain.

The theory proposes that the substantia gelatinosa (lamina II of the dorsal horn) serves as a gate that can be opened and closed. When the gate is closed, synaptic transmission to second-order afferents is inhibited and sensory input is blocked from reaching the sensory cortex. When the gate is open, synaptic transmission is not inhibited and sensory input reaches the higher centers. Input along large-diameter, nonnociceptive first-order afferents stimulates substantia gelatinosa, inhibiting synaptic transmission in the dorsal horn. Input along small-diameter, nociceptive fibers (A-delta and C) inhibits substantia gelatinosa, thus allowing for synaptic transmission and the propagation of impulses to higher centers.

Conventional TENS devices used in athletic training selectively depolarize large-diameter afferents. These devices reduce pain in many situations, suggesting that a gating mechanism may indeed exist.

Melzack and Wall also recognized that the analgesic effects of treatments such as electroacupuncture and acupressure could not be explained by the gate control theory. These treatments result in transient, localized pain. Thus, the small-diameter nociceptive afferents are active. The gate control theory also proposed that a central control mechanism exists that can modulate nociceptive input at the dorsal horn through tracts descending from brain centers. At the time the gate control theory was published, little was known about the anatomy of tracts descending to, and the interneurons found in, the dorsal horn. Subsequent research has confirmed the existence of overlapping analgesic systems and the existence of descending control over synaptic transmission in the dorsal horn.

ENDOGENOUS OPIOIDS AND NEW THEORIES

In the 1970s the endogenous opioids were discovered. Endogenous means "originating from within the body." An opioid is a peptide that exerts opiatelike effects by interacting with opiate receptors of cell membranes. These transmitter substances are made by the body and occupy receptor sites that are responsible for the effects of opiate drugs.

These discoveries were followed by the development of new pain control theories. Castel (1979) published three models of endogenous pain control systems: an ascending influence (Level I) model, a descending influence (Level II) model, and a beta-endorphin mediated (Level III) model. These models are the basis of the pain control theories presented in the rest of this chapter and serve as the theoretic foundation for many of the modality applications presented in this text.

Ascending Influence Pain Control (Level I) Model

The first pain control model is similar to the gate control theory in that it proposes that large-diameter, first-order afferent input inhibits synaptic transmission in nociceptive pathways in the dorsal horn (figure 4.12). The model proposes that the large-diameter afferents branch to synapse on enkephalin interneurons. When stimulated, the enkephalin interneurons release enkephalins into the first-order–second-order afferent synapses of the nociceptive pathways. Enkephalin is believed to inhibit the release of substance P, thus prohibiting synaptic transmission and blocking pain at the first synapse of the nociceptive pathway.

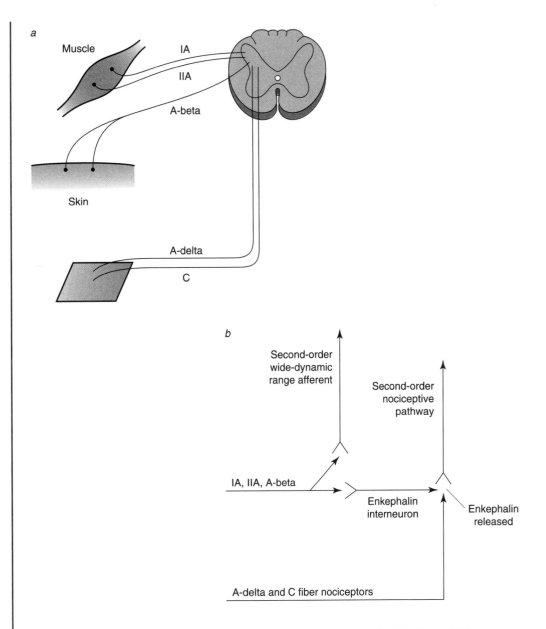

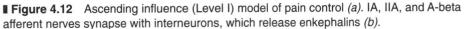

■ Figure 4.12   Ascending influence (Level I) model of pain control *(a)*. IA, IIA, and A-beta afferent nerves synapse with interneurons, which release enkephalins *(b)*.

The first-order nociceptors project to laminae I, II, and V. Large-diameter afferents project to laminae II and IV. The enkephalin interneurons are found in lamina II (substantia gelatinosa) and are known to project to lamina I. Thus, although the gate control theory was limited by the neuroscience of the times, the notion that noxious input is modulated at the dorsal horn under the influence of substantia gelatinosa (lamina II) activity is very plausible.

Descending Influence Pain Control (Level II) Model

Like Melzack and Wall, Castel also proposed that higher brain centers can modulate synaptic transmission in the dorsal horn. One model proposes that noxious input transmitted in the spinomesencephalic tract to the periaqueductal gray can trigger a descending pain control system (figure 4.13). When the stimulus reaches the

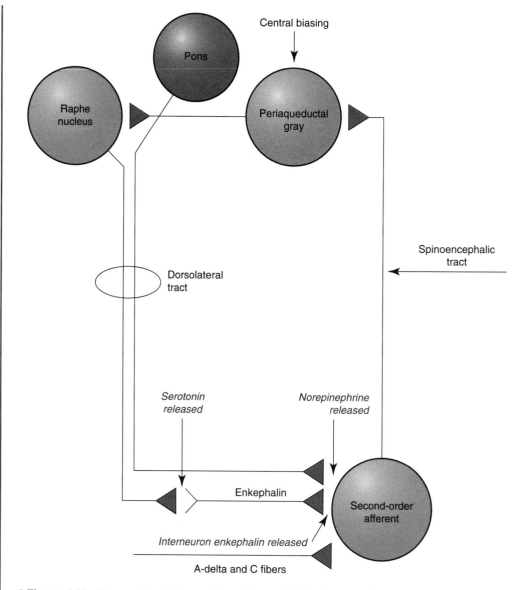

▌Figure 4.13   Descending influence (Level II) model of pain control.

periaqueductal gray, third-order neurons to the raphe nucleus are activated. The dorsal lateral tract descends from the raphe nucleus with fibers that synapse on enkephalin interneurons in lamina II. These fibers release serotonin, which depolarizes the enkephalin interneuron, leading to the release of enkephalin into the first-order–second-order afferent synapse of the nociceptive pathway.

This model plausibly explains the analgesic effect of acupressure and some forms of TENS (as occurs with local noxious stimulation). The neuroanatomy of this model has been established. However, the circumstances in which this descending system is most active and how best it can be activated by the certified athletic trainer's interventions have not been fully elucidated.

Additionally, some fibers in the dorsolateral tract originate in the pons. These fibers terminate in the dorsal horn and release norepinephrine, which inhibits nociceptive neurons. However, the mechanisms that trigger these fibers to modulate pain pathway transmission in the dorsal horn are not clear.

Beta-Endorphin Mediated Pain Control (Level III) Model

Dynorphin and beta-endorphin (BEP) are large peptide chains that are also active in the body's pain control system. BEP is a 31 peptide chain. In the pituitary, BEP is derived from a prohormone, proopiomelanocortin (POMC). Castel (1979) proposed that BEP released from the anterior pituitary resulted in an opioid-induced analgesia. However, the anterior pituitary secretes chemicals into the plasma to be circulated in the body. Because of the size of the molecule, little BEP is believed to leave the circulation for the cerebral spinal fluid. Thus, although plasma BEP may peripherally affect pain sensation, concentrations found within the blood–brain barrier probably do not originate in the anterior pituitary.

BEP is found in concentrations in discrete areas of the brain. Neurons projecting from the hypothalamus to the periaqueductal gray have high concentrations of BEP. BEP has a relatively long half-life. Stimulation of BEP release at the periaqueductal gray may result in a protracted activation of the dorsolateral tract (figure 4.14). It has been proposed that long-term (20–40 min) stimulation of small-diameter afferents may trigger a BEP-mediated analgesic response (Mannheimer and Lampe 1984).

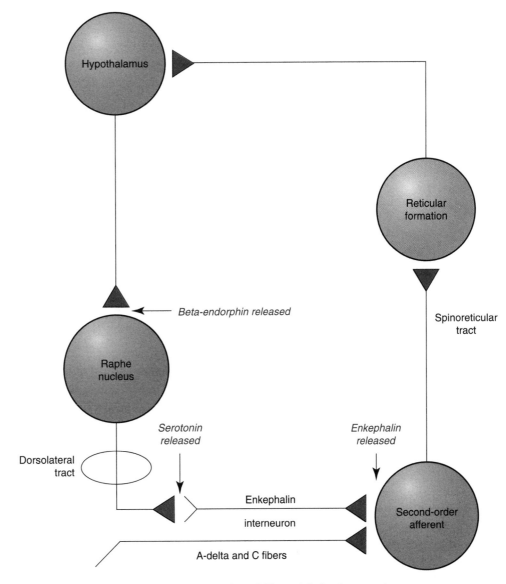

▌Figure 4.14 Beta-endorphin mediated (Level III) model of pain control.

The study of these systems is difficult. Assay of cerebrospinal fluid (CSF) requires a spinal tap, a procedure best reserved for medical rather than research purposes. Thus, the precise means of stimulating BEP release within the blood–brain barrier remains to be fully described.

Dynorphin is somewhat more widely distributed than BEP. The function of dynorphin has not been fully described; however, it may suppress the response to noxious mechanical stimulation. Electroacupuncture has been shown to stimulate the release of dynorphin, but it is not known if other modalities produce a similar response.

ADDITIONAL CONSIDERATIONS: SLOWING OF FIRST-ORDER AFFERENT CONDUCTION AND CENTRAL CONTROL

The theories presented here have expanded our understanding of pain control mechanisms and have led to the development of more scientifically based treatment rationales. However, these theories do not explain the analgesic effects of all modalities or pain management strategies. For example, these theories do not explain the analgesic response to cold or ultrasound. Thus, we are left to seek other explanations.

Cold slows nerve conduction velocity in first-order afferent fibers. There is some controversy as to whether fiber type affects the temperature at which blocking occurs (Mannheimer and Lampe 1984). However, three things are apparent: (1) Cryotherapy techniques used in athletic training decrease first-order afferent conduction, (2) a decrease in conduction along nociceptive pathways is most likely responsible for the analgesic response to cold application of greater than 10 min, and (3) the previously presented pain control models do not offer a plausible explanation to the analgesic response to cold applied for periods of 10 to 20 min, because these models are based upon an increase, rather than a decrease, in neural input to the dorsal horn.

Other modalities may also alter nerve conduction velocity. Ultrasound and some forms of electrotherapy have been reported to relieve pain by decreasing conduction in nociceptive, afferent fibers. These concepts are addressed later in this book as each modality is discussed.

There are still gaps in our understanding of the body's pain control systems. Melzack and Wall's notion of a central control of pain continues to intrigue researchers and clinicians. As noted in the opening of this chapter, there are many influences on the perception of and reaction to noxious stimuli. We all have observed individuals who can block out pain or alter their pain experience. Relaxation and imagery are but two techniques to facilitate conscious, "central" control of pain.

Placebo responses to treatments are also poorly understood. However, a belief that a treatment will relieve suffering may become a self-fulfilling prophecy. The placebo response confounds the investigation of therapeutic modalities used in athletic training and must be addressed by researchers in this area. However, another aspect of the placebo response is often overlooked by certified athletic trainers. Stated simply, a treatment is more likely to be effective if the individual and the athletic trainer believe it will be effective. Do not neglect the power of positive thinking in treating an injured athlete, whether you are applying a therapeutic modality or planning a rehabilitation program.

The mechanisms by which we can control our pain experience through conscious effort and subconscious processes are not fully understood. However, it is clear that the pain control systems described in this chapter are connected to a more complex process of neuromodulation that defines the pain experience.

SUMMARY

1. *Describe the multidimensional nature of pain.*

   Pain can be conceptualized as having two dimensions: intensity and affective–motivational. The intensity component is pain sensation. Where does it hurt and how badly? The affective–motivational component relates to how an individual responds to pain. For example, is the person angry or withdrawn? Providing care involves more than asking about the intensity of the pain. The athletic trainer must respect each person's response to pain.

2. *Explain the role of pain in preserving health and well-being.*

   Pain signals that something is wrong with the body and is usually the motivation to seek medical care. Without pain, diseases and injuries go undetected and therefore untreated.

3. *Discuss how the pain response can assist in evaluating the injured athlete.*

   Understanding the pain response following injury can help you make an accurate diagnosis. The causes, timing, locations, and severity of pain often narrow the possibilities and allow the sports medicine team to focus on special tests and examination procedures that lead to a rapid and accurate diagnosis.

4. *Describe how pain is sensed and how the "pain message" is transmitted to the central nervous system.*

   Free nerve endings are the body's pain receptors or nociceptors. When free nerve endings are stimulated, impulses are transmitted to the brain by specific nerves and neural pathways. Impulses are transmitted from the free nerve endings to the spinal cord by A-delta and C fiber primary or first-order afferent nerves. A-delta fibers are more rapidly conducting, whereas input on C fibers allows for more precise localization of the pain. The pain message is carried from the primary afferents up the spinal cord by second-order afferent nerves. The pain message can be carried on wide, dynamic range, second-order nerves or on nociceptive-specific nerves. The nociceptive-specific nerves carry only pain information, whereas the wide, dynamic range fibers carry all types of neural input. The second-order afferent fibers terminate at multiple brain centers. The thalamus, periaqueductal gray region, and reticular formation all play important roles in accurately assessing the pain message and mediate the individual's response to pain.

5. Discuss contemporary theories on modulating the pain message in the central nervous system.

   In 1965, Melzack and Wall published the gate control theory of pain, which proposed that the pain message could be blocked at the spinal cord with appropriate external stimuli. With advances in neuroanatomy and neurophysiology, the basic concept of pain modulation has been refined. Castel developed three models or levels of pain control, which form the basis for the presentation of pain modulation through therapeutic modality application in this text. The Level I model, a refinement of gate control theory, proposes that pain can be modulated in the dorsal horn of the spinal cord through stimulation of enkephalin interneurons by increased sensory input from large-diameter, first-order afferent nerves. The Level II model proposes that nerves descending from the raphe nucleus can trigger the release of enkephalin and modulate pain, and that this descending pathway is stimulated by noxious input transmitted in the spinalencephalic pathway to the periaqueductal gray.

This model offers a plausible explanation for pain relief induced by painful procedures such as acupressure. The Level III model proposes that prolonged stimulation of small-diameter afferent nerves can trigger the release of beta-endorphin by connections between the hypothalamus and the raphe nucleus. Because beta-endorphin has a long half-life, this transmitter substance can stimulate the descending pathway for long periods. This model may explain how acupuncture and perhaps superficial heat relieve pain.

CITED REFERENCES

Berne RM, Levy MN: *Physiology*, 3rd ed. St. Louis, Mosby, 1993.

Castel JC: *Pain Management: Acupuncture, and Transcutaneous Electrical Nerve Stimulation Techniques*. Lake Bluff, IL, Pain Control Services, 1979.

IASP: Pain terms: A list with definitions and notes on usage recommended by the IASP subcommittee on taxonomy. *Pain* 6:249-252, 1979.

Knight KL: *Cryotherapy in Sports Injury Management*. Champaign, IL, Human Kinetics, 1995.

Jessell TM, Kelly DD: Pain and analgesia. In Kandel ER, Schwartz JH, Jessell TM (Eds), *Principles of Neural Science*. Norwalk, CT, Appleton and Lange, 1991.

Mannheimer JS, Lampe GN: *Clinical Transcutaneous Electrical Nerve Stimulation*. Philadelphia, Davis, 1984.

Melzack R: *Pain Measurement and Assessment*. New York, Raven Press, 1983.

Melzack R, Wall P: Pain mechanisms: A new theory. *Science* 150:971-979, 1965.

Pollard CA: Preliminary validity study of the pain disability index. *Percept Mot Skills* 59:974, 1984.

ADDITIONAL SOURCES

Bonica JJ: *The Management of Pain*. Philadelphia, Lea & Febiger, 1990.

Calliet R: *Pain Mechanisms and Management*. Philadelphia, Davis, 1993.

Calliet R: *Soft Tissue Pain and Disability*, 2nd ed. Philadelphia, Davis, 1988.

Kendell E, Schwartz J, Jessell T: *Principles of Neuroscience*. Norwalk, CT, Appleton & Lange, 1991.

CHAPTER FIVE

Persistent Pain

OBJECTIVES

After reading this chapter, the student will be able to

1. describe the differences between acute and persistent pain, and

2. identify common causes for persistent pain in active individuals, including

   - diagnostic errors,

   - faulty plans of rehabilitation,

   - rest–reinjury cycle,

   - chronic regional pain syndrome,

   - myofascial pain, and

   - depression and somatization.

A 15-year-old basketball player developed patellofemoral pain during preseason. She was evaluated by the team physician and treated by the school's certified athletic trainer. She completed a rehabilitation program and returned to competition within 3 weeks, at varsity level. She subsequently developed a rotator cuff strain, was evaluated by an orthopedic surgeon, and again received treatment by the certified athletic trainer. She decreased her activity during Christmas break and recovered. One month later she developed low back pain. She was evaluated by the team physician and treated by the certified athletic trainer. She failed to improve, and she received additional treatment in a local sports medicine center. A modified plan of therapeutic exercises failed to resolve her low back pain, and she was reevaluated by an orthopedic surgeon. Reevaluation again suggested that she was suffering from mechanical low back pain. Her treatment was modified but the pain did not improve.

The athletic trainer was becoming frustrated about this athlete's situation. She always arrived in the training room on time and always complied with her rehabilitation. Finally, the athletic trainer discussed the situation with the basketball coach, learning that the athlete moved into the school district the previous year with her mother. Her parents had recently divorced and her father now lived far away. Her older sister had earned a basketball scholarship to a major university. The coach believed that the family expected this athlete to follow her sister and attend college on an athletic scholarship. The coach also noted that the injured athlete did not really fit in with her teammates socially but often attended games with a small group of friends who were active in the school's band and chorus programs.

The athletic trainer consulted with the team physician, and they subsequently sought the advice of the school psychologist. The team physician arranged a meeting with the athlete's mother, the athlete, the physician, and the school psychologist. The meeting confirmed the circumstances relayed by the basketball coach, revealing that the athlete felt so pressured to perform well in basketball that she felt guilty about exploring her interest in singing. Her mother stated her support for her daughter and indicated that although an athletic scholarship would be nice, it was not necessary in order for her daughter to attend college. Both mother and daughter were open about the difficult adjustments they were trying to make following the divorce and move to a new area.

The mother and daughter agreed that family counseling might help them, and they were referred to a local family counselor and psychologist. The athlete decided to continue to play basketball but also became more active in the school's fine arts programs. Under the guidance of the team physician and certified athletic trainer, she continued to be treated for mechanical low back pain. She was independent in her back care within 3 weeks.

The case study presents a situation where an athlete sought medical care because of pain that affected performance. The certified athletic trainer and team physician used pain to diagnose the injuries and plan treatments. However, psychological factors can also produce pain (Heil 1993; Peppard and Denegar 1999). The appropriate treatment of some physically active individuals will require the recognition of psychological factors, intervention, and, when necessary, referral for definitive psychological care. Somatization and depression are common psychological problems that can result in unexplained somatic pain.

In the previous chapter, pain was identified as a cardinal sign of inflammation and warning that something is wrong with the body, and the relationship between inflammation and tissue healing was described. Logic suggests that when the inflammatory response subsides and tissues heal, pain should disappear. However, sometimes pain persists.

Chronic pain is pain that lasts beyond the normal time frame for healing. Some have suggested a specific length of time, 6 months, for example (Donley and Denegar 1994; Stone 1987), before lasting pain is labeled as chronic. Because the term *chronic pain* implies that the pain is mysterious and untreatable, the term *persistent pain* is more appropriate. Persistent pain is a symptom of an often treatable problem. The sports medicine team should exhaust the possibilities of diagnosis and treatment before labeling a physically active person as suffering from chronic pain.

Persistent pain is a significant challenge to the sports medicine team, and it is frustrating to the physically active individual as well. Therapeutic modalities are very useful in some, but not all, cases of persistent pain.

This chapter introduces the problem of persistent pain, identifying sources of persistent pain in the context of clinical exam findings and touching on the treatment of persistent pain. However, uses of specific modalities to treat persistent pain are discussed in chapter 13, after each modality is introduced in intervening chapters.

FINDING THE CAUSE

Most injured individuals treated by a certified athletic trainer respond well to treatment and return to competition within a predictable time frame. However, some fail to respond to treatment, and their symptoms persist beyond the normal time required for tissue repair and maturation. Others present with complaints of pain without an identifiable pathology. Are these problems due to a failure to heal? Does pain linger even though tissue has healed? Is the injury imaginary? The certified athletic trainer must try to answer these questions, being ever mindful that pain is a symptom that something is wrong (figure 5.1).

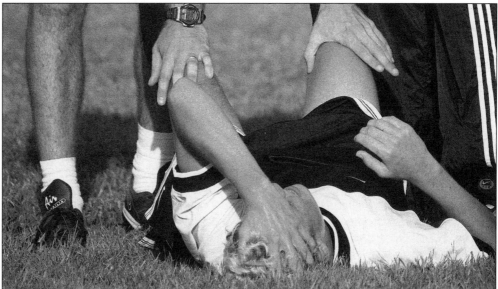

■ **Figure 5.1** Pain is a symptom that something is wrong.

The causes of persistent pain span a spectrum from physical to principally psychological (figure 5.2). The physical causes involve a diagnostic error, a failure to correct faulty biomechanics, an inappropriate treatment plan, or a rest–reinjury cycle. However, physical pain may also be a symptom of somatization and depression. The causes of chronic regional pain syndrome and myofascial pain syndrome are complex and not fully understood. However, psychological stress appears to contribute to or exacerbate these conditions.

THE DIAGNOSIS

When pain persists, the certified athletic trainer should reevaluate the injury and complaint of pain as though it were a new problem. Sometimes persistent pain stems from a problem that was not recognized on initial examination. Thus, the first step in reevaluation is to reconsider the original diagnosis.

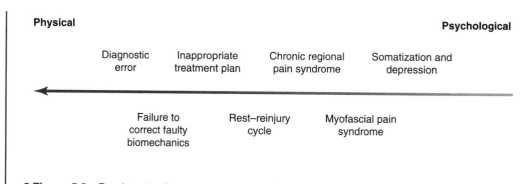

Physical   **Psychological**

| Diagnostic error | Inappropriate treatment plan | Chronic regional pain syndrome | Somatization and depression |

| Failure to correct faulty biomechanics | Rest–reinjury cycle | Myofascial pain syndrome |

■ **Figure 5.2**   Persistent pain spans a spectrum from physical to principally psychological.
Adapted from *Athletic Therapy Today* 1997.

In the following case, the new diagnosis required a much different plan of care. Appropriate treatment of this runner's stress fractures resulted in complete resolution of the persistent foot pain. Although she presented with many signs and symptoms consistent with plantar fasciitis, the persistence of the problem led to a complete review of her case and, ultimately, a correct diagnosis.

Case Study

A women's cross country runner was diagnosed by a team physician as having bilateral plantar fasciitis. She received daily treatments with ultrasound followed by massage and stretching before training and ice massage after workouts. Because her foot pain did not improve, she was referred to an athletic trainer who found that some of her symptoms were not consistent with plantar fasciitis. The athletic trainer discussed the athlete's situation with the team physician and an orthopedic surgeon; the orthopedic surgeon requested additional diagnostic imaging, which revealed bilateral navicular stress fractures (Denegar and Siple 1996).

This case illustrates two very important lessons. First, the application of therapeutic modalities is part of a comprehensive plan of care. Failures can occur in evaluation, treatment, or rehabilitation. When the physically active do not respond to treatment, you must explore the reasons.

Second, persistent pain problems are often complex. Modalities can mask symptoms and delay definitive care, but they can also allow pain-free therapeutic exercise. You must be capable of evaluating and treating persistent pain problems as well as symptoms of acute inflammation. This chapter provides a hierarchy of persistent pain problems that is a model for evaluation of physically active individuals.

BIOMECHANICS

Evaluating the injured person's movement mechanics is also an essential part of a comprehensive physical exam. Failure to identify biomechanical flaws may leave the major cause of persistent pain untreated. Certified athletic trainers commonly encounter individuals who are suffering from medial tibial stress syndrome or shin splints. Modalities may help reduce pain, but modality application does not cure the injury. Often the cause of the problem is excessive subtalar pronation, and recognizing and controlling excessive subtalar pronation may alleviate persistent shin pain with running. Thus, the solution to the problem lies in identifying and correcting the underlying cause of pain, rather than simply treating the pain.

Many other repetitive microtrauma injuries are related to movement mechanics, such as patellofemoral pain, iliotibial band friction syndrome, and Achilles tendinitis. In the upper extremity, improving scapular stabilization may be the key to relieving persistent shoulder pain.

PLAN OF CARE

Persistent pain after injury or surgery can sometimes be attributed to an incomplete or inappropriate treatment plan. Failure to address scapular stabilization in individuals with shoulder instability and impingement is one example. Another example is an aggressive postoperative regimen of therapeutic exercises following patellar bone–tendon–bone ACL reconstruction that results in patellar tendinitis. In the second case the exercise regimen must be modified to prevent persistent anterior knee pain.

Many treatment and rehabilitation programs for specific musculoskeletal injuries are discussed in the next book in this series: *Therapeutic Exercise for Athletic Injuries*. However, because therapeutic modalities are used to treat persistent pain, this chapter discusses the plan of care as a source of persistent pain.

REST–REINJURY CYCLE

Athletic excellence requires individuals to put forth maximum effort and push through pain in their training. When injured, physically active individuals generally will accept a period of rest until the pain is relieved. The absence of pain, however, is often interpreted as a sign that the tissue is healed and that the athlete is ready to return to unrestricted practice and competition. If the tissue is not ready, reinjury occurs and the rest–reinjury cycle begins (Peppard and Denegar 1994). Rehabilitation extends beyond specific treatments and therapeutic exercises and must include a gradual return to functional exercises.

Recognizing persistent pain involving a rest–reinjury cycle will allow the certified athletic trainer to educate the injured individual about the differences between conditioning and reconditioning after injury. Reconditioning requires careful control of exercise intensity, frequency, and duration. The exercise program must allow the person to stay within the exercise tolerance window. Exercise that results in pain severe enough to alter movement patterns must be avoided, and intensity and duration must be limited to avoid postexercise pain.

A good rule is that the injured individual should be able to do tomorrow what was done today. In other words, if someone is too sore to repeat yesterday's therapeutic and functional exercises, the exercise tolerance limit was exceeded and the rehabilitation process slowed. As a well-structured rehabilitation program progresses, the exercise tolerance window widens and the individual becomes more tolerant of exercise-induced pain. Training should be specific, structured, and, when possible, supervised. Coaches and strength and conditioning specialists can help the injured athlete progress in gradually more demanding sport-specific exercises and general reconditioning.

The certified athletic trainer should carefully evaluate the use of therapeutic modalities in all cases of persistent pain. This is especially important when a rest–reinjury cycle is involved. Physically active individuals frequently respond well to modality application for pain control, but they may continue to seek the treatments that allowed them to return to practice and competition following the initial injury. The certified athletic trainer can perpetuate the rest–reinjury cycle by continuing palliative care without educating the injured individual and his or her coaches about the problem and restricting the athlete's exercise program.

COMPLEX REGIONAL PAIN SYNDROME

Complex regional pain syndrome (CRPS), also commonly labeled reflex sympathetic dystrophy (RSD), is a symptom complex characterized by pain that is disproportional to the injury. CRPS involves hypersensitivity to touch and movement, joint stiffness and muscle guarding, edema, erythema, hyperhydrosis, and osteopenia (Gieck and Burton 1986). The etiology of this condition is not fully understood, making treatment a challenge. CRPS may occur after even minor injury or following surgery; it can occur immediately or may be delayed. The individual may experience a normal postinjury or postoperative course for several days before the early signs of CRPS appear. In some cases, the onset of CRPS may not appear until symptoms are nearly resolved.

Ladd and colleagues (1989) introduced the term *reflex sympathetic imbalance (RSI)*, a related disorder involving pain that is out of proportion to the injury. Although disproportional pain is the hallmark symptom of CRPS, other signs and symptoms may not be present initially. These authors suggested that RSI can be diagnosed solely based on the presence of disproportional pain, thus expediting recognition of many causes of complex regional pain syndrome. Early recognition increases the likelihood of successful treatment. If disproportional pain is present, the sports medicine team should not wait until other symptoms are present before considering a diagnosis of CRPS and initiating appropriate treatments.

CRPS progresses through three stages over several months. When it is recognized and treated early, the prognosis for recovery is good. However, CRPS can become a permanent, disabling condition if not recognized early in its development. Treatments and exercises that exacerbate pain should be discontinued, and the individual should follow up with his or her physician as soon as possible. Because CRPS can develop into a permanent and disabling condition, all members of the sports medicine team must be able to recognize its early signs. When pain appears out of proportion to what is expected with a specific injury, or at specific points in recovery from injury or surgery, the certified athletic trainer and team physician must explore the possibility of CRPS.

Medical management of CRPS may include medications as well as injections to block sympathetic pathways. The certified athletic trainer must work with the medical team to design a comprehensive plan of care. Therapeutic modalities can be very useful in treating CRPS; however, no treatment should be administered that is painful for the injured individual. Moist heat, cold, and massage must be used with caution. Biofeedback, TENS, gentle massage and joint mobilization, and pain-free therapeutic exercises are usually better tolerated than more vigorous treatment approaches. As the condition improves, the therapeutic exercise regimen can be progressed and more vigorous stimulation will be tolerated. The bottom line is that early recognition of CRPS is critical, and treatments that cause pain exacerbate the problem and must be avoided.

MYOFASCIAL PAIN

As previously noted, when pain persists beyond the time frame for tissue repair, the certified athletic trainer should review the situation systematically and thoroughly, looking for diagnostic and treatment errors, rest-reinjury cycles, and CRPS. If this review does not identify the cause of persistent pain, myofascial pain syndrome (MFPS) or somatization must be considered.

MFPS is characterized by pain emanating from the muscles and connective soft tissues. It is commonly associated with the cervical and lumbar spine; however, persistent joint pain can result in myofascial pain patterns in the extremities as well.

Causes of MFPS

There is no single cause of MFPS, making the condition difficult to diagnose and treat. Several factors can contribute to its development, including trauma and repetitive microtrauma with recurrent painful episodes, posture, stress, and fatigue.

In sports, repetitive microtrauma can trigger MFPS. For example, physically active individuals with long histories of knee and shin pain such as medial tibial stress syndrome or patellofemoral pain can develop secondary, or Type II, MFPS (Denegar and Peppard 1997), challenging you to treat the primary injury as well as the secondary MFPS. These athletes will generally complain of very localized tenderness over inflamed tissue and a more general aching pain in the affected limb. Further evaluation will often reveal soft tissue tightness and trigger points in a pattern characteristic of MFPS. With experience, you will be able to locate sensitive trigger points and identify characteristic patterns related to specific areas of the body. Trigger points manifest bilaterally, and those on the contralateral side may be the most sensitive. Figures 5.3 and 5.4 depict common trigger points associated with knee, hip, elbow, back, shoulder, foot/ankle, and forearm/upper extremity pain.

A single traumatic episode can result in MFPS. Often patients in the sports medicine center, some of which are physically active and others not, will complain of neck pain, shoulder pain, and headaches several months following automobile accidents. Often the only injury sustained was a "minor" whiplash or low back strain. Acute pain that resolved within 3 weeks and a lingering aching pain that worsens with fatigue are common findings. Increased pain while working on a keyboard, while driving, and while performing other activities that place the individual in a forward-head position and stress the paraspinal musculature is a common complaint. Neck and shoulder pain is frequently accompanied by headaches. The pain often affects the individual's ability to participate in sports. In these cases, MFPS is the primary problem.

Poor posture, faulty movement mechanics, and stress play a role in the development of MFPS. A general lack of fitness and occupations that lead to postural deficits are associated with Type I MFPS affecting the trunk and neck (Denegar and Peppard 1987). Some sports such as cycling and swimming can also lead to muscle imbalances and poor posture. Often people alter movement patterns in an attempt to avoid pain, and these natural adaptations stress tissues that are not well conditioned, exacerbating the pain. Conversely, faulty movement mechanics can cause repetitive microtrauma injuries that lead to Type II MFPS. If excessive pronation is the cause of medial tibial stress syndrome or patellofemoral pain, neither the primary problem nor Type II MFPS will resolve until running mechanics are addressed, unless, of course, the individual quits running. Thus, you should assess posture and movement mechanics in all cases of MFPS.

Stress is common in our lives, and the demands of sport and pressure to succeed add to stress. Student-athletes strive to balance schoolwork, social life, family commitments, and the demands of sports. Other physically active people often squeeze training and competition in between job and family commitments. Individuals respond to the stresses of daily life differently. However, many individuals treated for MFPS in the back, neck, and shoulders "hold" their stress in the affected area. Many do not appreciate how much tension resides in these areas until it is relieved through treatment. Some learn to manage pain when they appreciate how their response to life events affects them. Some clinicians are very effective at helping individuals understand their response to stress and assisting with stress management. All members of the sports medicine team must be able to recognize when physical responses to stress contribute to persistent pain and must be able to assist individuals with stress management (figure 5.5).

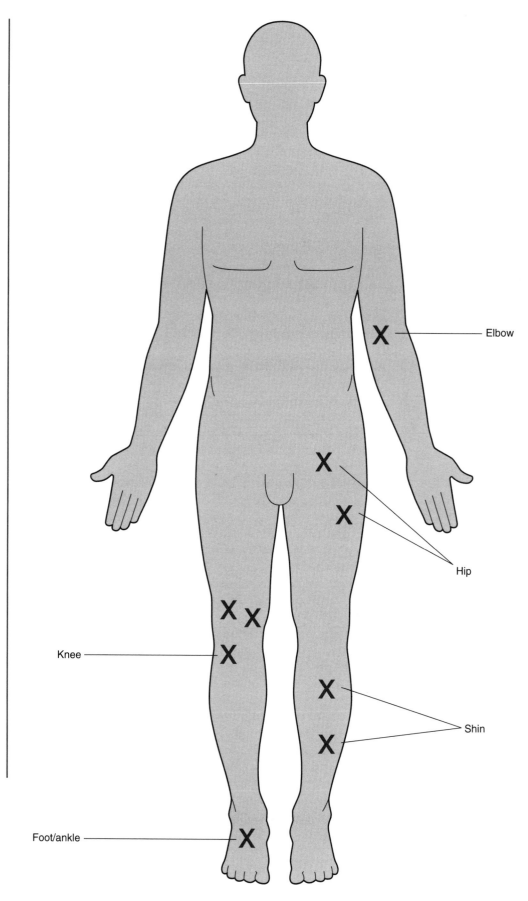

▌Figure 5.3 Common trigger points associated with knee, hip, elbow, shin, and foot/ankle pain.

Reprinted from *Athletic Therapy Today* 1997.

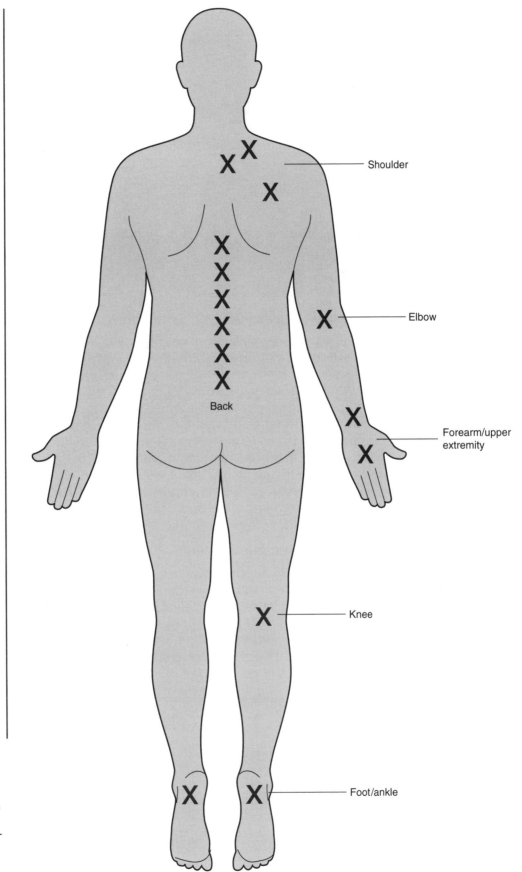

Shoulder

Elbow

Forearm/upper
extremity

Back

Knee

Foot/ankle

▌Figure 5.4 Common trigger points associated with shoulder, elbow, back, knee, foot/ankle, and forearm/upper extremity pain.

Reprinted from *Athletic Therapy Today* 1997.

Figure 5.5 Some physically active individuals may need help understanding their response to stress. All members of the sports medicine team should recognize when a stress response contributes to persistent pain.

Recognizing Myofascial Pain Syndrome

The individual with myofascial pain will complain of pain that has persisted for several months or recurrent painful episodes. Myofascial pain is generally localized to a region but is not focal. MFPS is characterized by tension in the muscles and fascia with exquisitely tender trigger points. The person will usually complain of an aching, burning sensation that is worse with overuse and fatigue. Symptoms often radiate from the neck and shoulder to an upper extremity and from the low back and sacroiliac region to a lower extremity. The radiating symptoms do not usually follow a dermatomal distribution and can usually be reproduced by stimulating the most sensitive trigger points. If you suspect MFPS, explore for contributing factors previously discussed. MFPS is a diagnosis of exclusion. Each case must be systematically reviewed to rule out other causes of persistent pain before the individual is treated for MFPS.

Modality Application and MFPS

There is not a single cause of MFPS and, therefore, there is not a single remedy. Orthotics to correct faulty biomechanics, therapeutic exercise and postural retraining, stress management, manual therapy, and therapeutic modalities can be used to treat MFPS.

The physical principles and physiological responses to contemporary therapeutic modalities are presented later in this book. Touch is important in the evaluation of MFPS (figure 5.6), and chapter 10 includes an extensive introduction to manual therapies. Manual therapy, superficial heat, cold, ultrasound, and TENS may be combined to treat MFPS. Development of a plan of care for the individual with MFPS is presented in chapter 13.

DEPRESSION AND SOMATIZATION

When pain fails to resolve despite additional diagnostic testing, the individual should be reexamined and multiple treatment approaches explored. The pain of a knee sprain signals the need for medical attention and treatment, but pain in the absence of physical injury also signals a need for treatment. The experienced sports medicine team must be able to read the signals and provide appropriate care.

One in eight individuals will require treatment for depression. However, only one half to one third of patients with major depressive disorders are recognized by

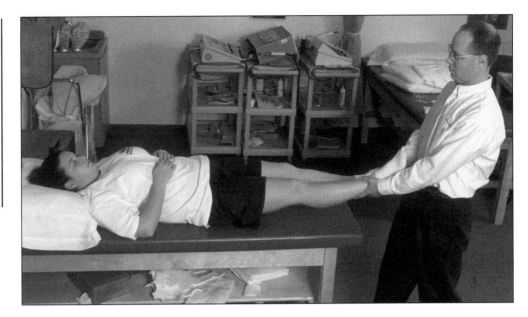

■ **Figure 5.6** Touch is important in the evaluation of MFPS, and manual therapies can be effective in its treatment.

physicians (Depression Guidelines Panel 1993). Many physically active individuals with depressive disorder are referred to certified athletic trainers and physical therapists for treatment of their somatic complaints. The close working relationship between the certified athletic trainer and the physically active person allows the athletic trainer greater opportunity to identify pain of psychological origin.

MAJOR DEPRESSIVE DISORDER

A major depressive disorder is diagnosed by the presence of at least five of the following symptoms (Depression Guidelines Panel 1993; Peppard and Denegar 1999). One of the first two must be present. The symptoms must be present nearly daily, for most of each day, for 2 weeks.

Signs and Symptoms of Major Depressive Disorder

- Depressed mood
- Markedly diminished interest in or pleasure derived from almost all activities
- Significant weight loss or weight gain
- Insomnia or hypersomnia
- Psychomotor agitation or retardation
- Fatigue or loss of energy
- Feelings of worthlessness or guilt

- Impaired concentration and indecisiveness
- Recurrent thoughts of death or suicide

Features most associated with younger individuals
- Overeating
- Oversleeping
- Mood that responds to events
- Extreme sensitivity to interpersonal rejection
- Complaints of heaviness in the arms and legs

SOMATIZATION DISORDER

Somatization is the presentation of somatic symptoms by someone with psychiatric illness or psychological distress (Lipowski 1988). A diagnosis of somatization disorder requires a history of many physical complaints, including four pain symptoms, two gastrointestinal symptoms, one sexual symptom, and one pseudoneurological symptom that are not explained by medical conditions or intentionally caused (American Psychiatric Association 1994). Undifferentiated somatoform disorder (somatization) is defined as one or more physical complaints, without identifiable cause, that last for more than 6 months (American Psychiatric Association 1994). The region and nature of the symptoms often mimic those of musculoskeletal injury. When a rehabilitation plan of care is initiated but the individual fails to improve, and other causes of persistent pain are ruled out, a diagnosis of somatization should be considered.

Indications of Somatization

Indications that somatization may be present include the following (American Psychiatric Association 1994; Lipowski 1988):

- Increased demand on the athletic trainer's time, including lengthy visits, frequent appointments, and multiple telephone calls

- Frequent requests for treatments that require special attention

- Behaviors that demonstrate a need for special attention

- Anger when the athletic trainer indicates that the condition has improved sufficiently to warrant discontinuation of treatment and a return to sports

- Individual's history inconsistent with the physical exam

Individuals with somatization disorder can be very demanding and difficult; however, recognition and appropriate care are to everyone's benefit. In treating somatization, the care provider should (1) provide care for a bona fide injury, (2) develop a sound relationship to prevent the individual from fleeing and entering a pattern of "doctor shopping" (seeking care from one doctor after another in search of a physical cause of symptoms), and (3) avoid doing harm by dismissing the individual as a malingerer or symptom magnifier.

You should not provide psychological counseling unless qualified to do so. However, many physically active individuals have benefited from informal counseling provided by members of the sports medicine team. The young physically active person often needs to talk to someone who will listen without prejudging. Listening to young athletes and reassuring them that their fears and concerns are common can help them cope during a difficult situation.

The skilled and appropriately trained certified athletic trainer can help individuals control their stress response through such techniques as biofeedback, muscle relaxation, thought stopping, deep breathing, or imagery (Peppard and Denegar 1994; Peppard and Denegar 1999). Proficiency at these techniques requires formal instruction and practice, and you should not employ techniques with which you are not proficient.

Regardless of your attempts to provide excellent care, a limitation of success must be recognized. Not all injured people get better. Physical causes of the problem should be sought; however, it is often easier to continue to search for physical causes than confront psychological ones. The search for psychological causes begins with communication. Listening and interpreting nonverbal communication require training, skill, practice, and patience.

Somatic pain of psychological origin is a symptom, a crying out. The sports medicine team is well prepared to treat the pain of physical injury and illness, but detecting emotional pain requires skill as well. Sometimes all that an individual needs is a sympathetic ear and reassurance that the stresses he or she is experiencing are normal. Sometimes the skilled athletic trainer can assist with stress management and arousal control. Definitive psychological care may ultimately be required; certainly depression and somatization warrant medical and psychological attention. The sports medicine team must develop the skills to identify these problems and refer individuals to appropriate resources.

SUMMARY

1. *Describe the differences between acute and persistent pain.*

   Acute pain, a warning that something is wrong and requires medical attention, is associated with musculoskeletal injury. Pain that persists beyond the normal time required for tissue repair is less well understood. Often, when an individual's pain lasts for weeks or months, it is labeled chronic pain. Because the term *chronic* implies a sense of hopelessness, the term *persistent pain* was introduced to identify situations where lasting pain is a signal that something is wrong and will respond to appropriate treatment. Chronic pain is complex and very poorly understood; however, often the causes of the persistent pain can be identified and effectively treated.

2. *Identify common causes for persistent pain in active people, including diagnostic errors, faulty plans of rehabilitation, rest–reinjury cycle, complex regional pain syndrome, myofascial pain, and depression and somatization.*

   Persistent pain can result from a number of causes. This chapter begins with physical causes and progresses to psychological causes of persistent pain. Physical causes include diagnostic errors and faulty plans of care. Failure to identify the problem or effectively address identified problems can lead to persistent symptoms. Physically active individuals often associate the absence of pain with complete recovery, which can lead them to overstress healing tissues and experience reinjury. This phenomenon can repeat, setting up a rest–reinjury cycle. Complex regional pain syndrome, also labeled reflex sympathetic dystrophy, is characterized by pain out of proportion to the extent of an injury as well as hypersensitivity to touch and movement, joint stiffness and muscle guarding, edema, erythema, hyperhydrosis, and osteopenia. Complex regional pain syndrome is progressive and the prognosis for complete recovery worsens if diagnosis and treatment are delayed. Myofascial pain, which may result from many causes, is a diagnosis of exclusion characterized by tender trigger points, increased tension in muscles, and often a pattern of referred pain. Physical symptoms can result from psychological dysfunction. The somatic pain experienced by those suffering from depression and somatization is a signal that care is needed. Unfortunately, somatic symptoms stemming from psychological dysfunction are more difficult to interpret. If other sources of persistent pain are ruled out, the sports medicine team should consider psychological causes before making the diagnosis of chronic pain.

CITED REFERENCES

American Psychiatric Association: *Diagnostic and Statistical Manual of Mental Disorders*, 4th ed. Washington, DC, American Psychiatric Association, 1994.

Denegar CR, Peppard A: Evaluation and treatment of persistent pain and myofascial pain syndrome. *Athl Ther Today* July:38-42, 1997.

Denegar CR, Siple BJ: Bilateral foot pain in a collegiate distance runner. *J Athl Train* 31:61-64, 1996.

Depression Guidelines Panel: *Depression in Primary Care: Vol 1. Detection and Diagnosis. Clinical Practice Guidelines, Number 5*. Rockville, MD, U.S. Department of Health and Human Services, Public Health Services, Agency for Health Care Policy and Research, 1993.

Donley PB, Denegar CR: Managing pain with therapeutic modalities. In Prentice WE (Ed), *Therapeutic Modalities in Sports Medicine*, 3rd ed. St Louis, Mosby, 1994.

Gieck J, Buxton BP: Reflex sympathetic dystrophy. *Athl Train, JNATA* 22:120-125, 1986.

Heil J: *Psychology of Sport Injury*. Champaign, IL, Human Kinetics, 1993.

Ladd AL, DeHaven KE, Thanik J, Patt RB, Feuerstein M: Reflex sympathetic imbalance. *Am J Sports Med* 17:660-667, 1989.

Lipowski ZJ: Somatization: The concept and its clinical application. *Am J Psychiatry* 145:1358-1368, 1988.

Peppard A, Denegar CR: Depression and somatization and persistent pain in the athletic patient. *Athl Ther Today* Nov:43-47, 1999.

Peppard AP, Denegar CR: Pain and the rehabilitation of athletic injury. *Orthop Phys Ther Clin North Am* 3:439-462, 1994.

Stone LA: Pain in neuromuscular disorders. In Ecternach JL (Ed), *Pain*. New York, Churchill Livingstone, 1987.

ADDITIONAL SOURCE

Travel JG, Simons DG: *Myofascial Pain and Dysfunction: The Trigger Point Manual*. Baltimore, Williams & Wilkins, 1983.

CHAPTER SIX

Impact of Injury and Pain on Neuromuscular Control

OBJECTIVES

After reading this chapter, the student will be able to

1. identify the three components of neuromuscular control,

2. differentiate between neuromuscular control deficits and muscle atrophy as causes of muscular weakness, and

3. discuss the effects of swelling, pain, and joint instability on neuromuscular control.

A fit, physically active, 22-year-old collegiate rugby player enters the athletic training room for a preoperative consultation to review a postoperative rehabilitation plan of care. He injured his right knee 5 months ago while skiing and was diagnosed with a torn ACL. He delayed surgery because of a heavy work schedule but is to undergo a patellar bone–tendon–bone allograft reconstruction in 2 days. He states he has been working out regularly to build muscle strength and maintain overall fitness. Examination of the knee reveals a positive Lachman's test, full knee range of motion, and excellent muscular development of the quadriceps and hamstrings.

On the day following surgery, he has extreme difficulty contracting his vastus medialis during a quadriceps set and is initially unable to perform a straight leg raise (figure 6.1). Why are the quadriceps so weak? Less than 24 hr has passed since surgery, certainly too little time for muscle to atrophy. You determine that this athlete is experiencing a loss of neuromuscular control and use neuromuscular electrical stimulation to assist in neuromuscular reeducation. Within a couple of days, you observe substantial improvement.

This case study illustrates that pain, swelling, and joint instability can impair neuromuscular control. The certified athletic trainer must be able to detect and correct deficits in neuromuscular control to progress a rehabilitation plan into strength, power, and sport-specific retraining.

The three previous chapters introduced the inflammatory response, acute pain, and persistent pain. These chapters, and this introduction to neuromuscular control, form the foundation for the application of therapeutic modalities. This chapter identifies the causes of impaired neuromuscular control and introduces basic concepts of neuromuscular reeducation. Chapter 8 presents techniques of neuromuscular electrical stimulation, and chapter 12 presents the role of biofeedback in restoring neuromuscular control. Additional treatment strategies are discussed in detail in the next text in this series, *Therapeutic Exercise for Athletic Injuries*.

Five components of a progressive rehabilitation program were identified in the first chapter (figure 1.3). Therapeutic modalities are commonly applied to control pain and interrupt the pain–spasm cycle. Pain control and appropriate postinjury care to minimize swelling will help restore range of motion. The next priority in rehabilitation is to return neuromuscular control, the last component of the rehabilitation program affected by modality application (figure 6.2).

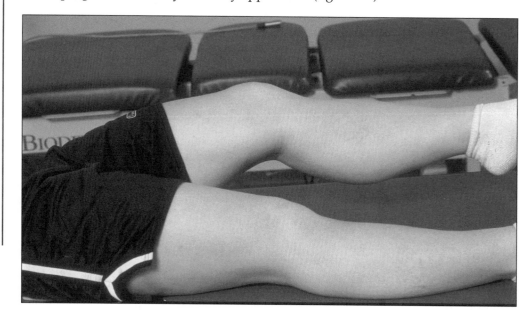

❚ Figure 6.1 Straight leg raise with extensor lag.

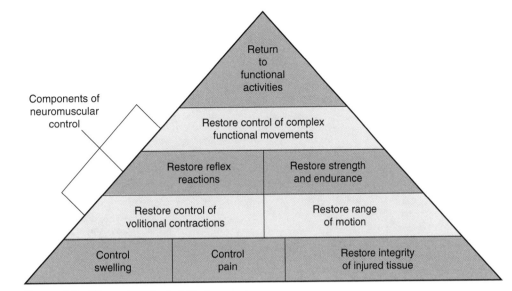

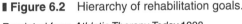

Figure 6.2 Hierarchy of rehabilitation goals.

Reprinted from *Athletic Therapy Today* 1998.

Neuromuscular control is an elusive concept in the rehabilitation paradigm. Unlike pain, range of motion, strength, endurance, and power, neuromuscular control is difficult to measure and quantify. From a practical and clinical perspective, there are three components of neuromuscular control. The first is consciously controlled, voluntary muscle contraction (or volitional contraction). Individuals who suffer significant knee injuries, experience patellofemoral pain, or undergo knee surgery will lose neuromuscular control of the quadriceps as a result of pain and swelling. A loss of volitional control of muscle is illustrated in the opening case study, where the rugby player was unable to contract the quadriceps muscle (quadriceps set) or perform a straight leg raise. This athlete demonstrated a disruption of the body's ability to recruit strong, volitional muscle contraction, because normal neuromuscular control had been compromised.

INTEGRATION OF COMPONENTS OF NEUROMUSCULAR CONTROL INTO A REHABILITATION PLAN OF CARE

Neuromuscular control was identified in chapter 1 (see figure 1.3 on p. 7) as the third priority in a rehabilitation plan of care. By recognizing that neuromuscular control consists of three components the certified athletic trainer can integrate activities to restore neuromuscular control throughout a progressive plan of care (figure 6.3).

The second component of neuromuscular control involves restoring reflex responses. For example, when the lateral ligaments of the ankle are stressed, mechanoreceptors in the joint capsules and ligaments respond with a volley of sensory input (see chapter 4). The increase in sensory input recruits the ankle evertors to resist ankle inversion. Because the reflex loop synapses are found in the dorsal horn, the reaction is a spinal reflex-generated muscle contraction (figure 6.4). When ligaments are damaged, the sensory input from the mechanoreceptors is altered and the reflex control over the muscles inhibited. This loss of reflex response is most associated with the concept of proprioception. However, proprioception is really the afferent component of neuromuscular control. Furthermore, in tasks such as balancing, the individual's ability to recruit skeletal muscle to maintain stance is based on sensory input from mechanoreceptors, Golgi tendon organs, and muscle spindles. Thus, these assessments really measure neuromuscular control rather than isolated proprioceptive function.

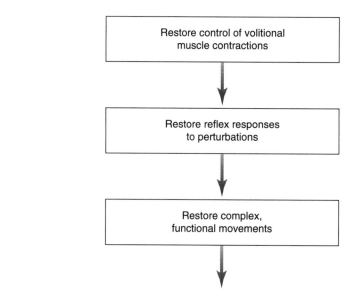

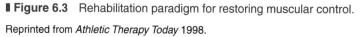

■ Figure 6.3   Rehabilitation paradigm for restoring muscular control.

Reprinted from *Athletic Therapy Today* 1998.

The final component of neuromuscular control relates to complex, functional movements. When one becomes proficient in athletics, complex integration of afferent input is required to precisely control movement through efferent pathways. Conscious effort is absent once the movement begins. For example, when attempting to learn to play golf, the player is consciously aware of each movement. As the player becomes proficient, he or she executes the swing without conscious control. However, injury can disrupt the ability to perform well-practiced, functional movement patterns. The individual who is unable to perform a straight leg raise will also demonstrate abnormal stair climbing patterns and running gait, indicating disrupted neuromuscular control of functional and sport-specific movements.

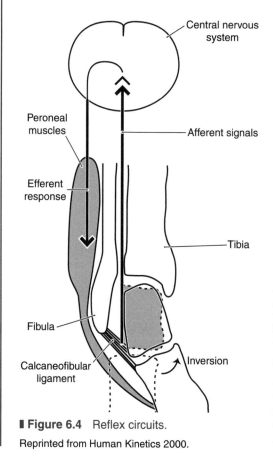

■ Figure 6.4   Reflex circuits.

Reprinted from Human Kinetics 2000.

NEUROMUSCULAR CONTROL AND MUSCLE ATROPHY

Muscles generate force when motor nerves send impulses to the muscle fibers they innervate. The more muscle fibers stimulated to contract, the more force is generated. The cross section of muscles also influences the amount of force a muscle can generate. When muscle is not used for a period of time the cross section diminishes, or atrophies, which is a relatively slow process. When the ability to recruit muscle fiber contraction in a coordinated manner is impaired, neuromuscular control has been lost, a process that can occur quite quickly.

Thus, a loss of neuromuscular control should not be confused with muscle atrophy. Several weeks of muscle disuse, such as cast immobilization, will result in atrophy as well as loss of neuromuscular control. Fortunately, the importance of early motion following musculoskeletal injury is widely recognized, and prolonged immobilization is used only when absolutely necessary.

WHY IS NEUROMUSCULAR CONTROL LOST?

The case study at the beginning of this chapter provides a clinical example of lost neuromuscular control. Inhibition of quadriceps function following knee injury is commonly encountered in clinical practice. The relationship between knee injury and neuromuscular control of the quadriceps has received considerable attention in the medical literature. However, much more study is needed for us to fully understand the impact of musculoskeletal injury on neuromuscular control and refine therapeutic approaches to restoring neuromuscular control.

Clinical observations and scientific investigations suggest that more than one factor contributes to decreased neuromuscular control following musculoskeletal injury. This chapter further explores the impact of swelling, pain, and altered mechanoreceptor input on the ability to consciously perform volitional muscle contractions.

Activities to restore pattern-generated movements and reflexive muscle contractions usually do not involve therapeutic modalities. These therapeutic strategies are addressed in *Therapeutic Exercises for Athletic Training*. However, volitional control over isolated muscles, such as occurs when a straight leg raise is used to recruit the quadriceps, or when controlled functional motions such as bending and stair climbing are initiated, can be restored by therapeutic modality application. Furthermore, conscious control of muscle must be restored before reflex patterns and more complex movement patterns can be retrained. Thus, successful rehabilitation often requires you to identify and correct deficits in volitional control over skeletal muscles.

SWELLING

Swelling within the joint capsule of the knee decreases quadriceps function. Certified athletic trainers observe this phenomenon following knee injury, and researchers have studied it. By infusing saline solution into the knee, researchers have been able to inhibit quadriceps function as measured through EMG (Kennedy, Alexander, and Hayes 1982; Spencer, Hayes, and Alexander 1984). Vastus medialis activity can be inhibited by as little as 30 ml of fluid (Spencer, Hayes, and Alexander 1984). This small increase in fluid volume would appear as very mild effusion upon clinical exam. Larger increases in volume affect the function of the other quadriceps muscles. A 200 ml increase can severely limit the ability to perform a straight leg raise even in the absence of knee injury. Neuromuscular inhibition appears to persist as long as joint capsule volume remains elevated (Kennedy, Alexander, and Hayes 1982).

The reason joint effusion inhibits quadriceps femoris function is not fully understood. However, much of the knee joint capsule is innervated by articular branches of the femoral nerve (figure 6.5). In particular, the articular branch of the femoral nerve to the vastus medialis supplies a large portion of the anteromedial joint capsule. Swelling within the capsule may stimulate stretch receptors, which in turn trigger reflex inhibition of the motor neuron pool. The suprapatellar pouch accommodates increases in joint fluid volume more than do other parts of the joint capsule. The tendency of fluid to accumulate in this area of the knee may partially explain why the vastus medialis is most affected by swelling within the knee joint.

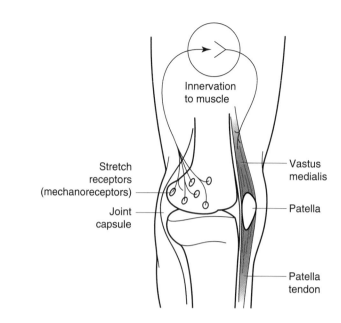

Figure 6.5 Swelling within the capsule may stimulate stretch receptors (mechano-receptors), which in turn trigger reflex inhibition of the motor neuron pool.

PAIN

Pain also appears to impact neuromuscular control. Individuals who have sustained injury to the lower extremity often limp to protect damaged tissue and minimize pain. The altered movement patterns represent alterations in neuromuscular control. Could the observed gait deviation be due to swelling and altered mechanoreceptor input? Perhaps, but careful observation suggests that pain contributes to neuromuscular control deficits. Individuals with little or no swelling and no history of trauma may exhibit decreased neuromuscular control.

For example, some individuals with patellofemoral pain (PFP) experience little or no swelling. The connective tissues housing mechanoreceptors have not been damaged, nor are these receptors stimulated due to swelling. However, if you ask the person with PFP to tighten the quadriceps muscle and you palpate the vastus medialis, it will feel softer than the fully tightened quadriceps of the uninjured leg (figure 6.6), because the individual is unable to effectively recruit the vastus medialis.

Observations such as these support the notion that pain contributes to the loss of neuromuscular control. Unfortunately, it is difficult to study the impact of joint pain

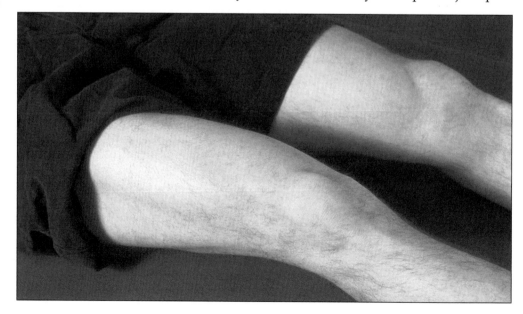

Figure 6.6 Decreased tone in quadriceps.

on neuromuscular control in a research laboratory. Ethical and methodological considerations restrict the induction of joint pain, so clinical observation remains the best evidence that pain alters neuromuscular control.

Despite the lack of research evidence, clinical observation offers insights into successful clinical practice. For example, in the physically active suffering patellofemoral pain, when knee pain inhibits vastus medialis function, patellar mobility increases. With greater patellar mobility, there is more irritation of the joint tissues and more pain. Thus, a cycle is created that gradually turns into patellofemoral pain syndrome. With sufficient irritation, swelling will also develop, further compromising neuromuscular control and exacerbating the cycle.

This phenomenon explains why some athletes who present with the signs and symptoms of patellofemoral pain syndrome have no history of knee injury. Other factors, such as changes in training routine, and biomechanical problems, such as subtalar hyperpronation and genu varus, clearly are contributors. However, these factors do not explain the loss of neuromuscular control of the quadriceps. Thus, it appears that pain decreases neuromuscular control.

The role of pain in the loss of neuromuscular control is an important consideration during therapeutic exercise. When active exercise is painful, normal neuromuscular patterning is disrupted. Painful exercise inhibits muscle groups, perpetuates abnormal motor control, and slows recovery from injury. With the exception of passive stretching of muscle and connective tissue, therapeutic exercise must remain pain-free if neuromuscular control is to be reestablished and maintained.

ALTERED INPUT

The proprioceptors in the skin, muscles, tendons, and joints provide the central nervous system (CNS) with a constant flow of somatosensory information. The CNS responds by generating appropriate motor commands to allow the body to move safely through a changing environment.

For example, when the ankle is inverted toward the limits of the range of motion, afferent input is generated in three ways: (1) The mechanoreceptors within the ligaments and joint capsule alert the CNS to the precarious position of the ankle; (2) muscle spindles within the muscles that evert the ankle (peroneus longus and brevis) signal that the muscle is rapidly stretching; and (3) skin receptors signal the distortion and stretch of the skin over the lateral ankle. The CNS processes these afferent signals and responds by activating the motor pathways that cause the evertors to contract and by inhibiting motor activity in the antagonistic muscles to counteract the sudden inversion of the ankle. Thus, the proprioceptors sense the potential for ankle joint injury, and the CNS responds through a dorsal horn synaptic reflex loop to prevent joint injury.

LIGAMENT AND JOINT CAPSULE INJURY

The sensory input from mechanoreceptors can trigger muscle contractions through the spinal reflex loops. Moreover, the continuous flow of sensory input from mechanoreceptors is essential to the performance of coordinated movements. Mechanoreceptors are most active at the anatomical limits of the physiological range of motion. Damage to ligaments and joint capsules alters mechanoreceptor input in the damaged tissue and subsequently impacts neuromuscular control. Swelling that limits full range of motion also alters mechanoreceptor activity. These changes in the pattern of sensory input from mechanoreceptors decrease neuromuscular control. For example, researchers studying quadriceps musculature in patients with ACL-deficient knees found 10% to 30% decreases in pain-free, isokinetic force production despite minor atrophy and little morphological change (Lorentzon et al. 1993).

It has been suggested that following ACL injury, input from capsular mechanoreceptors facilitates hamstring function and inhibits recruitment of the quadriceps (Solomonow et al. 1987). Certainly the observant athletic trainer can detect altered movement patterns in physically active people following knee injuries as well as in those with more chronic knee instability. The evidence suggests that these changes in neuromuscular control persist after pain and swelling have resolved.

Much of our understanding of the impact of swelling and pain on neuromuscular control has come from the study of knee injury. However, alterations in kinesthetic awareness and slowed reflex contractions have been observed following injury to other joints.

Ankle Injuries

Neuromuscular control is lost following sprains of the lateral ligaments of the ankle. Researchers have reported deficits in position sense (Freeman 1965) and balance in single-leg stance (Gross 1987). In addition, the response of the peroneal muscles is slowed following ankle sprain (Lofvenberg et al. 1995). One of the goals of treatment following an ankle sprain is to restore neuromuscular control of the muscles surrounding the ankle. This is accomplished through a return to pain-free weight bearing as early as possible, depending on the severity of the injury, and a progressive program of balance and coordination exercises (figure 6.7).

Shoulder Injuries

Pain, disruption in ligamentous stability, and swelling appear to inhibit the rotator cuff, especially supraspinatus, and perhaps the scapular stabilizers. The stabilizing function of these two muscle groups is essential for normal, pain-free shoulder function. For many years, individuals with rotator cuff tendinitis and glenohumeral impingement were treated with rotator cuff strengthening exercises. Some improved

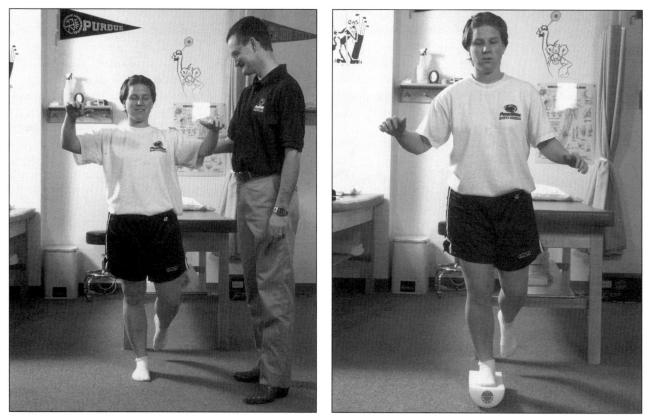

■ Figure 6.7   Single-leg balance *(a)* and balance on foam roller *(b)*.

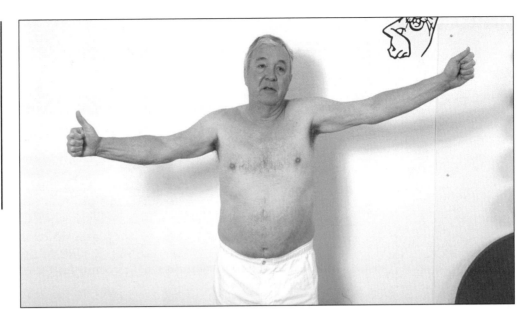

Figure 6.8 Shoulder hiking in an effort to abduct the arm is a common manifestation of impaired neuromuscular control.

rapidly, whereas others improved very slowly. Closer examination of those who failed to respond to rotator cuff strengthening revealed that many demonstrated impaired neuromuscular control of the rotator cuff, the scapular stabilizers, or both (figure 6.8).

Injury to the ligaments and capsule of the glenohumeral joint compromises the sense of shoulder positioning and movement detection. Clinically these injuries compromise the athlete's ability to keep the shoulder out of positions likely to cause dislocation and further injury.

Training with visual and EMG biofeedback effectively addresses neuromuscular control deficits and speeds recovery. Pain, instability, and swelling appear to affect the shoulder muscles in much the same manner as occurs with the quadriceps following knee injury. Strengthening alone does not relieve shoulder pain or promote recovery following shoulder dislocation. The injured individual must relearn proper control of the glenohumeral and scapular stabilizers—in other words, reestablish neuromuscular control.

The impact of swelling, pain, and instability in other joints on neuromuscular control warrants further study. Certainly, there is a component of neuromuscular retraining following any injury; however, it may be more easily accomplished in some parts of the body than others. One area receiving greater attention is the lower back, where pain may alter neuromuscular function of paraspinal muscles. Certainly this loss of neuromuscular control represents a significant challenge in treating a physically active person with a history of back injury and pain.

THE ROLE OF THERAPEUTIC MODALITIES IN RESTORING NEUROMUSCULAR CONTROL

Subsequent chapters discuss neuromuscular electrical stimulation and EMG biofeedback, the modalities most commonly used to help individuals regain volitional control of muscle contraction. There are no direct modality applications used to retrain protective reflex responses or control of complex movements. However, several therapeutic modalities may be used to permit pain-free exercises aimed at restoring these components of neuromuscular control. When rehabilitation is viewed as a hierarchy of goals and modalities are viewed as a means of achieving specific goals, the relationship between modality application and efforts to restore neuromuscular control becomes evident.

SUMMARY

1. *Identify the three components of neuromuscular control.*

    Neuromuscular control can be divided into three components: (1) conscious, volitional control over isolated muscle contraction, (2) protective reflex patterns, and (3) control over complex, functional movements.

2. *Differentiate between neuromuscular control deficits and muscle atrophy as causes of muscular weakness.*

    Muscles generate force when motor nerves send impulses to the muscle fibers they innervate. The more muscle fibers stimulated to contract, the more force is generated. The cross section of muscles also influences the amount of force a muscle can generate. When muscle is not used for a period of time, the cross section diminishes, or atrophies, which is a relatively slow process. When the ability to recruit muscle fiber contraction in a coordinated manner is impaired, neuromuscular control has been lost, which can occur quite quickly.

3. *Discuss the effects of swelling, pain, and joint instability on neuromuscular control.*

    Impaired neuromuscular control is common following musculoskeletal injury. Research has demonstrated that swelling alone can impair neuromuscular control. Most of the work has involved the knee, where relatively small amounts of fluid infused into the joint diminish the ability to contract the quadriceps muscle. Pain results in protective muscle spasm and loss of function. The precise mechanisms by which pain affects neuromuscular control have not been fully explained. However, observations of individuals without demonstrable swelling or instability often reveal inhibition of neuromuscular control. Joint instability has also been shown to alter neuromuscular control. Injuries to ligaments and joint capsules damage the mechanoreceptors and alter the proprioceptive feedback to the CNS. Control of muscle activity depends on sensory feedback, and disruption of this loop manifests as loss of neuromuscular control.

CITED REFERENCES

Freeman MAR: Instability of the foot after injuries to the lateral ligaments of the ankle. *J Bone Joint Surg* 47B:669-677, 1965.

Gross MT: Effects of recurrent lateral ankle sprains on active and passive judgment of joint position. *Phys Ther* 67:1505-1509, 1987.

Kennedy JC, Alexander IJ, Hayes KC: Nerve supply to the human knee and its functional importance. *Am J Sports Med* 10:329-335, 1982.

Lofvenberg R, Karrholm J, Sundelin G, Ahlgren O: Prolonged reaction time in patients with chronic lateral instability of the ankle. *Am J Sports Med* 23:414-417, 1995.

Lorentzon R, Elmqvist L, Sjostrom M, Fagerlund M, Fuglmeyer AR: Thigh musculature in relation to chronic anterior cruciate ligament tear: Muscle size, morphology and mechanical output before reconstruction. *Am J Sports Med* 17:423-429, 1993.

Solomonow M, Baratta R, Zhou BH, Shoji H, Bose W, Beck C, D'Ambrosia R: The synergistic action of the anterior cruciate ligament and thigh muscles in maintaining joint stability. *Am J Sports Med* 15:207-213, 1987.

Spencer JD, Hayes KC, Alexander IJ: Knee joint effusion and quadriceps reflex inhibition in man. *Arch Phys Med Rehabil* 65:171-177, 1984.

ADDITIONAL SOURCES

Basmajian J, Deluca C: *Muscles Alive: Their Function Revealed by Electromyography*. Baltimore, Williams & Wilkins, 1985.

Smith LK, Weiss EL, Lehmkuhl LD: *Brunnstrom's Clinical Kinesiology*, 5th ed. Philadelphia, Davis, 1996.

CHAPTER SEVEN

Cold and Superficial Heat

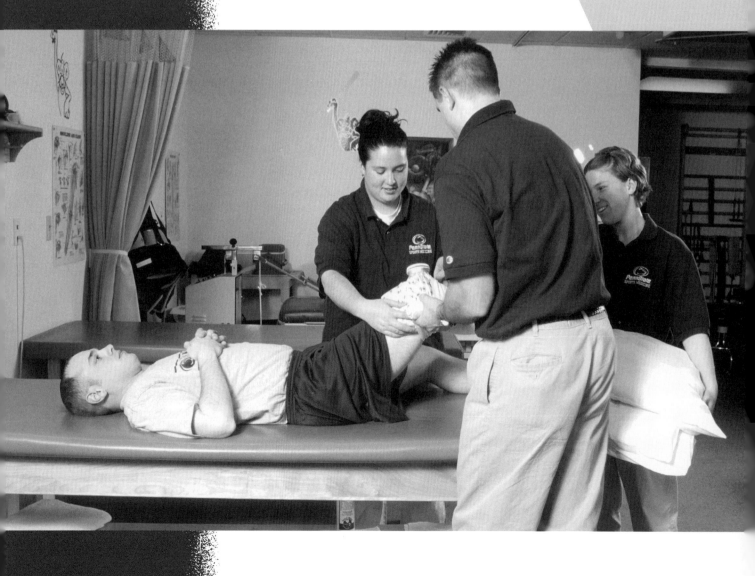

OBJECTIVES

After reading this chapter, the student will be able to

1. describe the four energy transfer mechanisms related to therapeutic modalities;

2. describe the common methods of applying superficial heat and therapeutic cold;

3. describe the thermal changes that occur with superficial heat and local cold application;

4. discuss the effect of superficial heat and local cooling on blood flow, muscle, and the nervous system;

5. discuss the indications for cold application and the impact of cooling on acute inflammation;

6. describe the common indications for the application of superficial heat;

7. identify contraindications and precautions in applying superficial heat and therapeutic cold; and

8. differentiate between superficial heating and deep heating modalities.

A 43-year-old club hockey player is referred to your care for treatment of an acute recurrence of low back pain. The player states that he twisted his back when he collided with two opponents in a game early this morning. He experienced immediate pain and chose not to continue playing because there were only a few minutes left in the game. He was evaluated by his personal physician because he began experiencing increased pain and muscle spasm while at work. He was provided with analgesic medications and referred for treatment of "mechanical low back pain."

On presentation he is in obvious discomfort but states that the pain is well localized to the mid–lumbar spine. He denies radicular symptoms or significant medical problems except for one previous episode of back pain he experienced while cutting wood last year. He received treatment on three occasions consisting of superficial heat, manual therapies, and therapeutic exercise, and his back pain resolved within 2 weeks.

You determine that relieving pain and muscle spasm is the first priority. Which modality is the best choice? Are any treatments contraindicated? Which treatments will facilitate completion of therapeutic exercises at home? This chapter addresses the application of cryotherapy and superficial heat as therapeutic modalities.

Cold and superficial heat are probably the most commonly applied therapeutic modalities. These modalities conduct heat to or away from the body. The application of cold decreases temperature of the skin and deeper tissues; however, the application of heat increases temperature only in the superficial tissue. Deeper heating can be accomplished with ultrasound and diathermy, which are discussed in chapter 9. This chapter is limited to modalities that cool tissue or warm superficial tissue.

Despite the simplicity and widespread use of cold and superficial heat, the mechanisms that bring about the desired effects are not fully understood. Although these modalities are applied to help individuals recover from injury, these modalities can also cause injury. Thus, this chapter presents fundamental concepts of energy transfer, the indications and contraindications of cryotherapy and superficial heat, and physiological responses to these modalities.

ENERGY TRANSFER

Thermal energy can be transferred to or from the body by four mechanisms: conduction, convection, radiation, and conversion. Conduction is the transfer of heat through the direct contact between a hotter and a cooler area (Michlovitz 1990). When heat or cold is applied directly to the skin, the amount of temperature change depends primarily on the temperature difference between the two surfaces and the length of time the two surfaces are in contact. Surface cooling begins immediately; however, the deeper the tissue, the longer cooling takes. When a larger surface area is heated or cooled, temperature at the center of the area being treated changes somewhat more rapidly.

Convection is the transfer of heat by the movement of air or liquid between regions of unequal temperature. For example, a convection oven circulates heated air around the food being cooked. In athletic training, a whirlpool or a fluidotherapy unit can be used to heat or cool via convection. As with conduction, the rate and extent of temperature change are determined primarily by the differences in temperature between the medium and the tissue, the length of exposure, and the size of the area treated.

Radiant energy is emitted from surfaces with temperatures above absolute 0° (Michlovitz 1990). Thus, the body emits radiant energy. However, the body can also absorb radiant energy, and radiant energy can heat the superficial tissues. The obvious example of radiant heating is sun bathing. At one time infrared or baker's lamps were commonly used for superficial heating in athletic training and physical therapy. Although less common today, these modalities are quite useful for warming large areas.

The amount of heating caused by radiant energy relates primarily to the output of the infrared bulb, the distance between the bulb and the skin, and the length of exposure.

The relationship between the heating effect and the distance between the bulb and the skin is stated as the inverse square law (figure 7.1). The inverse square law implies that the change in heating effect varies with the inverse square of the distance between the bulb and skin. For example, if a lamp were lowered from 60 cm above the skin to 30 cm, the distance would be reduced by $\frac{1}{2}$. The inverse of $\frac{1}{2}$ is 2, and the square of 2 is 4. Thus, the heating effect is increased fourfold when the height of the lamp is reduced by $\frac{1}{2}$.

This relationship assumes that the radiant energy strikes the skin perpendicularly. If the light strikes the skin at an angle, some is reflected, reducing the heating effect. This relationship is defined by the cosine law, which states that the heating effect varies with the cosine of the angle formed between the beam of radiant energy and the perpendicular (figure 7.2). For example, if the light forms a 30° angle with

a   *b*

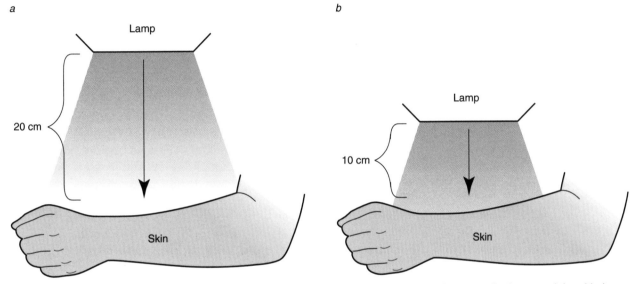

∎ Figure 7.1   The inverse square law: Heating effect equals *x (a)*. When the distance between the lamp and the skin is reduced by half *(b)*, the heating effect is increased to 4*x* (the inverse of $\frac{1}{2}$ equals 2, and 2^2 equals 4).

a   *b*

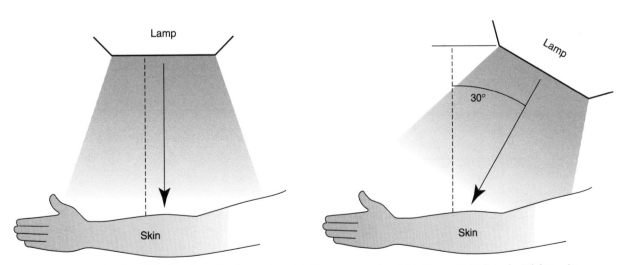

∎ Figure 7.2   The cosine law: The heating effect equals *x (a)*. The angle of the light does not deviate (= 0°) from the vertical. The cosine of 0 equals 1; thus, the heating effect equals 1*x*. The light strikes the skin at a 30° angle *(b)*. The cosine of 30° is 0.86. Thus, the heating effect is only 86% of the effect when the light was beaming straight down.

the perpendicular, the heating effect is reduced by the cosine of 30°, which is 86. Thus, the heating effect is reduced 14%.

Conversion implies that energy is changed from one form to another, so this concept does not relate to the application of cold and superficial heat. However, it does relate to two modalities discussed later and is included here for completeness. Ultrasound machines deliver acoustic (sound) energy to tissues where it is reflected and absorbed. When sound energy is absorbed into the tissues, it is converted to thermal energy. A similar phenomenon occurs when the tissues are exposed to continuous electromagnetic energy as with diathermy. These two modalities increase tissue temperature through conversion of energy within the body.

COLD APPLICATION

The application of cold for therapeutic purposes, termed *cryotherapy*, and the therapeutic combination of cold and exercise, *cryokinetics*, are common in athletic training. These treatments are cost-effective and time proven. Cryotherapy has also been extensively studied by athletic trainers, and much of what we know can be attributed to Dr. Ken Knight (1995). Yet questions remain as to how localized cooling affects the body.

METHODS OF APPLICATION

Therapeutic cooling can be accomplished by several means. The most simple is an ice pack (figure 7.3), where crushed ice in a plastic bag is placed or wrapped on the skin to cool tissues. This is an inexpensive treatment that also allows for compression and elevation of the injured part. Commercial cold packs can also be applied; however, crushed ice applied directly to the skin is preferable for several reasons. Some commercial cold packs do not conform well to the skin. In addition, cold packs stored in a freezer may be considerably colder than crushed ice, which is maintained at 32° F (0° C). Because of the greater temperature difference between the cold pack and the skin, cooling is greater and more rapid and may result in cold injury to the skin (frostbite). Because of the differences between ice and the materials used in commercial cold packs, an insulating layer of plastic or cloth must be used between commercial cold packs and the skin in order to protect it. Ultimately, greater cooling is achieved with crushed ice, especially if an elastic bandage is applied over the ice pack (Knight 1995).

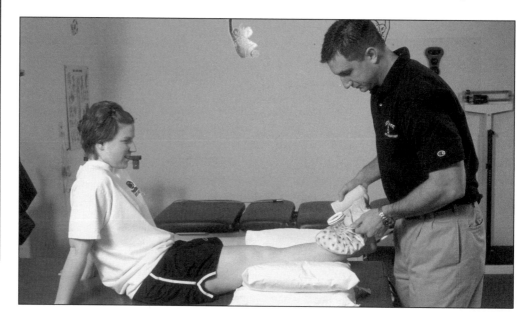

■ **Figure 7.3** Application of an ice pack.

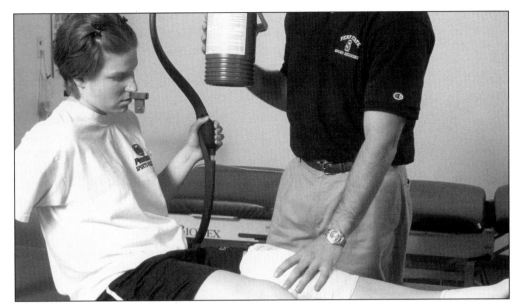

■ **Figure 7.4** Polar Care unit.

Cold water circulating units (figure 7.4), also called Polar Care units or cryocuffs (a term derived from the trade name Cryo/Cuff), are similar to ice packs in that a cold surface is placed on or near the skin. Cold water is pumped into a cuff, which is then placed on or near the skin to withdraw heat from the tissue. However, a cuff filled with cold water results in less tissue cooling than the direct application of an ice pack. Perhaps the best use of cryocuffs is under wraps and braces used postoperatively. Although the wound dressing insulates the skin against the cold, the cold water circulating unit appears to effectively decrease postoperative pain and lessen the need for analgesic medications. The cold water circulating unit provides hours of mild cooling without the need to remove braces and wraps and without the mess of ice packs.

Ice massage offers another inexpensive form of cryotherapy (figure 7.5), whereby water frozen in a paper or Styrofoam cup can be used to cool and massage the skin. Ice massage should not be applied as a first aid treatment or during the acute inflammatory response, because ice massage is incompatible with compression. However, ice massage reduces pain prior to therapeutic exercise and relieves postexercise discomfort. This technique can also be used to desensitize trigger points in the individuals who have myofascial pain syndrome and is readily available for home-based treatment.

■ **Figure 7.5** Ice massage.

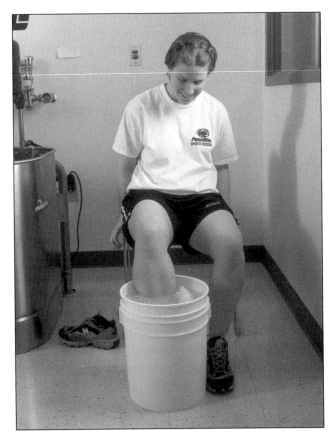

Cold water immersion and cold whirlpools are also used to administer cryotherapy (figure 7.6). Immersion in 40 to 50° F (4–10° C) water or a 50 to 60° F (10–15° C) whirlpool will cool tissue as well as an ice pack will. Warmer water is used in a whirlpool because the movement of the water continually breaks down the thermopane, the boundary layer of water around the foot that is warmer than the cold bath (figure 7.7). Loss of the thermopane allows tissues to cool more rapidly. These application methods offer a couple of advantages: The entire limb or joint can be cooled, and active exercise can be performed during the cooling process. However, cold water immersion is not ideal for first aid or during the acute inflammatory response, because the injured limb cannot be elevated.

One more method of cold application warrants brief mention. Vapocoolant sprays result in very superficial, rapid cooling through evaporation (figure 7.8). There is virtually no temperature change below the epidermis; however, vapocoolant sprays will numb an area briefly and may be effective in the management of tender trigger points associated with myofascial pain syndrome (Travel and Simons 1983).

COOLING AND REWARMING SKIN

When an ice pack is applied or a limb is immersed in an ice bath, the skin cools rapidly. After a few minutes, the rate of cooling slows and finally levels off a few degrees above the temperature of the ice pack or ice bath. When a compression wrap is applied over the ice pack, greater decreases in skin temperature are observed (Knight 1995).

When the cold is removed, a similar pattern of rewarming occurs. There is an initial rapid rise in temperature (which is of lesser magnitude than the sudden drop that occurs with cold application), followed by a more gradual return to preapplication

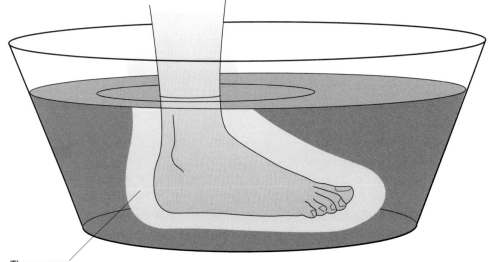

Thermopane

❚ Figure 7.7   The foot immersed in cold water. The skin warms the surrounding water, forming a thermopane or the boundary layer, which is warmer than the cold bath.

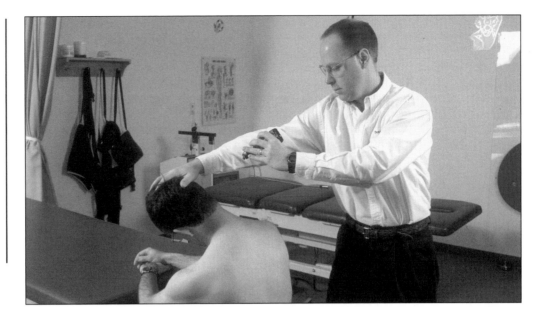

Figure 7.8
Vapocoolant spray.

temperature. At rest, the skin temperature can remain below preapplication levels for over 1 hr following 30 min of cold pack application. More rapid rewarming occurs when cooling is followed by physical activity.

COOLING AND REWARMING DEEPER TISSUES

In general, deeper tissues cool more slowly and to a lesser extent than skin. Measures of gastrocnemius muscle tissue temperature at a depth of 2.3 cm revealed slow cooling during a 22-min ice pack application (Hartviksen 1962). However, temperatures continued to drop for several minutes following the removal of the ice pack in subjects at rest, and cooling plateaued at approximately 82° F (28° C).

Research suggests that changes in intraarticular temperature follow a similar pattern as those observed in muscle (Haimovici 1982; Oosterveld et al. 1992). However, there is a greater temperature decrease in the joint than in the surrounding muscle (Wakin, Porter, and Krusen 1951). When the joint is held at rest, temperatures continue to drop after cold is removed (Bocobo et al. 1991; McMaster, Little, and Waugh 1978). Cold water immersion results in greater cooling of the intraarticular space than an ice pack (Bocobo et al. 1991), because a greater surface area of the joint is exposed to cold.

Deep tissues maintained at rest rewarm very slowly, and the rewarming of muscle and intraarticular spaces has been reported to exceed $2\frac{1}{2}$ hr (Knight 1995; Knight et al. 1980). The research into rewarming has implications for athletic training. For example, in treating an individual who will remain at rest following knee surgery, you can use ice to control pain and swelling. Research suggests that a 20- to 30-min ice pack application will cool tissues for 2 hr or more. Reapplication during the rewarming period will result in cooler tissue temperatures. Although there are not enough data to recommend a specific cooling–rewarming ratio, Knight (1995) recommended a rewarming period of at least twice the cooling period when applying ice directly to the skin. This is excellent advice.

Orthopedic surgeons have frequently used Cryo/Cuff (Aircast Inc., Summit, NJ) cold water circulating units following surgery. Although the cuff is applied over the surgical dressing, these units provide good pain relief. Because there is less tissue cooling, the unit can be applied for an extended period of time.

When the individual is active following cryotherapy, rewarming occurs much more quickly. Physical activity rapidly increases body temperature. Thus, deep tissue temperatures return to normal much more rapidly when cryotherapy is followed by exercise.

BLOOD FLOW: PHYSIOLOGICAL RESPONSE TO COOLING

Localized cooling results in a number of physiological responses. Cooling lowers the metabolic activity and oxygen demand of cells. Vasoconstriction and decreased local blood flow occur in superficial and deep tissues, although different mechanisms are involved. Superficial vasoconstriction occurs primarily through reflex mechanisms, whereas decreased metabolic activity is responsible for decreased blood flow in deep tissues.

IMPACT ON THE NERVOUS SYSTEM AND MUSCLE FUNCTION

Cold application also affects the nervous system, and individuals have described a progression of sensations during cold application. Initially, intense cold is perceived. This is followed by an aching pain, which gives way to sensations of pins and needles or warmth and finally numbness. Although not every individual will experience these sensations, this general description suggests that cold initially stimulates cold and pain receptors. Cooling of nerve fibers slows the conduction of neural impulses. Thus, after several minutes of cold, sensation is diminished because impulses cannot be transmitted from the periphery to the sensory cortex. The numbness or analgesia experienced during cryotherapy results in the first goal of rehabilitation: pain relief.

MUSCLE SPASM AND FUNCTION

Muscle function is controlled by the nervous system. However, we will examine muscle spasm and function separately because of their importance in athletic training. In addition to relieving pain and thus breaking the pain–spasm cycle, cold also reduces muscle spasm by directly affecting the muscle spindle.

Muscle spindles sense the stretch of a muscle. The spindles are innervated by gamma efferent fibers, which allow the spindle to adjust to changes in muscle length. When injury occurs, the body responds through reflex contraction of surrounding muscles. These involuntary contractions or spasms splint the injured area and prevent further injury. However, spasm occludes blood flow and exacerbates the pain–spasm cycle.

Cold application appears to decrease spasm through direct and reflex mechanisms. When cooled, the muscle spindles are less sensitive; thus, the muscle relaxes and spasm is relieved. However, decreases in muscle spasm begin to occur before the muscle cools significantly, suggesting that a reflex response to cold also occurs. Certainly, the antispasmotic effects of cryotherapy are an important consideration when selecting a therapeutic modality to treat musculoskeletal injuries.

Force production of muscle is decreased by cooling. Knight summarized the findings of several investigators and concluded that maximum isometric and isotonic strength and rate of force development are reduced when the muscle tissue is cooled below 59 to 64° F (15–18° C). Cooling to this level requires at least 20 min of application. Following cryotherapy, an individual should rewarm muscle tissue through rhythmic exercises before returning to activities that require maximal muscular efforts.

PROPRIOCEPTION AND SENSATION

Although cooling slows nerve conduction velocity and relieves pain and muscle spasm, the effects on proprioception, postural stability, and sensation are less evident. Studies of the effect of cryotherapy on balance and postural stability have reported conflicting conclusions. Ice bath immersion of the ankle and lower leg appears to temporarily reduce postural stability and balance (Gerig 1990; Rivers et al. 1995; Steinagel et al. 1996). However, ice pack application to the ankle and knee does not result in similar changes (McDonough et al. 1996; Thieme et al. 1996). Open kinetic chain repositioning is not altered following cold water immersion (LaRiviere and Osternig 1994).

Performance of maximal-effort jumping and agility tasks may also be affected by tissue cooling, although the results of studies are conflicting. Some investigators (Cross, Wilson, and Perrin 1995; Greicar et al. 1996) reported that cold adversely affects jumping and agility performance, whereas others (Evans et al. 1996; Shuler et al. 1996) found no performance differences after cryotherapy.

The previously mentioned research may appear confusing, and you may question when to apply cold in light of the potential to impact sport performance. However, when cold is used to treat athletic injury, these issues are of minimal concern. Individuals treated with cryotherapy are rarely capable of maximal-effort, functional exercise. For the few who are capable of such exercise but need to apply cold for pain management, a period of rewarming with safe, rhythmic exercises is advised. One must question, however, if jumping and agility exercises are appropriate for injured individuals requiring cryotherapy for pain management.

There is also conflicting information on the effect of cold on cutaneous sensation. Cooling of the forearm and hand appears to alter cutaneous sensation in the fingers and thumb (Provins and Morton 1960; Rubley 1997) However, cold water immersion does not alter cutaneous sensation of the foot (Ingersoll, Knight, and Merrick 1992). The differences in these findings are probably due to the greater sensitivity of the hand. Rewarming of the hand appears warranted before performing fine motor tasks.

INDICATIONS FOR THERAPEUTIC COLD

The primary reason for applying cold is pain relief. Cryotherapy is a simple, portable, and inexpensive means of relieving pain and muscle spasm following musculoskeletal injury. Cryotherapy can be used to manage pain during the acute inflammatory response, to allow for pain-free therapeutic exercise, and to manage some persistent pain patterns, particularly myofascial pain syndrome.

Cryotherapy and Acute Inflammation

During the acute inflammatory response, use of an ice pack or cold pack should be combined with compression, elevation, and protection of the injured tissues. This combination of treatments controls pain, limits swelling, and prevents further injury. Each component plays a role in increasing the injured individual's comfort and speeding recovery. However, these treatments must be combined for maximum effect, and cold application must be repeated. A 20- to 30-min cold application repeated every 2 hr is an effective and well-tolerated use of cold in the management of acute musculoskeletal injuries.

During the acute inflammatory response following tissue injury, cold reduces pain and minimizes secondary tissue injury. Pain relief is most likely due to a slowed nerve conduction velocity. Clinical observation and investigation suggest that cold decreases secondary injury. Knight (1995) referred to secondary injury as *hypoxic cell death.* He theorized that during an acute inflammatory response, disruption of capillaries and congestion due to edema decrease oxygenation of healthy cells close to the tissue damage. Hypoxia leads to cell death. Thus, following musculoskeletal injury there is a period of additional tissue damage, or secondary injury, due to hypoxia.

Certainly cooling of tissue lowers the metabolic activity and reduces oxygen demand. When oxygen demand is reduced through cooling, more cells survive this period of hypoxia. Because more cells survive there is less total tissue damage, a more rapid resolution of the signs and symptoms of acute inflammation, and a more rapid recovery.

In light of the hypoxic cell death model, the benefits of cold following acute injury are obvious. However, the neutrophils and macrophages in the area of tissue damage are very active, and there is a localized vasodilation. Is secondary injury solely the result of hypoxia, or is there another explanation?

In figure 3.4, cyclooxygenase was identified as the enzyme that converts arachidonic acid to endoperoxide. This conversion and neutrophil activity generate large quantities of oxygen free radicals. These free radicals and lysosomal enzymes are present to break down the damaged cells so that the area can be cleared for tissue repair. However, the free radicals also damage healthy cells. It is possible that secondary tissue injury is due more to the actions of free radicals and cell-damaging enzymes than to hypoxia.

This alternative explanation is speculative. Is it important? The benefits of cryotherapy in managing acute musculoskeletal injury are apparent. Thus, the athletic trainer may view this issue as academic, having little clinical relevance. However, it is worth exploring. First, this explanation may better explain why cold is effective. More importantly, further investigation may lead to additional therapeutic adjuncts, such as antioxidant therapy, that the sports medicine team can use to help injured athletes.

Compression and elevation are also important in acute injury management. Elevation lowers capillary hydrostatic pressure. Chapter 3 introduced a capillary filtration pressure system. When there is tissue injury, osmotic pressure exerted by free proteins in the interstitium disrupts normal pressure. Swelling will increase until a new pressure balance is reached. When the injured body part is elevated and capillary hydrostatic pressure is lowered, less fluid escapes from the capillary and a new filtration pressure balance is reached sooner.

Compression also can influence swelling by exerting an external force that tends to hold fluid within the capillary system. However, the pressure exerted by elastic wraps probably has little impact on swelling. Felt pads and tape exert greater pressures but may increase pain as tissue is squeezed between the force of the interstitial fluid volume and the external compression.

Although elastic wraps do not exert a great deal of pressure, the wraps do remind the individual to protect injured tissues and may reduce pain and protective muscle spasms. Protecting the injured tissues is very important through the first two phases of the inflammatory process. Others have used terms such as *rest* and *stabilization* rather than *protection*. Whichever term is used, the injured individual should avoid activity that increases pain during the acute inflammatory response.

CRYOKINETICS

Knight (1995) described the application of cold before or during exercise and coined the term *cryokinetics* ("cold and motion"). Cryokinetics involves cold application, usually consisting of cold water immersion, cold whirlpool, or ice massage, and active exercise. Cold is applied until analgesia is achieved (10–15 min). Once the painful area is numbed, a careful progression of exercises is initiated. When the numbing effects of the cold wear off, cold is reapplied. Several repetitions of cold application and exercise can be performed.

Cryokinetics can speed functional recovery. A pain–spasm cycle can persist beyond acute inflammation, and you may have to break the cycle before therapeutic exercises can progress. In addition, injury sensitizes the tissues. Following an injury, normal stresses may be perceived as painful despite ample time for tissue repair. Peppard (personal communication, 1977) described using cryokinetics to reset central bias. By using cold to control pain, you can progress the individual through increasingly demanding activities. When you carefully control the injured individual's activity progression, previously painful movements become pain-free, central bias is reset, and normal, painless functional movement patterns are restored.

Sound clinical judgment must be used in initiating cryokinetics. With relatively minor injuries such as a Grade I lateral ankle sprain, cryokinetics can be initiated 1 to 2 days following injury. Actions such as walking and jogging do not stress the lateral ligaments. Thus, the injured person can return to activity when his or her function allows, provided that the ankle is protected from forced inversion. However, if the ankle injury is more severe and involves injury to the syndesmosis (articulation between the distal tibia and fibula), walking and jogging must be delayed until the damaged ligaments heal. These activities greatly stress the syndesmotic ligaments and would delay healing and result in an unstable ankle.

In general, cold decreases sensation and relieves pain but does not provide anesthesia. If exercise during cryotherapy is painful, it should be discontinued. You can reapply the cold and resume exercises after numbness has returned or end the exercise session. Likewise, if the injured individual becomes too aggressive with a therapeutic regimen, pain, spasm, and swelling will increase the following day, and rehabilitation will be slowed for 1 to 3 days while the newly inflamed tissue recovers. Two good rules in any rehabilitation exercise program are (1) pain that alters normal movement patterns indicates that the individual is not ready to perform the exercise, and (2) the individual should be able to do tomorrow what was done today. Clinical experience will refine your ability to judge the appropriateness of an exercise for each individual, but these rules are commonsense guidelines for the progression of therapeutic exercise, especially cryokinetics.

CRYOTHERAPY IN THE TREATMENT OF PERSISTENT PAIN

Cryotherapy may also be effective in managing some persistent pain problems. For individuals with myofascial pain syndrome, characterized by very sensitive trigger points, cryotherapy offers a safe, cost-effective home treatment. Travel and Simons (1983) described the use of ethyl chloride spray and stretch in treating myofascial pain. Ice massage using brief stroking can produce similar responses.

Brief, intense cold to sensitive points may decrease pain by stimulating the nociceptive pathway (Level II pain model) described in chapter 4. A more prolonged ice massage decreases the sensitivity of free nerve endings and slows conduction velocity of afferent fibers. The numbing effect of the ice breaks local pain–spasm cycles, relieving the symptoms of myofascial pain.

Cryokinetics may also be useful in the management of myofascial pain. Therapeutic exercises to restore motion, improve posture, and reestablish pain-free, functional movement patterns are often better tolerated following cryotherapy.

Cold is not indicated in the treatment of all persistent pain problems. Complex regional pain syndrome may be exacerbated by cryotherapy; the intense stimulus of the cold can result in excruciating pain and worsen the problem.

CAUTIONS AND CONTRAINDICATIONS

Although therapeutic modalities are applied to make injured individuals more comfortable and speed rehabilitation, these treatments can also cause harm. Before applying any therapeutic agent, be certain relevant equipment is in proper working order, ensure that any electrical equipment (e.g., whirlpool) is powered by a circuit served by a ground fault interrupter, and identify known contraindications or conditions that warrant special caution.

Some medical conditions result in significant adverse reactions and contraindicate the application of cold (table 7.1). The most common condition in this category is vasospastic disorders, of which Raynaud's phenomenon is the most common. Raynaud's phenomenon is characterized by constriction of arteries and arterioles in an extremity. The restriction in blood flow results in a blue, gray, or purplish discoloration of the skin accompanied by burning or tingling sensations or numbness. Raynaud's phenomenon is most common in women. The symptoms and signs are transient; however, many individuals with Raynaud's phenomenon experience such discomfort that cold cannot be applied long enough to have a beneficial effect. Thus, cryotherapy is contraindicated.

Table 7.1   Indications, Contraindications, and Precautions for Cold

Indications	Contraindications	Precautions
Relieve pain	Raynaud's phenomenon	Application over superficial nerves
Control swelling and protect injured tissues (when combined with rest, elevation, and compression)	Cold urticaria	Diminished sensation
	Cryoglobinemia	Poor local circulation
	Paroxymal cold hemoglobinuria	Slow-healing wounds
Decrease muscle spasm		Medically unstable

Cold urticaria, an allergic reaction to cold exposure, also contraindicates cryotherapy. When cold is applied to someone susceptible to cold urticaria, an anaphylactic reaction occurs. Hives break out in the cooler area and are accompanied by intense itching. Failure to recognize the problem and discontinue the cryotherapy could result in a more systemic reaction and could affect respiration and consciousness.

Cold-induced hemoglobinuria (paroxymal cold hemoglobinuria) and cryoglobinemia are two rare conditions that also contraindicate cryotherapy. Hemoglobinuria occurs when the rate of red blood cell breakdown exceeds the rate at which hemoglobin combines with other proteins. The excess hemoglobin is excreted in the urine. The condition is characterized by darkened urine and back pain. Cryoglobinemia is a condition where an abnormal clumping of plasma proteins (cryoglobins) is stimulated by cold application. The symptoms include skin discoloration and dyspenia. These conditions may occur in conjunction with Raynaud's phenomenon or cold urticaria. Although these conditions are rare, you must keep them in mind. Initially cryotherapy is uncomfortable, but most individuals accommodate and tolerate it well. Be certain that discomfort during cryotherapy is not associated with any of these conditions.

Some other situations warrant caution. Some large nerves emerge from deep tissue and pass just below the skin and fatty layer. Because there is less tissue to insulate the nerve, it can be injured by cold or pressure during ice pack application. These injuries, referred to as cold-induced nerve palsy, are preventable. The ulnar nerve as it passes through the ulnar groove and the peroneal nerve as it passes through the posterior lateral aspect of the knee are most susceptible. The lateral femoral cutaneous nerve can also be injured by cold applied in the area of the femoral triangle.

Protect these nerves by applying a dry cloth over the nerve and limit cold application in the area to 20 to 30 min.

Special caution is warranted when using cryotherapy to treat individuals who are frail, are suffering from significant medical problems, have slow-healing wounds, or have diminished circulation or sensation. The first law of therapeutics is "Do no harm." Thus, if you are uncertain about the safety of any modality application, do not administer the treatment.

SUPERFICIAL HEAT

Because the fatty layer of tissue beneath the dermis insulates the deeper tissues, modalities that heat the skin are classified as superficial heating modalities. These modalities have little to no effect on the temperature, metabolism, or blood flow below the skin except in areas with little fat, such as over the joints of the hand. Despite the limited effects on deep tissue temperature, these modalities are commonly used to decrease pain and muscle spasm. The remainder of this chapter addresses methods of application, physiological effects, and safety issues related to the application of superficial heat.

METHODS OF APPLICATION

The most common form of superficial heat is the moist heat pack, usually a hydrocollator pack (figure 7.9). Hot water tanks called hydrocollator units are found in most athletic training rooms and sports medicine clinics. These units heat packs that are filled with a gel that retains heat. By placing the packs into a hydrocollator tank (170° F, or 76.6° C), you have ready access to superficial heat. At that temperature, direct contact would burn the skin, so you should wrap the packs in terrycloth covers and towels for protection. When using heat packs with individuals who are at risk for skin injury (i.e., those with circulatory compromise) and in circumstances when a person lies on a hot pack, be certain to provide sufficient insulation.

Warm water whirlpools are another common form of superficial heat (figure 7.10). Whirlpools permit heating around an entire limb or joint. The motion of the water also massages the tissue, which may add to the analgesic and antispasmotic effects of superficial heating. Whirlpools also allow for active or passive motion during heating.

The temperature of the water must be maintained within a safe range. Water that is too hot can scald the skin, and whirlpool temperatures should never exceed 115° F (46° C). Because treatment in a whirlpool also stresses the body's ability to dissipate heat, whirlpool treatment can result in hyperthermia and heat illness. The larger the portion of the body immersed in the whirlpool, the greater the heat stress. Table 7.2 provides reasonable guidelines for maximum whirlpool temperatures for various areas of the body. If the whirlpool is located in a poorly ventilated area,

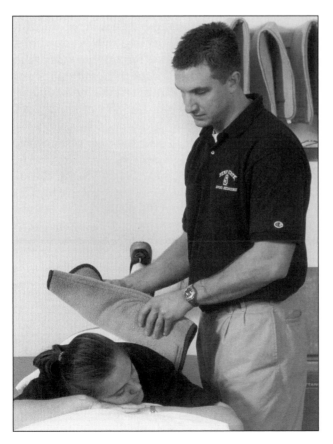

Figure 7.9 A hydrocollator pack application.

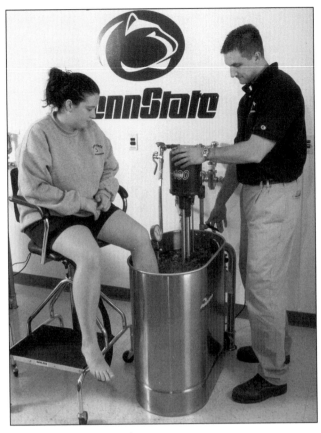

Figure 7.10 A warm water whirlpool.

greater caution is advised. The whirlpool should be visible from all areas of the athletic training room or clinic, and no one should use a whirlpool unsupervised. Use extra caution when treating individuals prone to heat illness or with medical conditions that compromise the body's ability to withstand hot, humid environments.

Thermal injury is not the only concern associated with whirlpool use. Bacteria thrive in warm, moist environments. Whirlpools should be thoroughly cleaned and disinfected after each use. Because many individuals are treated in some facilities, the whirlpool may not be properly cleaned between uses. Under these circumstances, identify individuals with open wounds and take extra precautions to prevent the spread of infections.

Moist heat packs and warm whirlpools are the most commonly applied superficial heating modalities. However, paraffin baths, heat lamps, and fluidotherapy are also classified as superficial heating devices.

Paraffin baths are filled with seven parts paraffin wax and one part mineral oil heated to 125 to 127° F (51.6–52.7° C). Because of the lower specific heat of the wax, higher temperatures are used than with whirlpool baths. Paraffin is most commonly used in treating the hand and wrist. The treated hand should be washed and then dipped into the paraffin (figure 7.11). The hand is then removed until the wax hardens. This procedure is repeated four to five times until there is a thick layer of warm wax around the treated area. The hand is placed in a plastic bag and wrapped in a towel or placed in an oven mitt; the plastic bag allows you to remove the wax at the end of treatment without making a mess, while the towel or the oven mitt hold heat longer. Generally the paraffin is left on for 20 to 30 min. Paraffin has limited application in athletic training but is valuable in treating hand pain and loss of hand function. Paraffin cannot be used if there is an open wound and should be used with caution if the individual has sensory or vascular compromise in the area to be treated.

Heat lamps were once commonly used to provide superficial heat. Because of cost and convenience, heat lamps have been replaced by moist heat packs. A heat lamp positioned over a moist towel will increase the temperature of the skin. The amount of heating depends on the strength of the bulb and the distance between the

Table 7.2 Maximum Whirlpool Temperature by Body Part*		
Body part	**°F**	**°C**
Wrist and hand	112	44.4
Foot and ankle	110	43.3
Elbow	108	42.2
Knee	106	41.1
Thigh	104	40.0
*Assuming well-ventilated whirlpool area and absence of medical conditions that require precaution in warm, humid environments.		

Figure 7.11 A paraffin bath.

lamp and the towel (see inverse square law, p. 103). The heat lamp provides the same benefits as a moist heat pack. However, each lamp can only be used on one person at a time, whereas many individuals can be treated simultaneously with inexpensive moist heat packs.

Fluidotherapy has been referred to as a dry whirlpool (figure 7.12). A fluidotherapy unit contains ground cellulose material that can be heated to 120 to 125° F (48.8–51.6° C) and then blown around the chamber with forced air. The result is heating through convection and a massage. Fluidotherapy allows passive or active movement during treatment. Individuals with properly dressed open wounds can be treated with fluidotherapy without the risk of contamination. In contrast to treatment of an extremity in a whirlpool, with fluidotherapy the treated limb does not sit in a gravity-dependent position.

TEMPERATURE INCREASES AND PHYSIOLOGICAL RESPONSES

Superficial heating increases the skin temperature several degrees. The intraarticular temperature of small joints such as the carpals can be increased to therapeutically

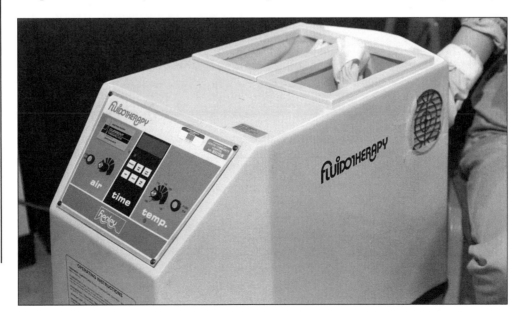

Figure 7.12
Fluidotherapy unit.

beneficial levels. The temperature of deeper tissues such as large muscles and deep joints rises insignificantly. For example, superficial heat placed over the hamstrings or the glenohumeral joint will not raise the temperature of those tissues sufficiently to have a therapeutic benefit.

If superficial heat has little effect on the temperature of injured tissue, why is it so commonly applied in athletic training and physical therapy? Much like cold, the primary clinical benefits of superficial heat are pain control and relief of muscle spasm. However, the mechanisms responsible for these physiological responses are not well understood.

Pain relief following heat application has been attributed to the gate control system. However, the gate control model proposes that input from large-diameter afferent fibers inhibits nociception, whereas small-diameter afferent input facilitates transmission of pain impulses. The sensation of heat is carried by small-diameter fibers (A-delta and C fibers), not large-diameter fibers (A-alpha and A-beta). Thus, the gating mechanism does not offer a plausible explanation for the analgesic effects of superficial heating. Is there an alternative explanation?

The Level III model presented in chapter 4 proposes that small-diameter afferent input stimulates a beta-endorphin–mediated activation of the descending analgesic pathway, which terminates on enkephalin interneurons. It has been suggested that longer stimulation (20–40 min) is required to elicit a beta-endorphin response. Clinical observation suggests that this theory may have merit. Athletic trainers often apply superficial heat for 20 to 30 min. Clinical observation suggests that shorter periods of heating do not result in as profound an analgesic response. Athletic trainers and others have also observed that superficial heat has a sedative effect. These observations provide empirical support for the Level III model as the mechanism behind the analgesic effects of superficial heating (figure 7.13).

The mechanism behind the antispasmodic effect of superficial heating is equally speculative. One explanation is that by relieving pain, superficial heating breaks the pain–spasm cycle. However, other factors may be involved. When heat is applied, the sensitivity of muscle spindles decreases, even though the temperature of the spindle is not affected. Thus, superficial heating may alter muscle spindle activity through a spinal reflex mechanism. Although speculative, this is the best explanation for the decrease in spindle sensitivity and relief of spasm associated with superficial heating.

Other physiological responses are associated with tissue heating, including increased metabolic activity, increased circulation, increased inflammation, increased tissue elasticity and decreased viscosity, and sweating. Although these responses occur in the dermis, deeper tissues are much less affected because of the insulating effects of adipose tissue. With the exception of very superficial joint structures, superficial heating does not alter deeper tissues. Thus, superficial heating does little to the metabolism or blood flow of deeper damaged tissues.

INDICATIONS FOR SUPERFICIAL HEATING

Certified athletic trainers primarily apply superficial heat to relieve pain and muscle spasm prior to therapeutic exercise. Superficial heating in a whirlpool or fluidotherapy unit also permits passive or active range-of-motion exercises. Active motion increases lymphatic drainage, which will reduce swelling. Local blood flow also increases.

Superficial heat can also be used to treat restrictions in superficial joints. The joints of the hand, wrist, foot, and ankle respond best because there is little adipose tissue over these joints. However, ultrasound results in a more vigorous heating and is the modality of choice for heating capsular tissue prior to mobilization and stretching.

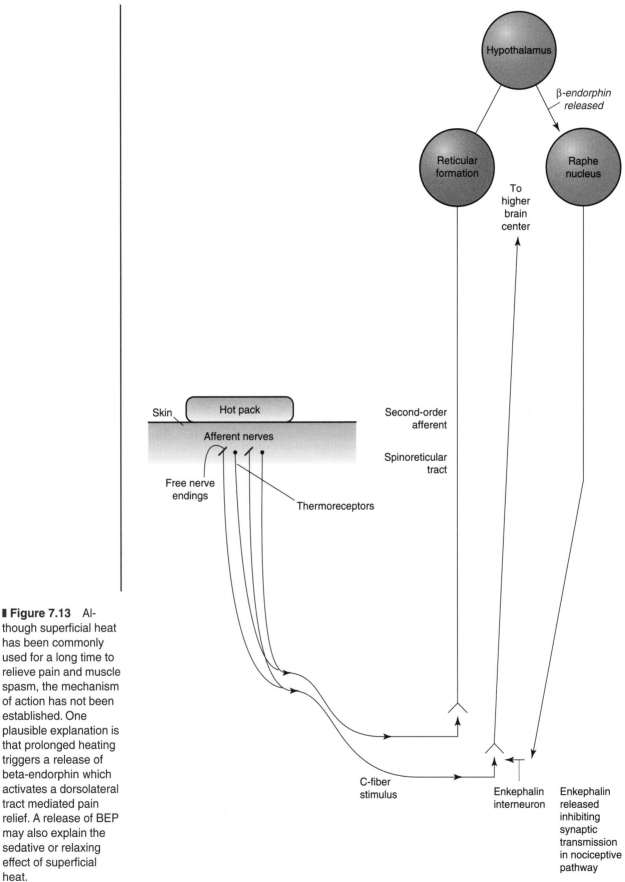

Hypothalamus

β-endorphin
released

Reticular
formation

Raphe
nucleus

To
higher
brain
center

Skin

Hot pack

Afferent nerves

Second-order
afferent

Spinoreticular
tract

Free nerve
endings

Thermoreceptors

C-fiber
stimulus

Enkephalin
interneuron

Enkephalin
released
inhibiting
synaptic
transmission
in nociceptive
pathway

■ **Figure 7.13** Although superficial heat has been commonly used for a long time to relieve pain and muscle spasm, the mechanism of action has not been established. One plausible explanation is that prolonged heating triggers a release of beta-endorphin which activates a dorsolateral tract mediated pain relief. A release of BEP may also explain the sedative or relaxing effect of superficial heat.

CAUTIONS AND CONTRAINDICATIONS

Unlike cold there are no rare complications associated with superficial heat (table 7.3). This does not imply, however, that superficial heat is completely safe. In fact, burns from superficial heating are far more common than cold-induced injuries. Burns, the primary risk of superficial heating, can be prevented by providing adequate insulation around moist heat packs, controlling whirlpool and fluidotherapy temperatures, and screening out individuals at risk for burns due to loss of sensation or circulatory problems. In addition, caution is needed when anyone lies on a moist heat pack, because heat cannot escape and builds up more rapidly. Extra insulation with toweling is necessary if the injured person is to lie on the heat pack.

Heat also stresses the cardiovascular system. The heat stress from a superficial heat application combined with a warm, humid environment can be lethal for someone with coronary artery disease or multiple medical problems. These problems are rarely encountered in athletic training. However, be ever mindful that modalities routinely used with young, healthy individuals are not safe for everyone.

Table 7.3   Indications, Contraindications, and Precautions for Superficial Heat

	Indications	Contraindications	Precautions
Superficial heating in general	Decrease pain Decrease muscle spasm	Diminished sensation Poor local circulation	Medically unstable Coronary heart disease
Modality-specific			
Whirlpool	Heat very superficial joint capsules	Open wounds	
Fluidotherapy	Heat very superficial joint capsules		
Paraffin	Heat very superficial joint capsules	Open wounds	

HEAT AND COLD: CONTRAST THERAPY

Contrast therapy, which consists of alternating applications of heat and cold, is also used to treat athletic injuries. The most common approach to contrast treatment consists of alternately immersing the foot, ankle, and leg in a cold water whirlpool or bath and a warm whirlpool (figure 7.14). The temperature of the cold bath and warm whirlpool should be within the ranges previously described in this chapter. The literature provides several recommendations (Walsh 1996; Bell and Prentice 1998) as to the length of time cold and heat should be applied as well as the number of cycles of heat and cold that should be completed during a treatment. A 1:3 or 1:4 min ratio of cold to warm appears reasonable based upon clinical observations and experience.

Several physiological effects have been proposed to explain the benefits of contrast therapy. Many have suggested that contrast therapy results in cycles of vasodilation and vasoconstriction, thus creating a pumping action to reduce swelling. However, the brief exposure to cold and the fact that superficial heating has minimal effect on deep blood flow suggest that there is little vascular response to contrast therapy.

Even though there is no good explanation for the effects of contrast therapy, this approach can be used to treat some physically active individuals. Contrast therapy seems most effective in reducing edema in subacute foot and ankle injuries. Typically

Figure 7.14 Contrast therapy.

the injuries I have treated have been several days old with swelling that limited range of motion, and contrast therapy along with active range of motion has reduced swelling. The sharp sensory contrast between heat and cold appears to reduce pain and therefore muscle spasm. The Level II pain model certainly offers a plausible explanation for the analgesic response to contrast. A decrease in pain and spasm, combined with active, pain-free range of motion, would in turn increase lymphatic drainage from the area and decrease swelling.

HEAT, COLD, AND CONTRAST THERAPY: DECIDING WHAT TO APPLY

Pain and muscle spasm indicate the use of cryotherapy, superficial heat, and contrast treatment. This raises the question, which is best? There is no simple answer, and you must consider several factors when selecting a modality, weighing the potential benefits against potential risks.

Contraindications are the first consideration in selecting a therapeutic modality. If the injured person suffers from Raynaud's phenomenon (cryoglobinemia, hemoglobinuria) or cold urticaria, then cold and contrast cannot be used.

Traditionally heat has been thought to be contraindicated following acute injury because of the associated increase in blood flow. However, superficial heat has little effect on deep tissue temperature and blood flow, and there is little evidence to suggest that heat combined with rest, compression, and elevation slows recovery. Nonetheless, cold is the treatment of choice in the management of acute injuries because it is a more effective analgesic and antispasmotic and may minimize secondary tissue injury. In the management of acute injuries, cold should be combined with protection of the healing tissues, compression, and elevation. Thus, cold pack application is preferred over cold water immersion or cold whirlpool, because these treatments place the limb in a gravity-dependent position.

If neither heat nor cold is contraindicated and the condition is not acute, you must consider other factors in choosing between cryotherapy, superficial heat, and contrast therapy. The most important considerations are the severity of pain and muscle spasm and patient preference. Cold is a better choice when pain and muscle spasm are severe. However, the preference of the individual is also important. If a certain treatment has helped a person in the past, he or she is likely to believe that the treatment will work again and is likely to actively participate in a plan of care that includes the specific treatment.

Compliance by the injured individual is especially important in a sports medicine clinic. The certified athletic trainer often must develop home treatment programs for individuals who are treated in the clinic only once or twice per week. Certainly someone who prefers not to be treated with cryotherapy is unlikely to use cold at home unless provided with a very convincing argument as to why such treatments are essential to their recovery. Thus, the ease of application and the probability of compliance with home treatment programs are also considerations when choosing between cryotherapy, superficial heat, and contrast therapy.

A Word on Counterirritants

The subject of counterirritants (analgesic balm) designed for superficial application does not fit with any specific chapter on therapeutic modalities. Although the topical application of some of these agents results in a sensation of heating, topical counterirritants do not result in clinically meaningful changes in tissue temperature.

The lack of a thermal response does not mean, however, that these agents are useless. The chemical stimulation of cutaneous sensory receptors will alter sensory input into the dorsal horn of the spinal column. The pain theories presented in chapter 4 offer some explanation for the soothing, analgesic benefits of counterirritants. The rubbing required for application and the stimulating effects of the counterirritant will increase large-diameter afferent input. Thus, the gate control theory and the Level I model offer plausible explanations for a favorable response to topical counterirritants.

SUMMARY

1. *Describe the four energy transfer mechanisms related to therapeutic modalities.*

   Thermal energy can be transferred to or from the body by four mechanisms: conduction, convection, radiation, and conversion. Conduction involves direct contact between a warm and a cool surface. Convection involves heating or cooling through movement of air or a liquid. Radiation involves exposure of a surface to radiant energy such as occurs with lying in the sun or under a heat lamp. Conversion involves converting one form of energy, such as ultrasound, to thermal energy.

2. *Describe the common methods of applying superficial heat and therapeutic cold.*

   Superficial heat can be applied with a hot pack, a heating lamp, a warm whirlpool, paraffin, or fluidotherapy. Therapeutic cold can be applied with an ice pack, ice massage, a cold whirlpool, cold water immersion, or a vapocoolant spray.

3. *Describe the thermal changes that occur with superficial heat and local cold application.*

   Superficial heat increases the temperature of the skin. Due to the insulating effects of adipose tissues, the superficial joint structures are the only deep tissues that are heated to a clinically significant degree. Cold application cools the skin and deeper tissues. Cooling of the skin occurs more rapidly than cooling of deeper tissues, and the skin is cooled to lower temperatures than the deeper tissues. However, a 20-min cold pack application will decrease muscle temperature approximately 7° F (3.9° C) at a depth of over 2 cm.

4. *Discuss the effect of superficial heat and local cooling on blood flow, muscle tone, and the nervous system.*

   Superficial heat increases cutaneous blood flow. However, because blood flow to deeper tissues such as muscle is regulated by metabolic demand rather than temperature, superficial heating has little effect on blood flow in deeper tissues. Therapeutic cold causes vasoconstriction in cutaneous and deep tissues. Both therapeutic cold and superficial heat can decrease muscle spasm. Therapeutic cold decreases the temperature of muscle spindles, relieving muscle spasm. Superficial heat has a similar effect; however, because superficial heating does not raise deep-tissue temperature, the decrease in muscle spindle activity is thought to occur through reflex mechanisms. A 15- to 20-min application of cold will decrease nerve conduction velocity. Because the rate at which impulses are carried by small-diameter primary afferent nerves is slowed, fewer pain messages reach the central nervous system and less pain is perceived. Superficial heat stimulates thermal receptors, increased input from which may trigger descending analgesic mechanisms mediated by the release of beta-endorphin.

5. *Discuss the indications for cold application and the impact of cooling on acute inflammation.*

   Cold is primarily used to relieve pain and muscle spasm. Cold may also limit swelling following musculoskeletal injury. Cold application will be maximally effective when combined with compression, elevation, and protection of injured tissues.

6. *Describe the common indications for the application of superficial heat.*

   Superficial heat is used to relieve pain and muscle spasm. The choice between using heat or cold depends on a number of factors, including contraindications, degree of pain and muscle spasm, and preference.

7. *Identify contraindications and precautions for applying superficial heat and therapeutic cold.*

   Some medical conditions result in significant adverse reactions and contraindicate the application of cold (table 7.1). The most common condition in this category is vasospastic disorders, of which Raynaud's phenomenon is the most common. Cold urticaria, an allergic reaction to cold exposure, also contraindicates cold application. Cold-induced hemoglobinuria (paroxymal cold hemoglobinuria) and cryoglobinemia are two rare conditions that also contraindicate cryotherapy. Hemoglobinuria occurs when the rate of red blood cell breakdown exceeds the rate at which hemoglobin combines with other proteins. Cryoglobinemia is a condition where an abnormal clumping of plasma proteins (cryoglobins) is stimulated by cold application. In addition, cold can injure superficial nerves such as the ulnar and common peroneal. Thus, extreme caution is required when cold is applied near or over these structures.

   Burns are the primary risk of superficial heating. These can be prevented by providing adequate insulation around moist heat packs and by controlling whirlpool, fluidotherapy, and whirlpool temperatures. Heat and cold stress the cardiovascular system, so special caution is warranted when superficial heat or cryotherapy is used to treat individuals who are frail, have significant medical problems (such as coronary artery disease), or have diminished circulation or sensation.

8. *Differentiate between superficial heating and deep heating modalities.*

   The superficial heating modalities described in this chapter have little effect on the temperature of deeper tissues such as muscle. Ultrasound and diathermy, however, can increase the temperature of deeper tissues by converting acoustic or electromagnetic energy to thermal energy in the tissues.

CITED REFERENCES

Bell GW, Prentice WE: Infrared modalities. In Prentice WE (Ed), *Therapeutic Modalities for Allied Health Professionals*. New York: McGraw-Hill, 1998, 201-239.

Bocobo C, Fast A, Kingery W, Kaplan M: The effect of ice on intraarticular temperature in the knee of the dog. *Am J Phys Med Rehabil* 70:181-185, 1991.

Cross KM, Wilson RW, Perrin, DH: Functional performance following ice immersion to the lower extremity. *J Athl Train* 30:231-234, 1995.

Evans TA, Ingersoll C, Knight KL, Worrell TW: Agility following the application of cold therapy (Abstract). *J Athl Train* 31:S-53, 1996.

Gerig BK: The effects of cryotherapy on ankle proprioception (Abstract). *J Athl Train* 24:S-119, 1990.

Greicar M, Kendrick Z, Kimura I, Sitler M: Immediate and delayed effects of cryotherapy on functional power and agility (Abstract). *J Athl Train* 31:S-33, 1996.

Haimovici N: Three years experience in direct intra-articular temperature measurement. *Prog Clin Biol Res* 107:453-461, 1982.

Hartviksen K: Ice therapy in spasticity. *Acta Neurol Scand* 38(suppl 3):79-84, 1962.

Ingersoll CD, Knight KL, Merrick MA: Sensory perception of the foot and ankle following therapeutic applications of heat and cold. *J Athl Train* 27: 231-234, 1992.

Knight KL: *Cryotherapy in Sport Injury Management*. Champaign IL, Human Kinetics, 1995.

Knight KL, Aquino J, Johannes SM, Urban CD: A re-examination of Lewis' cold-induced vasodilation in the finger and ankle. *Athl Train* 15:238-250, 1980.

LaRiviere J, Osternig LR: The effect of ice immersion on joint position sense. *J Sport Rehabil* 3:58-67, 1994.

McDonough E, Strauss K, Apel T, Ingersoll C, Knight KL: Cooling the ankle, lower leg and both affects dynamic postural sway (Abstract). *J Athl Train* 31:S-10, 1996.

McMaster WC, Little S, Waugh TR: Laboratory evaluations of various cold therapy modalities. *Am J Sports Med* 6:291-294, 1978.

Michlovitz SL: *Thermal Agents in Rehabilitation*, 2nd ed. Philadelphia, Davis, 1990.

Oosterveld FGJ, Rasker JJ, Jacobs JWG, Overmars HJA: The effect of local heat and cold therapy on the intraarticular and skin surface temperature. *Arthritis Rheum* 35:146-151, 1992.

Provins KA, Morton R: Tactile discrimination and skin temperature. *J Appl Phys* 15:155-160, 1960.

Rivers D, Kimura I, Sitler M, Kendrick Z: The influence of cryotherapy and Aircast bracing on total body balance and proprioception (Abstract). *J Athl Train* 30:S-15, 1995.

Rubley MD: *Cryotherapy, Sensation and Isometric Force Variability*. Unpublished thesis, Pennsylvania State University, State College, 1997.

Shuler DE, Ingersoll C, Knight KL, Kuhlman JS: Local cold application to the foot and ankle, lower leg, or both effects on a cutting drill (Abstract). *J Athl Train* 31:S-35, 1996.

Steinagel MC, Szczerba JE, Guskiwicz KM, Perrin DH: Ankle ice immersion effect on postural sway (Abstract). *J Athl Train* 31:S-53, 1996.

Thieme HA, Ingersoll CD, Knight KL, Ozmun JC: Cooling does not affect knee proprioception. *J Athl Train* 31:8-10, 1996.

Travel JG, Simons DG: *Myofascial Pain and Dysfunction: The Trigger Point Manual*. Baltimore, Williams & Wilkins, 1983.

Wakin LG, Porter AN, Krusen FH: Influence of physical agents and certain drugs on intraarticular temperature. *Arch Phys Med Rehabil* 32:714-721, 1951.

Walsh MT: Hydrotherapy: The use of water as a therapeutic agent. In Michlovitz SL (Ed), *Thermal Agents in Rehabilitation*, 3rd ed. Philadelphia, Davis, 1996, 139-167.

ADDITIONAL SOURCES

Knight KL: *Cryotherapy*. Champaign, IL, Human Kinetics, 1995.

Lehman JF: *Therapeutic Heat and Cold*, 4th ed. Baltimore, Williams & Wilkins, 1990.

Michlovitz SL: *Thermal Agents in Rehabilitation*, 3rd ed. Philadelphia, Davis, 1996.

CHAPTER EIGHT

Electrotherapy

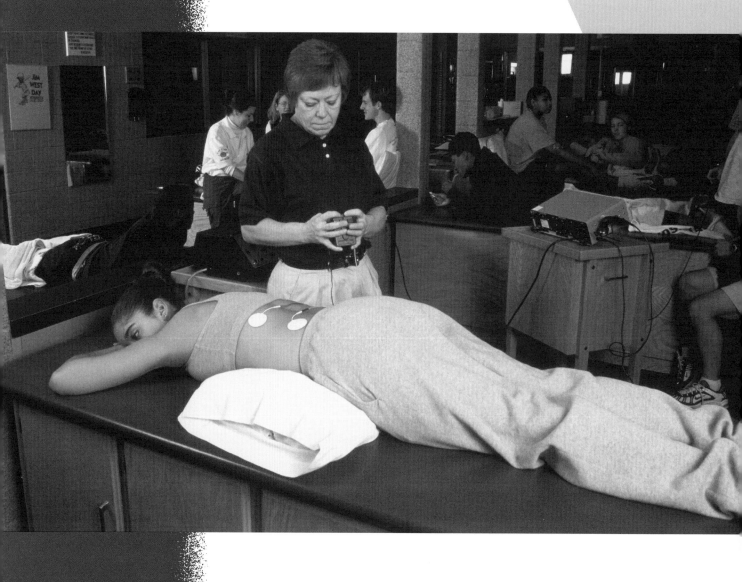

OBJECTIVES

After reading this chapter, the student will be able to

1. define volt, ampere, impedance, and resistance;

2. describe the differences between alternating, direct, and pulsatile current;

3. discuss the difference between TENS, iontophoresis, microcurrent, and stimulation of denervated muscle;

4. define parameters of pulsatile current including phase duration, amplitude, phase charge, and frequency;

5. describe the three types of pulsatile currents;

6. identify contraindications for the application of electrotherapy; and

7. discuss indications for treatment with electrotherapy.

A 30-year-old triathlete is referred to a sports medicine clinic for treatment of myofascial pain syndrome in the neck and shoulders. She has had recurring trouble with her neck and shoulder, mostly associated with prolonged training on her bicycle. Her pain became acutely worse 6 weeks after an accident in which the car she was driving was rear-ended. Her primary complaints are increased pain radiating into the right arm with cycling and working at her desk for prolonged periods (she is a practicing corporate lawyer). She also reports occasional headaches associated with her neck and shoulder pain, which have become more frequent. X-rays were taken of her neck recently, and the orthopedic surgeon who referred her was unable to identify a structural cause for her pain. Examination reveals a fit, physically active woman with a forward-head, protracted-shoulder posture. There are multiple tender trigger points in her neck and shoulders. Upper extremity sensation, motion, and strength are normal. The middle and lower trapezius and serratus are weaker than expected for her fitness level. A treatment plan is designed consisting of modalities for pain management, manual therapies, and exercises to strengthen the weak muscles and improve posture. She asks about using electrical stimulation for pain control and says that she received treatment in college from a certified athletic trainer for a back and hip injury sustained while running track. Because of her previous positive experience, electrotherapy is identified as the treatment of choice. Which type of electrotherapy is most appropriate to achieve the treatment goals? What are the optimal parameters of treatment? Is electrotherapy contraindicated? Chapter 8 answers these questions and provides the physical principles and physiological bases for the use of electrotherapy in sport rehabilitation.

The therapeutic use of electricity dates back to ancient times, when the Greeks used electric eels to treat physical ailments (Kahn 1987). Electrotherapy has continued to evolve and is very commonly applied by certified athletic trainers.

Four types of electrical current are used in health care: transcutaneous electrical nerve stimulation (TENS), iontophoresis, direct stimulation of denervated muscle, and low-level current (microcurrent). The most commonly used form is TENS, which involves applying an electrical current across the skin to depolarize nerve fibers. TENS can be used to stimulate afferent fibers to relieve pain or efferent fibers to cause muscle contraction. Most of this chapter is devoted to the application of TENS.

Iontophoresis is the use of a direct current to drive electrically charged ions through the skin. Iontophoresis is used to deliver medications that are electrically charged in solution into the tissues to treat musculoskeletal conditions and speed recovery.

Electrical current can also be used to stimulate muscle contraction following injury to the motor nerve. Certified athletic trainers do not encounter denervated muscle frequently, and there is little evidence of long-term benefit when electrical stimulation is used to treat denervated muscle. However, failure to elicit a contraction with TENS indicates damage to a motor nerve such as can occur with stretch of the brachial plexus and common peroneal nerve. Thus, this topic is covered briefly.

Low-level electrical current or microcurrent speeds healing in some slow-healing wounds. There is no evidence that electricity can speed normal tissue healing or recovery from injury in relatively healthy individuals. However, new knowledge suggests that small electrical currents (microcurrent) may be helpful in treating some musculoskeletal injuries.

This chapter provides a basic understanding of electrical currents and stimulators used in athletic training. The text identifies the parameters of the stimulus that the athletic trainer must control and discusses each type of stimulator along with indications and contraindications for clinical applications.

BASICS OF ELECTRICITY

Electrical current is the flow of electrons. Current (identified by the symbol I) is measured in amperes. One ampere (abbreviated A) is equal to the flow of 6.25×10^{18} electrons per second. Electrical charge is measured in coulombs (C). One coulomb equals 6.25×10^{18} electrons. Thus, 1 A equals the delivery of 1 C of electrical charge per second. Electrical current and electrical charge are both important in understanding the principles of electrotherapy.

Voltage and impedance are also important concepts. Voltage (V) is a measure of electromotive force. In order for electrons to flow, there must be a difference in the quantity of electrons between two points. Because electrons possess a negative charge, the difference in concentrations creates positive and negative polarity. Thus, electrons flow from negative to positive, creating an electrical current. The magnitude of the difference between the positive and negative poles is the electromotive force that will drive the current.

Definitions

coulomb (C)—Measure of electrical charge or a quantity of electrons. One coulomb = 6.25×10^{18} electrons.

ampere (A)—Measure of electrical current. One ampere equals the movement of 1 C per second.

volt (V)—Measure of potential difference or electromotive force. One volt equals the electromotive force required to drive 1 A of current across 1 Ω of resistance.

ohm (Ω)—Measure of resistance to the flow of electrons.

impedance—Resistance + inductance + capacitance.

resistance (R)—Opposition to the flow of electrical current by a material.

inductance—Opposition to electrical current created by electromagnetic eddy currents created when current passes through a wire.

capacitance—Ability of a material to store an electrical charge.

Before voltage can be quantified, impedance must be defined. Impedance is the force that resists the flow of electrons. Impedance is the sum of resistance, inductance, and capacitance. Resistance (R) is the opposition to the flow of electrons by the material through which the current travels. Inductance is opposition created by eddy currents that form around materials conducting current (figure 8.1). Inductance is of little importance in the discussion of electrotherapy in this chapter but is important in understanding how another modality, diathermy, works. Capacitance is the ability of a material to store an electrical charge. Capacitors are important in the function of many electrical devices. The human body can store electrical charge, and the concept of capacitance will be very important in understanding TENS.

Of the three components of impedance, resistance has the greatest influence in the application of electrotherapy. Resistance is measured in ohms (Ω). How does this relate to voltage? An electromotive force of 1 V is required to drive 1 A of current across a resistance of 1 Ω. Thus, current, voltage and resistance are closely related. This relationship, known as Ohm's law, states that voltage = current $\times$ resistance, or $V = I \times R$. Thus, if resistance increases, a greater voltage is required to drive the same current.

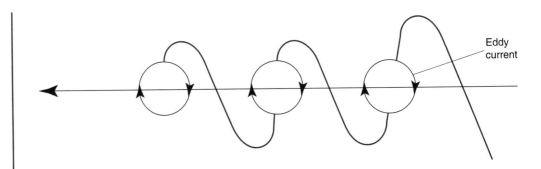

■ **Figure 8.1**   When current passes through a coiled cable, a magnetic field is generated that can affect surrounding tissues by inducing localized secondary currents, called eddy currents, within the tissue.

Ohm's Law

Ohm's law states that voltage = current × resistance. As resistance increases, more voltage is required to pass the same current through an electrical circuit. If resistance is held constant, a greater voltage will result in greater current.

When a certified athletic trainer applies electrotherapy, the body becomes part of an electrical circuit (figure 8.2). The electrical stimulator generates a voltage to overcome the resistance of the wires and tissues, and a current passes through the body along the path of least resistance. By understanding electrical charge, current, voltage, resistance, and capacitance, you are prepared to explore the differences between the types of electrical stimulators.

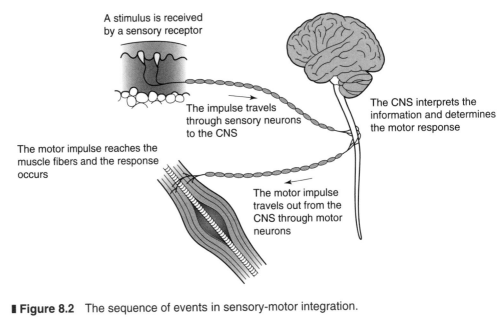

■ **Figure 8.2**   The sequence of events in sensory-motor integration.

Reprinted from Wilmore and Costill 1999.

TYPES OF ELECTRICAL CURRENT

The greatest distinguishing feature between the types of electrical stimulators is the type of current delivered. There are two types of continuous current: direct current (DC) and alternating current (AC) (figure 8.3). For example, household current is AC, whereas the current generated by a car battery is DC. In AC, the polarity at each end of the circuit is constantly being reversed, creating a sinusoidal pattern of positive and negative phases. In DC, the polarity of the poles remains constant, and thus current only flows in one direction.

In iontophoresis, DC is applied. If the goal of treatment is to contract denervated muscle, either AC or DC can be used. However, in all other forms of electrotherapy, the current is modulated into a noncontinuous, pulsed form. TENS and microcurrent stimulators deliver pulsatile current with very short (microsecond or 1/1,000,000 s) pulses separated by interpulse intervals. Pulsatile currents allow for higher peak currents while maintaining average current at levels that do not damage tissues.

Pulsatile currents can be classified into three types of waveforms: monophasic, biphasic, and polyphasic (figure 8.4). Monophasic pulsatile current is similar to DC in that it is either positive or negative. However, because of the interpulse intervals, monophasic pulsatile current is noncontinuous and cannot be classified as DC. Likewise, biphasic pulsatile current is similar to AC in that there are positive and negative phases, but interpulse intervals result in a noncontinuous current.

The great problem in terminology exists with the polyphasic pulsatile currents. "Russian current," so named because it was introduced in the West by Yadov Kots, (1977), a Soviet scientist, has multiple pulses between interpulse intervals. Russian current has been defined as a timing-modulated AC current (Robinson 1995); however, *polyphasic* is the label used in this text. Interferential polyphasic pulsatile current is created by interfering two alternating currents of different frequencies (figure 8.5). The resulting current has high peaks when the interfering waves are in phase and very small peaks when out of phase. The small peaks are insufficient to affect nerve tissues. Thus, when the interfering waves are out of phase, the impact on tissue is equivalent to that of an interpulse interval with monophasic and biphasic waveforms.

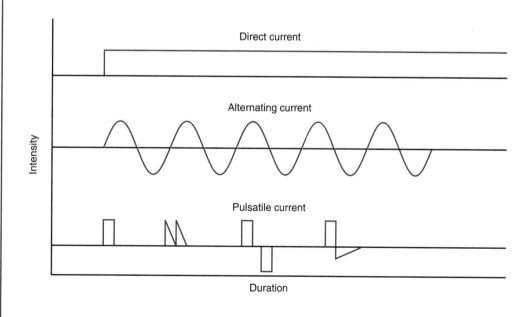

■ **Figure 8.3**   Direct, alternating, and pulsatile current.

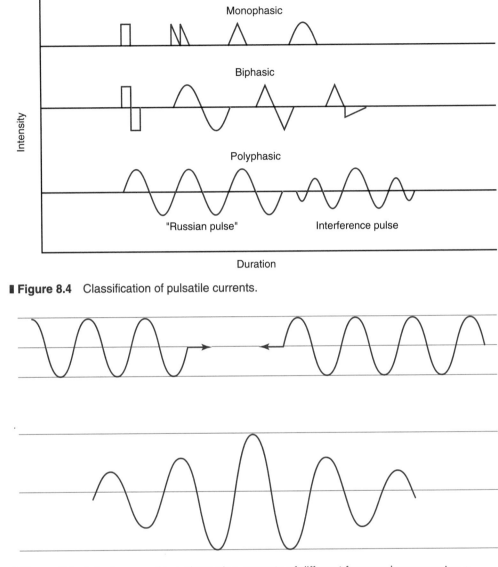

▌Figure 8.4   Classification of pulsatile currents.

▌Figure 8.5   Interference of two alternating currents of different frequencies generates a polyphasic pulsatile current. Pulses capable of depolarizing nerves are generated when two interfering AC waves are in-phase. When the two waveforms are out of phase, small amplitude pulses below nerve fiber rheobase result.

It is important to understand these waveforms and use proper terminology when discussing electrical stimulators. Consider the following true story. A member of the electrical engineering faculty at a college was referred for treatment by the team physician. This man had experienced an acute onset of mechanical low back pain while playing tennis. The certified athletic trainer elected to use TENS to treat the pain and muscle spasm. When the professor inquired what the athletic trainer was using, he was told that the unit was a high-volt, pulsed galvanic stimulator. This patient informed the athletic trainer that galvanic and DC are synonymous and that there was no such thing as pulsed, continuous current. He was, of course, correct.

In addition to helping you use proper terminology, understanding the various electrical waveforms will help you use TENS in the training room and clinic. Finally, and most importantly, understanding the basics of electricity and the physiological response to TENS will help you understand the differences between stimulators producing different forms of pulsatile currents.

PARAMETERS OF ELECTRICAL STIMULATION

Eight parameters can be adjusted on electrical stimulators: *phase charge* (which is determined by *phase duration* and *amplitude*), *frequency, waveform, polarity, duty cycle,* and *ramp.* Not all parameters can be adjusted on all stimulators and not all parameters are of concern for every application. This section defines each parameter and introduces the physiological effects of parameter adjustment.

PHASE DURATION, AMPLITUDE, PHASE CHARGE, AND FREQUENCY

Phase charge and frequency are the most important parameters for TENS. These parameters are also adjusted to stimulate denervated muscle and to stimulate tissue healing. Neither phase charge nor frequency is adjusted during iontophoresis, because DC is used.

Phase charge is a measure of electrons delivered in each phase of a pulsatile current. It is really not necessary to know the exact phase charge, and few electrical stimulators display it. However, phase charge is adjusted by altering phase duration and amplitude. Figure 8.6 depicts how increasing either phase duration or amplitude increases phase charge.

Why is phase charge so important? As mentioned previously, nerve fibers act as capacitors and store an electrical charge. If the electrical charge delivered is sufficient to overcome the capacitance of a nerve fiber, it will depolarize (figure 8.7). If the electrical charge does not exceed the capacitance of a nerve fiber, the electrical charge will leak out of the fiber during the interpulse interval and the nerve will not depolarize.

Figure 8.8 depicts the capacitance of the nerve fiber types introduced in chapter 4. Using a monophasic square wave, figure 8.9 illustrates the concept of phase charge being increased to overcome the capacitance of an alpha-beta fiber. Thus, in TENS application you can select the nerve fiber type or types to be depolarized.

If phase charge is so important, why is it not important to know the precise phase charge? If you adjust the phase duration and amplitude of TENS to cause a tingling sensation without muscle twitch, you have adjusted the phase charge to exceed the capacitance of A-alpha and A-beta afferent nerve fibers, but not alpha motor neurons. A muscle contraction indicates that the capacitance of the alpha motor neuron has also been exceeded. If TENS application results in a burning, needling

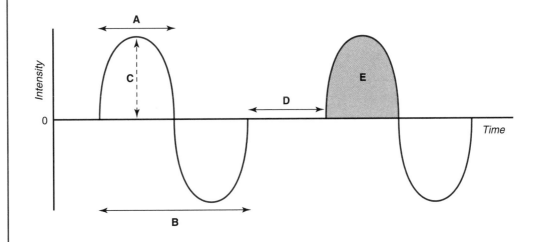

▌Figure 8.6 Phase charge, or number of electrons moved during each phase **E**, can be increased by increasing phase duration **A** or amplitude **C**. Pulse duration **B** and interpulse interval **F** are also shown.

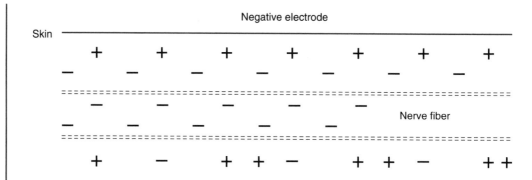

Figure 8.7 When the area surrounding a nerve becomes negatively charged by electrical current, the nerve fiber is no longer polarized in relation to the surroundings. When the nerve is depolarized, an impulse travels along the nerve to a synaptic junction.

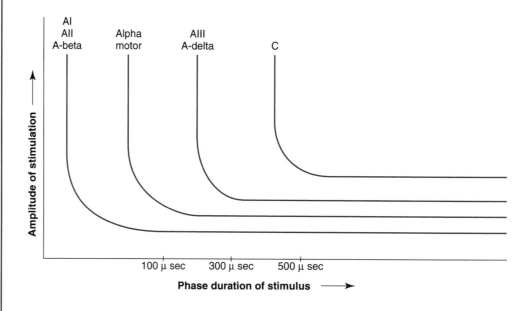

Figure 8.8 Estimated nerve fiber capacitance.

sensation, you have exceeded the capacitance of A-delta afferent. Thus, by soliciting feedback from the individual and observing for muscle twitch, you can alter phase charge by adjusting amplitude and phase duration.

Two concepts related to the adjustment of amplitude and phase duration are rheobase and chronaxie (figure 8.10). *Rheobase* is the minimum amplitude needed to depolarize a nerve fiber. If the peak amplitude of an electrical current fails to exceed rheobase, the nerve will not depolarize regardless of phase duration. During stimulation to promote wound healing, very low amplitudes are often used. Because of the low amplitude, no afferent fibers are depolarized; thus, no sensation is associated with the stimulation.

Chronaxie is the time required to depolarize a nerve fiber when the peak current is twice rheobase. Chronaxie is thought to occur at the break in the capacitance curve. Stimulation parameters with an amplitude twice rheobase and a phase duration slightly greater than chronaxie result in greatest comfort for the recipient of TENS. Later this chapter provides guidelines for parameter adjustment to elicit the desired response with the greatest comfort.

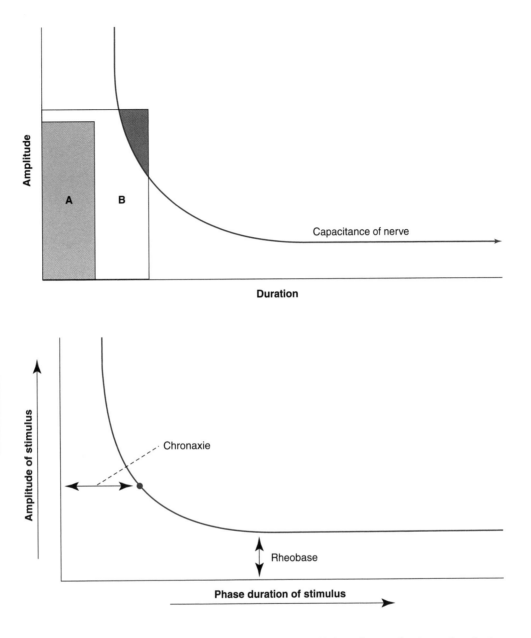

■ **Figure 8.9** Capacitance is the ability of a nerve to store an electrical charge. The pulse charge must exceed capacitance to depolarize the nerve. Pulse **A** lacks sufficient charge to overcome capacitance of the nerve. However, by increasing amplitude and phase duration (Pulse **B**), you increase phase charge to overcome capacitance and cause depolarization.

■ **Figure 8.10** Rheobase is the minimum amplitude required to depolarize a nerve fiber. Chronaxie is the phase duration required to depolarize a nerve fiber when the amplitude is 2 X rheobase.

Phase charge determines which nerve fiber will depolarize during stimulation, and frequency determines how often the nerve fibers will depolarize. Frequency of TENS and microcurrent stimulation is measured in pulses per second. The unit hertz (Hz) designates the frequency of AC but not pulsatile currents. Guidelines for TENS treatment frequencies have been developed primarily through clinical observation.

WAVEFORM

A variety of waveforms are produced by TENS used in athletic training. Historically, manufacturers have touted the benefits of using specific waveforms to treat pain and injury without presenting data to support their claims. Although there may be some individual preference based on comfort, the physiological response to TENS will be the same if the phase charge is equal, regardless of the waveform. Thus, it is more important to understand the limitations imposed by the various waveforms than it is to select a specific waveform for a particular application.

The waveform of the stimulus is important for iontophoresis. Iontophoresis units currently used by certified athletic trainers are DC devices. Direct current, broken into millisecond bursts, is being studied as an alternative delivery system for medications such as insulin. For lack of a better term, these stimulators have been labeled as *pulsed DC generators* to distinguish them from microsecond phase duration, monophasic pulsatile current generators, which lack sufficient phase duration to drive electrically charged particles across the skin.

Because of the high capacitance of muscle tissue, DC and low-frequency AC are used to contract denervated muscle. A TENS unit is not capable of depolarizing denervated muscle regardless of waveform. The impact of waveform on tissue healing is not well understood. Most researchers and clinicians have studied monophasic pulsatile currents in the treatment of slow-healing lesions such as decubitus ulcers. Much more study is needed to fully elucidate the effects of electrotherapy on tissue healing.

POLARITY

Like waveform, polarity is primarily of concern when you are applying iontophoresis. An electrode will have either a positive (anode) or negative (cathode) polarity. The active or treatment electrode must be of the same polarity as the ion in the solution to be driven into the tissue. Appropriate polarity selection may also influence the response to electrical stimulation of slow-healing wounds. Although monophasic pulsatile TENS allows you to select polarity, it does not impact the response to treatment.

DUTY CYCLE AND RAMP

Duty cycle and ramp are parameters that must be adjusted when applying TENS to stimulate alpha motor neurons and cause muscle contraction. Duty cycle refers to the pattern of "on" and "off" sequencing. For example, you may want to stimulate the quadriceps muscles following knee injury or surgery because the individual has lost volitional control due to pain and swelling. The stimulation must be patterned to allow the muscles to recover between contractions. You might select a 12 sec "on" time during which the quadriceps contract and a 12 sec rest between contractions. The duty cycle would then be 12 sec on and 12 sec off.

Ramp time is a period of time during which the amplitude of the stimulus is gradually increased (ramp up) or decreased (ramp down). The number of alpha motor neurons stimulated and thus the number of motor units recruited is directly proportional to the phase charge. Because the phase duration is fixed before treatment begins, a gradual rise in amplitude results in a gradual increase in phase charge. As phase charge increases, more motor units are recruited and the strength of contraction increases. Ramp up prevents a sudden, violent contraction that would be painful and potentially damaging. Ramp down has little impact on comfort and no impact on treatment safety. Ramp down is available on a limited number of TENS devices on the market. Figure 8.11 depicts the concepts of duty cycle and ramping.

Table 8.1 summarizes the eight parameters discussed as they relate to the four applications of electrical stimulation. Focusing on the parameter adjustment for each application will help you understand the concepts related to effective use of electrical stimulation. These concepts are reviewed and reinforced as each type of electrotherapy is addressed in the next section.

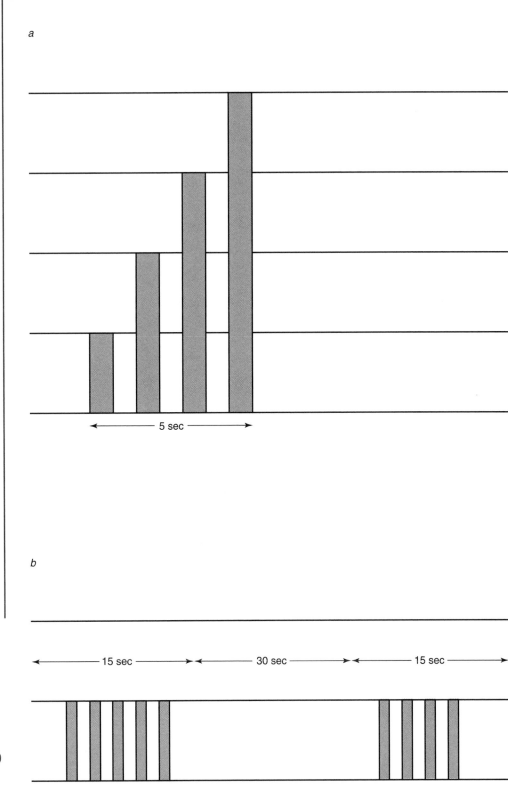

■ **Figure 8.11** Ramp and duty cycle. Ramping is a programmed increase in phase charge over several pulses (1–5 sec) *(a)*. Duty cycle involves periods of current flow ("on" time) interrupted by periods of no current ("off" time). In this illustration, the duty cycle is 15 sec on, 30 sec off *(b)*.

Table 8.1	Eight Parameters of TENS, Iontophoresis, Microcurrent, and Stimulation of Denervated Muscle							
	Phase charge	Phase duration	Amplitude	Frequency	Waveform	Polarity	Ramp	Duty cycle
TENS								
Pain control	P	IP*	IP**	P	AP	AP	NA	NA
Neuromuscular stimulation	P	IP*	IP**	P	AP	AP	P	P
Iontophoresis	NA	NA	S	NA	DC	P	NA	NA
Microcurrent	P$	IP$	IP$	TP	M	P?	NA	NA
Stimulation of denervated muscle	P#	IP#	IP#	P	AC/DC	AP	P?	P?

P = primary determinant of physiological response
IP* = component of variables controlling phase charge must exceed rheobase
IP** = component of variables controlling phase charge must be long enough to overcome capacitance of target tissue provided rheobase is exceeded
AP = any polyphasic waveform
NA = not applicable for this treatment application; adjust to 0 if necessary
S = maximum of 5 µA for safety
DC = direct current
AC = alternating current
P$ = small phase charges with low amplitude (< 600 µA and short phase duration), optimal parameters not established
P# = large phase charge required to overcome capacitance of muscle, long phase duration produced with low-frequency AC or DC, amplitude to tolerance
P? = optimal ramp and duty cycle not established

TRANSCUTANEOUS ELECTRICAL NERVE STIMULATION (TENS)

TENS refers to any modality that drives an electrical current across the skin (transcutaneous) to depolarize nerve fibers (nerve stimulation). TENS can be administered to relieve pain or to cause muscle contraction through stimulation of alpha motor neurons, often referred to as neuromuscular stimulation (NMS). TENS for pain relief and NMS are often thought of as separate concepts requiring different machines. As noted in the previous section, the parameters of the stimulus determine the treatment response. Many electrical stimulators can be adjusted to deliver optimal parameters for pain control and NMS.

This section reviews the physiological basis for pain control with TENS and NMS. Guidelines for parameter adjustment to achieve the desired effects follow. The origins and features of TENS devices with different waveforms are presented at the end to prepare you to use the variety of TENS devices found in sports medicine facilities.

TENS FOR PAIN RELIEF

Understanding how TENS relieves pain requires the integration of two basic concepts: the pain control models presented in chapter 4 and the concept of nerve fiber capacitance presented earlier in this chapter. When the parameters of the stimulation are adjusted to target the large-diameter A-alpha and A-beta afferent nerve fibers, the release of enkephalins into the dorsal horn is triggered through the ascending mechanism illustrated in the Level I pain model (figure 8.12). These afferents are sensory fibers. Depolarization results in a tingling sensation, but, because the capacitance of these afferents is less than that of the alpha motor neurons, pain is relieved without muscle contraction. Avoiding muscle contraction is desirable because of the

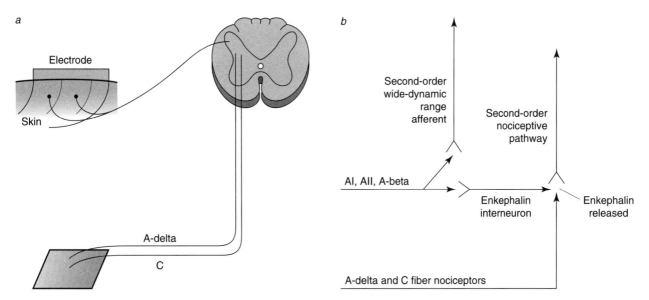

I Figure 8.12 Electrical current flowing through tissues cause large-diameter (AI, AII, A-beta) primary afferent nerves to depolarize *(a)*. Increased large-diameter primary afferent activity increases enkephalin release inhibiting transmission in the nociceptive pathway *(b)*.

discomfort associated with prolonged muscle twitch and the potential for muscle contractions to stress damaged tissue and slow repair.

TENS can also relieve pain by stimulating descending pathways as illustrated in the Level II model (figure 8.13). Long phase duration, high-amplitude stimulation of trigger points results in a burning, needling sensation through stimulation of A-delta afferents. Pain relief is believed to result because of stimulation of the fibers in the dorsolateral tract. Because the capacitance of A-delta afferents is greater than that of alpha motor neurons, very small treatment electrodes are used to prevent recruitment of large numbers of motor units and muscle contraction.

The Level I and II models provide the most plausible explanations for the analgesic responses to TENS stimulation. By selecting parameters to recruit the large-diameter or A-delta afferent fibers, the certified athletic trainer can stimulate the body's analgesic system. Because pain control is the first priority in rehabilitation, TENS can be a valuable adjunct in treating many musculoskeletal injuries.

Reference to the Level III model is notably absent from the previous paragraph. At one time it was believed that through appropriate parameter selection, C fiber afferents could be depolarized, triggering a release of beta-endorphin. Increased beta-endorphin concentrations in the cerebrospinal fluid have been reported following electroacupuncture (Clement-Jones et al. 1980), a technique where electrical currents are passed through acupuncture needles inserted into specific target sites and with long (0.2 sec) phase duration transcutaneous electrical impulses (Salar et al. 1981). However, the phase charge delivered through the needles was greater than that delivered by TENS and the transcutaneous stimulation differs substantially from that produced by commercially available TENS devices. There is no evidence that the TENS devices used by athletic trainers are capable of triggering a beta endorphin release and pain control through the mechanism described in the Level III model.

Later in this chapter and in chapter 9, the efficacy of several therapeutic modalities is called into question because of the lack of evidence that treatment with these devices improves clinical outcomes. The use of TENS for pain control has also been assessed, and both experimental studies (Denegar and Huff 1988; Denegar and Perrin 1992; Denegar et al. 1989) and clinical studies (Abram, Reynolds, and Cusick 1981; Melzack 1975; Rosenberg, Curtis, and Bourke 1978) have supported the use of TENS in pain control.

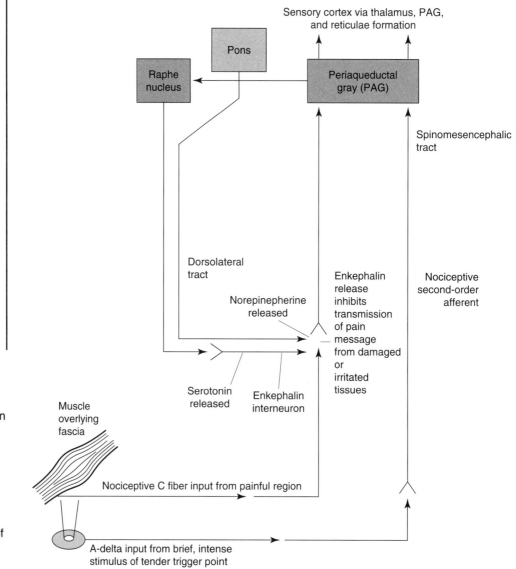

Figure 8.13 Sensitive trigger points associated with a myofascial pain pattern can be treated with TENS. Electrical stimulation with appropriate parameters stimulate a descending pain-inhibiting pathway. There is a sensation of being prodded with a hot needle.

Like other modalities, TENS is not a cure. For example, TENS alone is not effective in treating chronic low back pain (Deyo et al. 1990). This finding reinforces the concept that modalities should be used to achieve specific treatment goals, such as decreasing pain and muscle spasm to promote pain-free exercise. In sport rehabilitation, therapeutic exercise usually holds the key to recovery.

NEUROMUSCULAR STIMULATION (NMS)

Neuromuscular stimulation results in muscle contraction by depolarizing alpha motor neurons. NMS is particularly useful to overcome neuromuscular inhibition due to pain and swelling. After an injury or surgery, the individual loses the ability to fully contract some muscles. Through NMS, muscle contraction is stimulated and afferent feedback from the muscle is processed in the CNS. After several contractions, the injured individual can try to contract the affected muscles actively during the stimulation. Through this process of neuromuscular reeducation, the individual regains volitional control of the muscles and can progress in strength and functional retraining.

Originally NMS was developed to increase the strength of muscles in trained athletes. Kots (1977) claimed that NMS combined with intense training resulted in greater strength gains than training alone. However, there is little evidence that NMS is any more beneficial than volitional isometric contractions in building strength. In fact, because isometric strength gains are position specific, NMS is less effective than resistance through the normal range of motion.

NMS can also be applied to slow disuse atrophy in innervated muscle. At one time NMS was most commonly used to prevent disuse atrophy in postoperative care following ACL reconstruction. When intraarticular graft placement procedures were developed, fixation of the graft was difficult, and patients were placed in plaster casts for up to 6 weeks following surgery. NMS was found to limit disuse atrophy during cast immobilization. However, improved graft fixation now allows for range of motion and active quadriceps and hamstring contractions to be initiated soon after surgery, eliminating the need for NMS. Today, prolonged cast immobilization is reserved for unstable fractures. NMS is contraindicated in these cases, because active muscle contractions can alter alignment of the fracture site and delay healing. Thus, NMS in the management of musculoskeletal injuries is limited to neuromuscular reeducation. In fact, NMS could be reserved for treating individuals who demonstrate neuromuscular inhibition that fails to respond to biofeedback.

PARAMETERS

Armed with a theoretical model and a knowledge of the capacitance characteristics of the afferent and alpha motor nerves, you can easily select the appropriate parameter. Table 8.2 summarizes the phase duration, amplitude, frequency, duty cycle, ramp time, and treatment time characteristics for TENS for pain relief and NMS. Electrode placement considerations follow.

Pain control through ascending mechanisms requires stimulation of A-alpha and A-beta afferent fibers. Because of the low capacitance and short chronaxie of these fibers, a short phase duration is optimal. A phase duration between 40 and 120 microseconds (μs) is ideal for comfort.

A slightly longer phase duration can be used with lower amplitude, whereas higher amplitude is required with a very short phase duration. An optimal frequency has

Table 8.2 Characteristics of TENS for Pain Relief and NMS						
Application	**Phase duration**	**Amplitude**	**Frequency**	**Duty cycle**	**Ramp time**	**Treatment time**
Pain relief Level I or gate control model (conventional TENS)	< 120 μs	Adjust to comfortable tingle—no muscle twitch	80–120 pps; adjust to comfort	None; continuous stimulation desired	None	20 min to hours
Pain relief Level II model	200 + μs	To tolerance; burning, needling sensation desired	Low; 2–4 pps best tolerated	None; continuous stimulation desired	None	30–40 sec per point with very small electrode
Neuromuscular stimulation	200 + μs	To tolerance; comfortable muscle contraction desired	≈ 50 pps	10–15 sec on, 10 sec off; longer rest required for strong contractions	3–5 sec	Poorly defined; 10–15 repetitions, depending on individual response and tolerance
Note: pps = phase per second						

not been established, but 80 to 120 pps is generally comfortable. The stimulation can be applied continuously for as long as desired. Prior to therapeutic exercise or manual therapy, 20 min of TENS treatment, often combined with cold or superficial heat, is an effective analgesic and antispasmodic. For acute pain problems following injury or surgery, and for myofascial pain syndrome, TENS can be applied throughout the day. Individuals wear the TENS unit, turning it off when they are not in pain and resuming stimulation when pain returns. This gives individuals a measure of control over their pain and encourages their active participation in the plan of care. If TENS is to be used throughout the day, the electrodes should be removed and the skin cared for once or twice daily. When not in use, adhesive electrodes should be stored on plastic sheets and enclosed in packages so the conducting medium does not dry out.

Stimulation of A-delta afferent nerves to trigger the descending pain control system requires a longer phase duration because of the greater capacitance of the target nerves. Phase duration of 200 to 400 μs is optimal. The amplitude of the stimulus should be adjusted to elicit a burning, needling sensation. I have found that a low frequency (2–4 pps) is best tolerated while producing the desired pain relief. This treatment approach should be reserved for individuals with persistent pain patterns and sensitive trigger points. A very small treatment electrode should be used to deliver 30 to 40 sec of stimulation to each sensitive trigger point. Trigger points can be located through palpation or a "point finder," which passes a very low-level current through the tissue. The resistance of nonsensitized tissue is too great, and the circuit is not completed. However, trigger points have a lower resistance to electric, acoustic, and mechanical energy than surrounding tissue. When the electrode is placed over a trigger point, there is less resistance, the circuit is completed, and an audio or visual signal is emitted from the stimulator. With experience, you will become proficient at locating trigger points. A small electrode should be used to prevent contraction of the surrounding muscles. As with all TENS treatments for pain control, duty cycle and ramp should be set at 0.

The parameters for neuromuscular stimulation are adjusted to recruit the maximum number of fast twitch motor units. A motor unit consists of an alpha motor neuron and all of the muscle fibers it innervates. All muscle fibers within a motor unit are the same type. The fast twitch motor units are normally fired at a rate of 30 to 70 pps. Thus, selecting a frequency in this range ensures recruitment of fast- as well as slow-twitch units. The number of motor units recruited is correlated to the phase charge. Using a long phase duration, 200 to 400 μs, allows the amplitude of the stimulus to be maintained at comfortable levels. A ramp of 3 to 5 sec prevents injury and maximizes comfort. A duty cycle should be used to prevent fatigue. If the stimulation results in several seconds of maximal isometric force generation, a rest period of 50 sec or more is needed to replenish adenosine triphosphate stores. However, during neuromuscular reeducation, the individual cannot tolerate such strong contractions. In general, a 10 sec recovery is sufficient between isometric contraction during neuromuscular reeducation.

Electrode placement and size are generally a matter of common sense. When conventional TENS is applied for pain control, the electrodes are best placed over the site of pain. Over larger areas, such as the lower back, larger electrodes allow for lower current density and greater comfort. Use smaller electrodes over smaller areas (figure 8.14).

In very rare circumstances, it is not possible to place the electrodes over the site of pain. In these cases, the electrodes can be placed over the nerve roots associated with the area of pain or on the contralateral side over an area corresponding to the site of pain. These alternative electrode placements should be reserved for special cases, such as in the management of phantom limb pain or when there is extensive damage to the overlying skin.

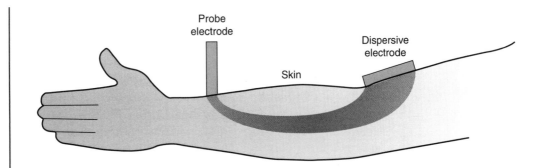

Figure 8.14 The small surface area of the probe electrode creates an area of high current density, resulting in perception of an intense electrical stimulus. The relatively large surface area of the dispersive electrode results in low current density and an excellent dispersion of the electrical stimulus.

The presence of sensitive trigger points dictates electrode placement when you are attempting to stimulate the dorsolateral tract. Trigger points are about the size of a pencil eraser, and small probes are best used for trigger point stimulation (figure 8.15).

When applying NMS, place the electrodes over the motor point of the target muscle. The motor point is the area where the alpha motor neurons pierce into the substance of the muscle and is generally located at the muscle belly. If a vigorous contraction is desired, a large phase charge is needed to depolarize the greatest number of motor units. Larger electrodes reduce current density and reduce the individual's discomfort.

Proper adjustment of these parameters and appropriate electrode placement will maximize the benefits of TENS. Waveform and polarity were not discussed along with the other parameter adjustments, because these factors have not been shown to affect the response to treatment, as further discussed in the next section.

TENS UNITS

A variety of TENS units are available to athletic trainers. TENS units are often identified by waveform or peak voltage output, which confuses users and complicates the basic concepts of parameter control. However, because TENS units do vary in waveform and peak output, it is important to review the characteristics of those most commonly used by athletic trainers. This section is organized by waveform, although many TENS devices offer a choice of waveform.

Biphasic Waveforms

Most small, personal TENS units produce a biphasic waveform. Some large clinical models such as the VMS II (Chattanooga Corp., Chattanooga, TN) also produce a biphasic waveform. The biphasic waveforms originated out of concerns for ion flux and skin

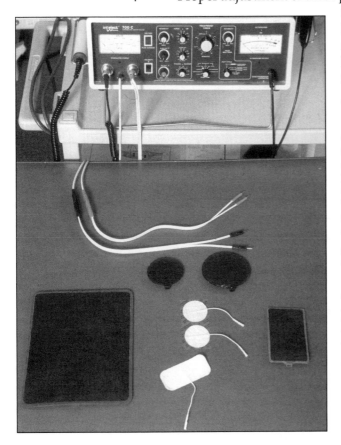

Figure 8.15 Small and large electrodes.

irritation associated with DC. The positive and negative phase in each pulse results in a zero net charge and no ion flux. The application for these TENS units depends on the limits of the adjustable parameters. Units that allow for a long phase duration, high amplitudes, and ramping and duty cycle adjustment can be used for pain control or neuromuscular stimulation. Some small units are intended for pain control. These TENS units do not generate sufficient electrical charge to contract large muscles such as the quadriceps and do not provide for ramping or appropriate duty cycle. Other small units (Respond II, Medtronic, San Diego, CA) are designed as neuromuscular stimulators; in terms of efficacy and patient comfort, the inability to control frequency and phase duration limits the use of these units for pain control. Consult the owner's or user's manual regarding the available parameter adjustments to determine the optimal application of each device.

Monophasic Waveforms

Despite early concerns, monophasic pulsatile waveforms do not cause ion flux. The pulse duration is too short to drive the movement of charged particles. Therefore, TENS units with monophasic waveforms do not cause skin irritation seen with the application of DC current.

The most common monophasic TENS units are high-volt stimulators, *high-volt* referring to peak voltages above 150 V. These units generate a twin peak monophasic waveform with very high peak voltage (and therefore high peak current) and very short phase duration (figure 8.16). The high-volt TENS units do not allow adjustment of phase duration. These TENS units are best used to stimulate large-diameter afferent nerves to trigger enkephalin release through an ascending pathway. The phase charge of these units is not sufficient to recruit strong contractions in large muscles, although the units could be used to enhance neuromuscular control of smaller muscles or muscle groups such as in the forearm.

One unique feature of high-volt units is a large electrode called a dispersive pad (figure 8.17a). At one time it was believed that the effect of treatment with monophasic current would differ depending on the polarity of the stimulus over the injured tissues. The large dispersive pad allowed for the injured area to be treated with one polarity while the electrical circuit was completed by an electrode at a distant site (figure 8.17b). Because a large electrode or dispersive pad was used, the current density at the

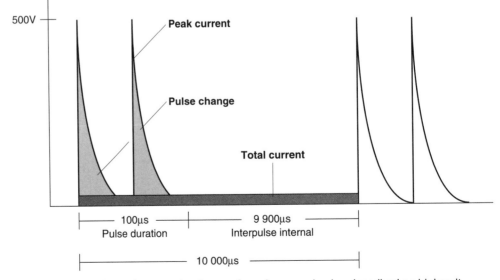

∎ Figure 8.16 Twin peak, monophasic waveform (commonly also described as high volt, pulsed galvanic stimulation; however, galvanic implies direct current and this is a pulsatile waveform).

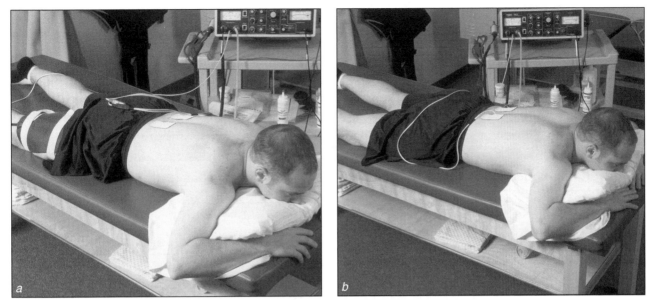

Figure 8.17 Setups using a dispersive pad (monopolar) *(a)* and a small electrode (bipolar) *(b)*.

distant sight was less than that over the treatment area. Thus, the individual receiving the treatment perceived greater stimulation at the treatment site.

This setup of high-volt stimulation is known as a monopolar setup because only one polarity is represented over the treatment area. Very little evidence suggests that a monopolar setup is more beneficial in treating musculoskeletal injuries than other types of TENS. In fact, attaching a small electrode in place of the dispersive pad secured over the treatment site is quite acceptable, a setup labeled bipolar.

The issue of monopolar and bipolar only relates to monophasic currents, because the polarity of the electrodes in biphasic and polyphasic waveforms is constantly reversing. There is nothing particularly special about the high-volt TENS units. In fact, a monophasic waveform with lower peak voltage and an adjustable phase duration is more versatile than the high-volt TENS units. High-volt TENS units are similar to biphasic waveform generators in that you must consult the owner's or user's manual to identify the limits to which parameters may be adjusted.

Polyphasic Waveforms

There are two types of polyphasic current: Russian and interferential. These electrical waveforms are derived from AC. The frequency of the AC that is modulated is labeled the carrier frequency. The carrier frequencies of these TENS devices fall into the range labeled as medium frequency (1000–10000 Hz), and therefore these devices are labeled as medium-frequency generators. Because higher frequency currents overcome tissue resistance more easily than lower frequencies, many practitioners have assumed that these currents reach target tissues more readily than monophasic or biphasic currents. However, polyphasic waveforms are not more comfortable or more effective in controlling pain and stimulating muscle contraction. This may be because electrical current follows a path of least resistance, or simply because with a very small increase in voltage, the same physiological effect can be elicited with monophasic and biphasic waveforms.

One limitation of polyphasic waveforms is that the phase duration of the stimulating current is fixed by the carrier frequency (table 8.3). Most TENS units generating polyphasic waveforms have a single carrier frequency. These units can be used for pain control or NMS, but the fixed carrier frequency often limits the versatility of the device.

Russian current modulates 2500 Hz AC (called the carrier frequency) into 10 μs packages, resulting in 50 packages per second. Alpha motor neurons are depolarized in response to the electrical charge delivered in the first phase. Thus, much of the electrical energy delivered with Russian current is wasted. The phase duration of a Russian current is 200 μs, and the amplitude can be adjusted to deliver a very

Table 8.3   Carrier Frequency and Phase Duration in Interferential Current

Carrier frequency (Hz)	Phase duration (μs)
2000	250
4000	125
5000	100

large phase charge. TENS units that generate Russian current are valuable as neuromuscular stimulators; however, the inability to adjust the frequency limits their application for pain control. Monophasic or biphasic waveforms with 200 μs phase duration and high amplitudes are equally effective for NMS.

Interferential current is created by interfering two alternating currents of different frequencies. When the two currents are in phase, the effect is summative and the resulting phase charge is sufficient to depolarize nerves. When the currents are out of phase, the resulting electrical charge is below rheobase, resulting in the physiological equivalent of an interpulse interval.

The most common carrier frequency on interferential generators is 4000 Hz. The interfering wave is always of higher frequency, and the difference between the two frequencies determines the treatment frequency. Thus, if the carrier frequency is 4000 Hz and the interfering frequency is 4080, the currents will be in phase 80 times per second, resulting in a treatment frequency of 80 pps. Another way of thinking about treatment frequency adjustment is that when you adjust the frequency delivered by an interferential TENS unit, you are really changing the frequency of the interfering AC.

The greatest limitation of interferential generators is the fixed carrier frequency. A carrier frequency of 2000 Hz results in phase duration of 200 μs and is ideal for NMS. With a 4000 Hz carrier frequency, the phase duration is 125 μs. The shorter phase duration is useful for pain control. Unfortunately, few interferential TENS units allow you to adjust the carrier frequency.

One other consideration is associated with IFC: electrode configuration. A four-electrode, or quadpolar, arrangement is used when interference of the alternating currents occurs within the tissues (figure 8.18). The current interference can also occur within the circuitry of the TENS device. This is referred to as premodulated IFC and allows for two- or four-electrode placement. Neither setup has been demonstrated to be more effective than the other.

Summary of Waveforms of TENS

The multiple waveforms and labels for TENS devices are confusing. However, the differences between TENS devices relate more to the limitations of application imposed by the waveforms rather than unique benefits created by them. Focus on the available parameter adjustments when considering a purchase or learning to operate new equipment.

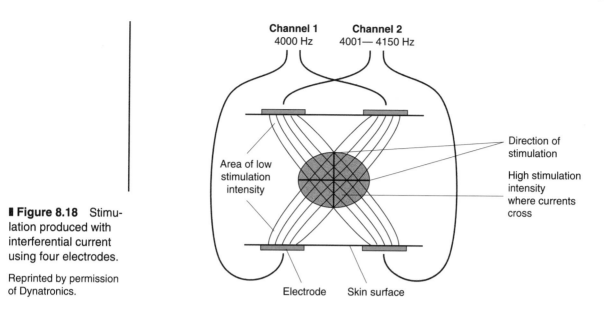

Channel 1
4000 Hz

Channel 2
4001— 4150 Hz

Direction of
stimulation

Area of low
stimulation
intensity

High stimulation
intensity
where currents
cross

Electrode   Skin surface

■ **Figure 8.18** Stimulation produced with interferential current using four electrodes.

Reprinted by permission of Dynatronics.

CONTRAINDICATIONS TO TENS APPLICATION

TENS is a very safe modality, because the TENS devices used by athletic trainers generate low levels of electrical energy and cannot damage tissue. There are three contraindications associated with TENS. The first is that electrodes should not be placed over the carotid arteries. Stimulation of this area alters baroreceptor regulation of blood pressure and can cause fainting. Although this is a very real concern, conditions that indicate electrode placement over the carotid arteries are rare.

The second contraindication is the presence of a cardiac pacemaker. Electrical interference from TENS could alter pacemaker regulation of cardiac function. However, halter monitoring of pacemaker function during TENS application suggests that TENS may be safe for patients with pacemakers. Certainly, you should consult with the individual's physician or cardiologist before using TENS. However, the presence of a pacemaker is not an absolute contraindication for TENS.

The third contraindication is pregnancy. TENS is used to ease the pain of labor and delivery without harming the infant. However, the safety of TENS application during fetal development has not been established. Because there is no proof that TENS does not cause birth defects or complications, pregnancy is an absolute contraindication to TENS.

In addition to these universal considerations, NMS is contraindicated in situations where active muscle contraction can impede healing or cause further damage. This commonsense consideration applies primarily to fracture care.

SUMMARY OF CLINICAL USE OF TENS

Before applying TENS, identify any contraindications and identify treatment goals to be facilitated by TENS. In most cases, the goal will be pain control. TENS may also be applied to help the physically active individual regain neuromuscular control through electrically induced muscle contraction.

Explain what the treatment should feel like and why it will help. Once the individual agrees to the treatment plan, select appropriately sized electrodes and secure them to the target area. Then turn on the TENS unit with appropriate parameter settings, including waveform (select monophasic, biphasic, or polyphasic as opposed to microcurrent or direct current options available on some units), frequency, phase duration, duty cycle (NMS only), and treatment time.

Once all adjustments are made, gradually increase the intensity of the current. Usually you are attempting to alleviate pain by stimulating large-diameter afferent nerves, in which case you will adjust the stimulation to produce a comfortable tingling sensation without muscle twitch. The TENS unit can now be left on for the desired length of treatment. Accommodation commonly occurs, where the individual perceives a decrease in the stimulus strength over time. Manufacturers have attempted to minimize accommodation through frequency modulation (programmed changes in frequency in a preset range) or scanning (programmed changes in stimulus pattern). However, the simplest approach is to instruct the individual to gently increase the stimulus or notify you that a greater intensity is needed to produce the same sensation of stimulation.

If the goal of treatment is pain control through stimulation of trigger points and the application of the Level II model, a burning, needling sensation is desired. The intensity of the stimulus should be adjusted to produce a tolerable but uncomfortable sensation. Effective treatment requires only 30 to 60 sec of stimulation per point. Because each trigger point differs in sensitivity, you must repeatedly adjust the intensity of the stimulus.

Neuromuscular stimulation requires electrical recruitment of muscle contraction. The sense of not having control of the muscle contraction can be difficult for some people. Thus, once the setup is completed you may need to adjust stimulus strength several times and provide encouragement to the injured person during the treatment. Second and third NMS treatments are often better tolerated and more effective as the individual becomes less apprehensive, although I have observed dramatic improvements in neuromuscular control with a single treatment.

IONTOPHORESIS

Iontophoresis, the use of an electrical current to drive charged particles across the skin, has been used for many years. Iontophoresis has been suggested for treating many conditions, including hyperhydrosis, excessive scarring, herpes simplex, muscle spasms, and fungus infections (Gangarosa, Payne, and Hayakawa 1989; Grice 1980; Grice, Satter, and Baker 1972; Haggard, Straus, and Greenberg 1939; Kahn 1987; Psaki and Carrol 1955; Shrivastera and Singh 1977; Sloan and Sotani 1986).

Modern electrical stimulators designed specifically for iontophoresis have made treatments safer than older devices. New devices used with specially designed electrodes control dosage and limit the risk of skin burns. The use of iontophoresis in athletic training is generally limited to administering dexamethasone, a steroidal anti-inflammatory, or lidocaine, an anesthetic. The use of acetic acid to dissolve calcium deposits has also been suggested. Further study of iontophoresis of acetic acid is needed to determine the efficacy of this treatment (table 8.4).

Little evidence substantiates the efficacy of iontophoresis in the treatment of musculoskeletal injuries, although many clinicians report success with iontophoresis, especially when using dexamethasone. You may be called upon to apply ionotophoresis and should be familiar with the equipment and treatment parameters.

Table 8.4   Medications Used by Certified Athletic Trainers in Iontophoresis

Medication	Polarity	Action
Dexamethasone	−	Anti-inflammatory
Lidocaine	+	Anesthetic
Acetic acid	−	Absorption of calcium deposits

INDICATIONS

The most common application of iontophoresis in sport rehabilitation is the use of dexamethasone to suppress inflammation, although there are no well-defined guidelines for such a treatment approach. The relationship between tissue repair and inflammation was emphasized in chapter 3, which pointed out that suppressing inflammation during tissue healing is inappropriate.

However, small amounts of necrotic tissue or mechanical stimulation sometimes cause persistent pain that fails to respond to rest and other treatment interventions. With age, the vascularity of tendon declines, which may compromise the body's ability to phagocytize necrotic tissues. In these circumstances there is empirical evidence that an injectable or iontophoretic steroidal anti-inflammatory medication can break a cycle of irritation and pain. These treatments can relieve symptoms for months or even permanently.

Lidocaine can be used to anesthetize a small area of skin and underlying tissues. The injection of lidocaine or other anesthetics into trigger points can be effective in managing myofascial pain syndromes. Iontophoresis offers a means of delivering the medication without needles. However, the treatment of multiple trigger points with iontophoresis would be extremely time consuming.

At one time it was common to mix lidocaine and dexamethasone for iontophoresis, to buffer the solution and thus minimize skin irritation. Iontophoresis must be conducted with water-soluble medications, but a direct current passing through water causes hydrolysis, lowering the pH of the drug solution. When lidocaine is used to buffer the free hydrogen ions, less change in pH occurs. Unfortunately, this practice also diminishes the delivery of dexamethasone into the tissues (figure 8.19). The use of buffered electrodes, which were marketed in the 1990s, minimizes the risk of skin irritation. Thus, there is no longer a need to mix lidocaine and dexamethasone.

An additional consideration with iontophoresis, which parallels concerns raised for phonophoresis, is the inability to precisely quantify the amount of medication delivered into the tissues. Continued investigation of the techniques is needed to provide treatment protocols with demonstrated efficacy.

TREATMENT PROCEDURES

The electrical stimulators used in athletic training for iontophoresis deliver DC. The substance to be driven into the tissue must carry an electrical charge in solution. The

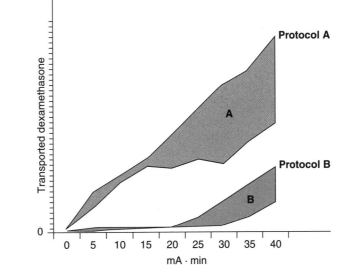

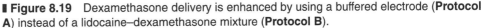

■ **Figure 8.19** Dexamethasone delivery is enhanced by using a buffered electrode (**Protocol A**) instead of a lidocaine–dexamethasone mixture (**Protocol B**).

The Effects of pH Buffering on Drug Delivery During Iontophoresis

Iontophoresis must be conducted using water-soluble drugs. However, a direct current passing through an aqueous solution causes the hydrolysis of water, thus creating potentially harmful changes in the pH of the drug solution.

$$OH^- \text{ raises pH}$$

$$H^+ \text{ lowers pH}$$

Because the most commonly used drug in iontophoresis is the negatively charged dexamethasone sodium phosphate, a potential problem is the accumulation of hydroxide ions, which are also negatively charged. If allowed to accumulate, they will be driven into the skin along with the drug ions. Depending on the length of the treatment, this can result in alkaline burns at the skin surface. Fortunately, there are ways to prevent these potentially dangerous pH changes. The method most frequently used in delivering dexamethasone sodium phosphate involved mixing the drug with lidocaine hydrochloride. When the two substances are mixed and iontophoresis is performed, the following electrochemical reactions occur:

$$DexPO_4^{-2} + 2Na^+ + OH^- + H^+ \underset{H_2O}{\longrightarrow} LidoH^+ + Cl^-$$

The hydrogen attached to lidocaine dislocates and then binds with the hydroxide ion. This recreation of water prevents the accumulation of hydroxide and the subsequent pH changes. Although this protocol does well to prevent most alkaline burns during iontophoresis of dexamethasone, it has been shown that it also greatly decreases the efficiency of drug delivery as compared to delivery of dexamethasone alone. This is because the chloride ions introduced by the lidocaine hydrochloride are much smaller, more mobile, negatively charged ions than those in dexamethasone. As a result, the current tends to drive in many more chloride ions than dexamethasone ions.

Another method of pH buffering has been introduced that does not decrease the efficiency of dexamethasone delivery. This method involves the use of a specially formulated ion exchange resin instead of lidocaine hydrochloride. The ion exchange resin, such as polyacrillin, can be incorporated into electrodes.

The polyacrillin does not introduce any small negatively charged ions like chloride, and cannot be delivered iontophoretically itself, because it is not water soluble. It does, however, have the ability to give up a hydrogen atom to neutralize the hydroxide ions created by the hydrolysis of water.

In a chemical equation, polyacrillin is represented by $P-CO_2H$. When used in the delivery of dexamethasone, the process is as represented below.

$$DexPO_4^{-2} + 2Na^+ + OH + H^+ + P-CO_2H \underset{H_2O}{\longrightarrow}$$

The hydrogen atom detaches from the polyacrillin and binds with the hydroxide ion, again recreating water and preventing harmful pH changes. Unlike the previous equation, however, the dexamethasone is now the *only* negative ion left in the solution. This allows for approximately three times more efficient drug delivery than when using lidocaine.

solution is placed in a treatment electrode that is buffered to minimize skin irritation (figure 8.20).

The maximum current delivered by the stimulator is 5 mA. Because DC is used, waveform duty cycle, frequency, phase duration, and ramp cannot be adjusted, and the only parameters of concern are polarity and dosage. The polarity of the treatment electrode should be the same as the ion to be driven into the tissue, because like charges repel. The unit of iontophoresis dosage is milliampere multiplied by minutes (mA · min). With buffered electrodes, the maximum dosage is 80 mA · min. The higher the dosage, the greater the amount of medication driven into the tissues. The dosage is determined by the amplitude of current that the recipient is able to tolerate multiplied by the length of the treatment. For example, if a 3 mA peak current is the most an individual can tolerate and the current is applied for 25 min, the dosage is 75 mA · min.

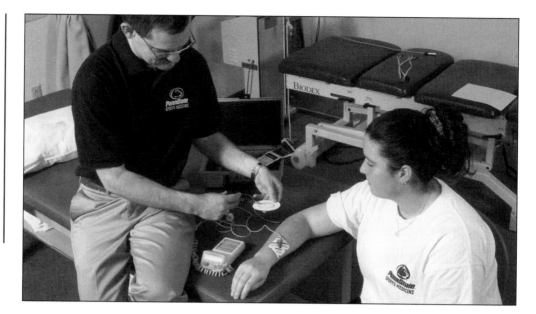

Figure 8.20 Electrode preparation for iontophoresis.

SAFETY

Safe application of iontophoresis requires proper equipment and clinical judgment. Iontophoresis carries all of the cautions and contraindications of TENS. In addition, medications to which the individual is allergic contraindicate iontophoresis. Even with modern electrodes designed for iontophoresis, skin irritation and chemical burns are possible. Instruct the recipient to report any sensation of burning, and if the individual does so, interrupt the treatment and inspect the skin. Terminate treatment if you have any concern that burning may be occurring. Some individuals, especially fair-skinned people, are very sensitive and cannot be treated with iontophoresis.

Although homemade electrodes and DC generators have been used for iontophoresis, it is strongly recommended that you use commercial stimulators and electrodes designed specifically for iontophoresis, to protect the individual as well as yourself. Proper equipment reduces the risk of skin injury substantially.

DIRECT STIMULATION OF DENERVATED MUSCLE

When the conduction of impulses to muscle by alpha motor neurons is disrupted, the individual loses control of the affected muscle. Alpha motor neurons conduct impulses from the spinal cord to the muscle and are also referred to as lower motor neurons, in contrast to the motor neurons of the spinal cord that are referred to as upper motor neurons. When the nerve to the muscle is not functioning, the muscle is denervated, or without innervation.

Denervation can be caused by injury or disease, but you will most likely encounter denervated muscle secondary to trauma. Severe knee sprains and dislocations can injure the peroneal nerve where it passes behind the head of the fibula, denervating muscles in the anterior tibial or lateral compartments of the leg. Injury to the brachial plexus can denervate the deltoid and other muscles of the arm.

Unlike upper motor neurons of the spinal cord, to which injury results in permanent paralysis, alpha motor neurons can regenerate and active control of the muscle can be restored. This reinnervation process is very slow and does not always occur.

However, because reinnervation is possible, clinicians have attempted to maintain the muscle through electrically stimulated contractions. The efficacy of electrical stimulation of denervated muscle has not been established. Electrical stimulation does not bring about reinnervation; however, a regularly stimulated muscle may recover force-generating capacity sooner if reinnervation occurs.

Although lower and upper motor neuron lesions are uncommon, it is important to understand the difference between these types of lesions. It is also important to understand that with lower motor neuron injury, the parameters of stimulation required for NMS will not elicit a contraction because the capacitance of muscle is much greater than that of the alpha motor neuron. Therefore, when NMS fails to elicit a contraction of the target muscle, one must suspect a lower motor neuron injury. If this diagnosis is confirmed, a low-frequency AC or DC current must be applied to overcome the capacitance of the muscle. The stimulation of denervated muscle carries the same contraindications as TENS.

The stimulation is uncomfortable because of the depolarization of small-diameter afferent nerves. Work closely with the directing physician in treating individuals with lower motor neuron lesions, and obtain the necessary equipment should stimulation of denervated muscle be requested.

MICROCURRENT

Microcurrent is a form of electrotherapy in which the stimulus amplitude is in the microamperage (millionth of an ampere) range. Microcurrent stimulators have been referred to as microcurrent electrical nerve stimulators (MENS) and low-intensity stimulators (LIS). MENS is a poor name because the peak amplitude generated is usually below the rheobase of even A-beta afferent fibers. Thus, the electrical current does not result in nerve depolarization. Moreover, the theoretical basis underlying the application of microcurrent does not involve nerve fiber depolarization.

A substantial body of evidence shows that electrical stimulation has physiological effects that are not related to nerve fiber depolarization. Electrical stimulation has been shown to speed repair in slow-healing surface wounds such as decubitus ulcers in humans (Barron, Jacobson, and Tidd 1985; Gentzkow 1993; Kloth and Feeder 1988; Wolcott et al. 1969; Wood et al. 1993). Enhanced repair in deeper tissue has been reported in animal models with the use of indwelling electrodes (Akai et al. 1988; Akai, Wadano, and Yabuki 1991; Nessler and Mass 1985; Kenney and Dahners 1988; Litke and Dahners 1992; Owoeye et al. 1987). Exciting work on the effects of microcurrent on edema formation in the acute inflammatory phase is ongoing; however, this work is limited to animal models.

There is also great interest in the use of pulsed ultrasound and pulsed electromagnetic fields to facilitate healing of nonunion and slow-healing fractures. The effects of these stimulators will be discussed in the next chapter.

Although the effects and potential benefits of microcurrent stimulation warrant continued investigation, the work completed so far has limitations. There is no evidence that using electrical stimulation facilitates the normal repair response in healthy humans. Whether microcurrent has application in the treatment of musculoskeletal injuries sustained by physically active people has yet to be determined. There is some testimonial evidence to the benefits of microcurrent in the treatment of these injuries; however, controlled investigations using delayed onset muscle soreness as a model for musculoskeletal injury suggest that microcurrent may relieve pain but does not speed recovery (Denegar et al. 1992). Some reports even question the pain-relieving effects of microcurrent (Lerner and Kirsch 1981; Weber, Servedino, and Woodall 1994). I have found cold, superficial heat, and TENS to be more effective in relieving pain than microcurrent.

Where does the evidence leave the certified athletic trainer who must decide whether to apply microcurrent? At this time, the only application of microcurrent shown to be effective is in treatment of slow-healing skin lesions, a condition that a

Table 8.5 Indications and Contraindications for Electrotherapy

	Indications	Contraindications
TENS	Pain control	Electrode placement over carotid artery
Neuromuscular stimulation	Restore neuromuscular control Retard atrophy	Cardiac pacemaker (unless approved by MD; Monitoring may be necessary.) Pregnancy
Iontophoresis	With dexamethasone: chronic inflammation	Electrode placement over carotid artery
	With lidocaine: local anesthesia	Cardiac pacemaker (unless approved by MD; Monitoring may be necessary.)
		Pregnancy
		Medications to which individual is allergic or hypersensitive
Stimulation of denervated tissues	Lower motor neuron lesion	Same as TENS
Microcurrent	Slow-healing wounds	Same as TENS

certified athletic trainer is not prepared to treat. The prospects for other uses of microcurrent will depend on future research findings. Clearly, electricity can alter tissue responses. However, research based on animal models and the use of indwelling electrodes does not provide answers about using surface electrode stimulation in humans to facilitate deep-tissue repair or alter capillary membrane permeability to minimize swelling.

Microcurrent stimulation is safe, although the cautions identified for TENS should be observed. The major challenge is developing a theoretical basis and substantiating the clinical efficacy of microcurrent in the treatment of musculoskeletal injuries. Throughout your career you should continue to review the research literature and critically assess whether there is enough evidence to warrant the application of any modality, including microcurrent stimulation. Table 8.5 summarizes the indications and contraindications for the forms of electrotherapy discussed in this chapter.

SUMMARY

1. *Define volt, ampere, impedance, and resistance.*

   Voltage is a measure of potential electrical difference or electromotive force. One volt is required for 1 A of current to pass through 1 Ω of resistance. Electrical current, measured in amperes, is the flow of electrons. One ampere equals the flow of 1 C (6.25×10^{18} electrons) per second. Resistance, measured in ohms, is the opposition to the flow of electrical current through a material. Impedance is resistance + inductance + capacitance.

2. *Describe the differences between alternating, direct, and pulsatile current.*

   There are two classifications of continuous currents: alternating (AC) and direct (DC). TENS units deliver electrical currents that are noncontinuous, or pulsed. Pulsatile currents are classified as monophasic, biphasic, or polyphasic.

3. *Discuss the difference between TENS, iontophoresis, microcurrent, and stimulation of denervated muscle.*

These are the four applications of electrotherapy in athletic training. TENS can be used to control pain or recruit muscle contraction through depolarization of the alpha motor neurons. Iontophoresis is the use of a direct current to drive medications that carry an electrical charge in solution through the skin. Microcurrent is a low-level current that speeds healing of slow-to-heal skin wounds. Stimulation of denervated tissue can be used when the alpha motor neuron has been damaged. In this case, electrical current is used to directly depolarize the sarcolemma, which requires a much greater electrical charge than does depolarization of an alpha motor neuron.

4. *Define parameters of pulsatile current, including phase duration, amplitude, phase charge, and frequency.*

Pulsatile currents are characterized by pulses of electrical current interrupted by interpulse intervals. Phase duration refers to the length of time required to complete each pulse. Amplitude is the current or voltage (voltage equals current if resistance is unchanged) in the electrical circuit. Phase charge, the number of electrons moved during each phase of an electrical pulse, is the primary determinant of which nerve fibers will be depolarized during TENS. Frequency is the number of pulses delivered per second for pulsatile currents, or cycles per second for AC.

5. *Describe the three types of pulsatile current.*

Pulsed currents may have a single phase that can be either positive or negative; these are classified as monophasic pulsatile currents. Pulsed currents may have a positive and negative phase, in which case they are classified as biphasic pulsatile currents. Two types of pulsatile current have multiple phases and are classified as polyphasic: Russian current and interferential current. Russian current delivers 10 μs bursts of AC before each 10 μs interval where no current is flowing. The very short bursts cannot really be classified as continuous current. Interferential current, created by the interference of two AC waves, never has a true interpulse interval. However, when the two interfering AC waves are out of phase with each other, this results in destructive interference. During this time there is too little current to have a physiological effect. Thus, physiologically there is an interpulse interval, and interferential currents are classified as polyphasic.

6. *Identify contraindications for the application of TENS, iontophoresis, and microcurrent.*

Pregnancy, use of a pacemaker, and placement of electrodes over the carotid arteries are commonly cited contraindications for TENS and microcurrent. TENS and microcurrent have not been proven to affect fetal development, and TENS is sometimes used in labor and delivery. However, because these modalities have not been proven safe during pregnancy, they should not be used to treat pregnant women. TENS and microcurrent may be safely used to treat individuals with cardiac pacemakers, provided that treatment is prescribed and monitored by a physician. An additional contraindication for iontophoresis is use of medications to which an individual may have adverse reactions. Caution should also be used to prevent chemical burns of the skin due to ion flux during treatment, of greatest concern in fair-skinned people.

7. *Discuss indications for treatment with TENS, iontophoresis, and microcurrent.*

TENS is indicated in pain management. Neuromuscular stimulation (TENS applied to depolarize alpha motor neurons) can also be used to restore neuromuscular control. In athletic training, iontophoresis is most commonly conducted with the anti-inflammatory medication dexamethasone. This is indicated in cases of chronic inflammation. Microcurrent may be indicated in the treatment of slow-to-heal skin wounds such as decubitus ulcers.

CITED REFERENCES

Abram SE, Reynolds AC, Cusick JF: Failure of naloxone to reverse analgesia from transcutaneous electrical stimulation in patients with chronic pain. *Anesth Analg* 60:81-84, 1981.

Akai M, Oda H, Shirasaki Y, Teteishi T: Electrical stimulation of ligament healing: An experimental study of the patella ligament of rabbits. *Clin Orthop & Related Res* 235:296-301, 1988.

Akai M, Wadano Y, Yabuki T, Oda H, Sirasaki Y, Tateishi T: Effect of a direct current on modification of bone and ligament repair process: Experimental investigation of a rabbit model. *J Jpn Orthop Assoc* 65:196-206, 1991.

Barron JJ, Jacobson WE, Tidd G: Treatment of decubitus ulcers: A new approach. *Minn Med* 68:103-106, 1985.

Clement-Jones V, Tomlin S, Rees LH, McLoughlin L, Besser GM, Wen HL: Increased beta-endorphin but not met-enkephalin levels in human cerebrospinal fluid after acupuncture for recurrent pain. *Lancet* 946-948, 1980.

Denegar CR, Huff CB: High and low frequency TENS in the treatment of induced musculoskeletal pain. *J Athl Train* 23:235-237, 1988.

Denegar CR, Perrin DH: Effects of transcutaneous electrical nerve stimulation, cold and a combined treatment on pain, decreased range of motion and strength loss associated with delayed onset muscle soreness. *J Athl Train* 27:200-206, 1992.

Denegar CR, Perrin DH, Rogol AD, Rutt R: Influence of transcutaneous electrical nerve stimulation on pain, range of motion and serum cortisol concentration in females with induced delayed onset muscle soreness. *J Orthop Sports Phys Ther* 11:100-103, 1989.

Denegar CR, Yoho AP, Borowicz AJ, Bifulco N: The effects of low volt, microamperage stimulation on delayed onset muscle soreness. *J Sport Rehabil* 1:95-102, 1992.

Deyo RA, Walsh NE, Martin DC, Schoenfeld LS, Ramamurthy S: A controlled trial of transcutaneous electrical nerve stimulation (TENS) and exercise for chronic low back pain. *N Engl J Med* 322:1627-1634, 1990.

Gangarosa L, Payne L, Hayakawa K: Iontophoretic treatment of herpetic whitlow. *Arch Phys Med Rehabil* 70:336-340, 1989.

Gentzkow GD: Electrical stimulation to heal dermal wounds. *J Dermatol Surg Oncol* 19:753-758, 1993.

Grice K: Hyperhydrosis and its treatment by iontophoresis. *Physiotherapy* 66:43-44, 1980.

Grice K, Satter H, Baker H: Treatment of idiopathic hyperhydrosis with iontophoresis of tap water and poldine methylsulfate. *Br J Dermatol* 86:72-78, 1972.

Haggard H, Straus M, Greenburg L: Fungus infections of hands and feet treated with copper iontophoresis. *JAMA* 112:1229, 1939.

Kahn J: *Principles and Practices of Electrotherapy.* New York, Churchill Livingstone, 1987.

Kenney TG, Dahners LE: The effect of electrical stimulation on ligament healing in a rat model with a dosage study. *Trans Orthop Res Soc* 13:348, 1988.

Kloth LC, Feeder JA: Acceleration of wound healing with high voltage, monophasic, pulsed current. *Phys Ther* 68:503-508, 1988.

Kots YM: *Electrostimulation.* Paper presented at the Canadian–Soviet Exchange Symposium on Electrostimulation of Skeletal Muscles, Concordia University, Montreal, 1977.

Lerner FN, Kirsch DL: Micro-stimulation and placebo effect. *J Chiropractic* 15:101-106, 1981.

Litke DS, Dahners LE: The effects of low level direct current electrical stimulation on ligament healing in a rat model: A dosage study. *Trans Orthop Res Soc* 17:669, 1992.

Melzack R: Prolonged relief of pain by intense transcutaneous somatic stimulation. *Pain* 1:357-373, 1975.

Nessler JP, Mass DP: Direct current electrical stimulation of tendon healing in vitro. *Clin Orthop Rel Res* 217:303-312, 1985.

Owoeye I, Spielholz NI, Fetto J, Nelson AS: Low-intensity pulsed galvanic current and the healing of tenotomized rat Achilles tendon: Preliminary report using low load-to-breaking measurements. *Arch Phys Med Rehabil* 68:415-418, 1987.

Psaki C, Carroll J: Acetic acid ionization: A study to determine the absorptive effects upon calcific tendinitis of the shoulder. *Phys Ther Rev* 35:84-87, 1955.

Robinson AJ: Basic concepts in electricity and contemporary terminology in electrotherapy. In Robinson AJ, Snyder-Mackler L (Eds), *Clinical Electrotherapy*, 2nd ed. Baltimore, Williams & Wilkins, 1995.

Rosenburg M, Curtis L, Bourke DL: Transcutaneous electrical nerve stimulation for the relief of postoperative pain. *Pain* 5:129-133, 1978.

Salar G, Job I, Mingrino S, Bosia A, Trabucchi M: Effect of transcutaneous electrotherapy on CSF beta-endorphin content in patients without pain problems. *Pain* 10:169-172, 1981.

Shrivastera S, Singh G: Tap water iontophoresis for palmar hyperhydrosis. *Br J Dermatol* 96:189-195, 1977.

Sloan J, Sotani K: Iontophoresis in dermatology. *J Am Acad Dermatol* 15:671-684, 1986.

Weber MD, Servedino FJ, Woodall WR: The effects of three modalities on delayed onset muscle soreness. *J Orthop Sports Phys Ther* 20:236-242, 1994.

Wolcott LE, Wheeler PC, Hardwicke HM, Rowley BA: Accelerated healing of skin ulcers by electrotherapy: Preliminary clinical results. *South Med J* 62:795-801, 1969.

Wood JM, Evans III PE, Schallreuter KU, Jacobson WE, Sufit R, Newman J, White C, Jacoboo M: A multicenter study on the use of pulsed low intensity direct current for healing chronic stage II and III decubitus ulcers. *Arch Dermatol* 129:999-1009, 1993.

ADDITIONAL SOURCES

Gersh MR: *Electrotherapy in Rehabilitation*. Baltimore, Davis, 1992.

Nelson RM, Currier DP: *Clinical Electrotherapy*, 2nd ed. Norwalk, CT, Appleton & Lange, 1991.

CHAPTER NINE

Ultrasound, Diathermy, and Electromagnetic Fields

OBJECTIVES

After reading this chapter, the student will be able to

1. describe how therapeutic ultrasound is generated by the treatment unit;

2. identify and describe the use of effective conducting media for ultrasound treatments;

3. define dose, duty cycle, treatment duration, and frequency as parameters of therapeutic ultrasound;

4. describe the thermal effects of therapeutic ultrasound;

5. describe the treatment parameters and physiological effects of pulsed ultrasound;

6. discuss the technique and efficacy of phonophoresis;

7. identify indications, contraindications, and precautions for treatment with therapeutic ultrasound and diathermy; and

8. describe the differences between therapeutic ultrasound and diathermy.

Two individuals are awaiting treatment. The first is a 22-year-old track athlete who sustained a strain of the biceps femoris 3 weeks ago. The second is a 36-year-old tennis player diagnosed with tendinitis of the long head of the biceps brachii. The certified athletic trainer uses ultrasound at the start of treatment for each; however, the treatments are not the same. Treatment of the track athlete takes longer and the ultrasound is delivered at a lower frequency. The certified athletic trainer also uses a gel pad between the ultrasound head and the skin when treating the shoulder but not the leg. Why were these treatments different? This chapter examines current uses of ultrasound and how new information is transforming old recipes into more effective treatments with ultrasound.

This chapter focuses on therapeutic ultrasound and, to a much lesser extent, the therapeutic use of electromagnetic fields. Ultrasound is commonly used by certified athletic trainers and physical therapists. With appropriate parameter adjustment, ultrasound can be applied to heat deeper tissues, including muscles, tendons, ligaments, joint capsules, and scar tissue. Unlike the superficial heating modalities discussed in chapter 7, ultrasound energy penetrates through the skin and subcutaneous fat. Thus, ultrasound can be considered a deep-heating modality.

Not all of the purported benefits of ultrasound are attributable to thermal effects. When ultrasound is pulsed, little heating occurs. Responses to pulsed ultrasound are due to the effect of the sound energy at the cellular level as opposed to tissue heating.

Sound energy also has been used to drive medication through the skin. This process, known as phonophoresis, is commonly used in athletic training despite very little evidence of efficacy. These issues are explored in greater detail later in this chapter.

Electromagnetic fields also can be applied to heat deeper tissues. At one time diathermy was a popular deep-heating modality. Because diathermy is more cumbersome to apply and has more contraindications than ultrasound, diathermy is rarely found in the modern athletic training room. However, a brief discussion of diathermy is included to introduce treatments with pulsed electromagnetic fields.

Many certified athletic trainers are familiar with pulsed ultrasound. However, in the past several years both pulsed ultrasound and pulsed electromagnetic field devices have been developed to facilitate bone healing, and the use of these modalities in treating physically active individuals has increased. Therefore, diathermy and treatment with electromagnetic fields are discussed in this chapter to provide background on what is known and yet to be answered regarding the impact of these modalities on tissue healing.

THERMAL EFFECTS OF ULTRASOUND

Ultrasound differs from the modalities discussed in the previous two chapters in that it transmits energy that falls within the acoustic, rather than electromagnetic, spectrum. Ultrasound is used in medicine for imaging and for loosening joint replacements requiring revision as well as for therapeutic benefits. Different frequencies of

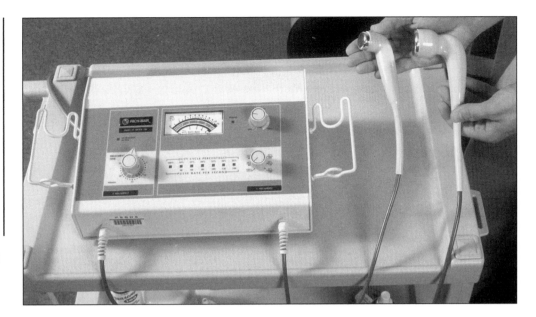

Figure 9.1 Modern ultrasound unit with multiple frequencies and sound heads.

ultrasound are used for each application. The ultrasound units used in athletic training and physical therapy emit sound energy at frequencies between 800 KHz (800 000 Hz) and 3 MHz (3 000 000 Hz). Modern high-quality ultrasound units can transmit sound waves at frequencies of 1 and 3 MHz. Some units are adjustable to 1, 2, and 3 MHz (figure 9.1). The importance of frequency and the applications of ultrasound at various frequencies will be discussed in detail. Initially, it is important to understand that therapeutic ultrasound uses acoustic energy, delivered at very specific high frequencies, for therapeutic purposes.

Ultrasound machines use electrical current to create a mechanical vibration in a crystalline material housed in the "head" of the unit. Vibration of the crystalline material produces a wave of acoustic energy (ultrasound) (figure 9.2). The crystalline material is usually lead zirconate titanate, although natural crystals and other synthetics have been used. The sound energy emitted from the ultrasound head travels through tissues and is absorbed.

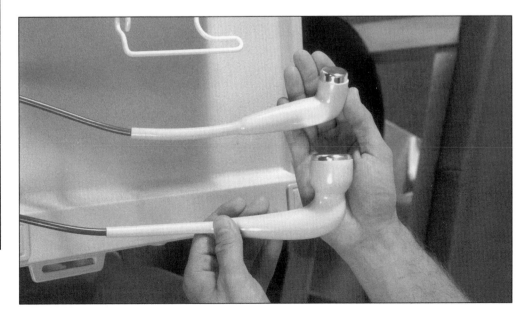

Figure 9.2 Components of an ultrasound unit.

Ultrasound is now used extensively for diagnostic imaging. Ultrasound of 1 MHz to 10 MHz is used to image deep structures such as the abdomen and superficial structures such as the eye, respectively. Ultrasound is also routinely used for prenatal examination. Through ultrasound some correctable birth defects can be indentified and the sex of the fetus can also be determined.

CRYSTAL QUALITY AND SIZE: BEAM NONUNIFORMITY RATIO AND EFFECTIVE RADIATING AREA

Two terms describe the size and quality of an ultrasound crystal. Effective radiating area (ERA) is the area that receives at least 5% of the peak sound energy. This is essentially the size of the area to which sound energy is conducted when the head of the ultrasound unit contacts the skin. The ERA is somewhat smaller than the surface area of the sound head.

The beam of sound energy emitted from a crystal is not uniform but rather is characterized by areas of high intensity and lower intensity (figure 9.3). Beam nonuniformity ratio (BNR) is the ratio between the peak intensity of the ultrasound beam (across the ERA) divided by the average intensity of the ultrasound beam; the lower the BNR, the more uniform the intensity of the sound wave.

$$BNR = \frac{\text{spacial peak intensity}}{\text{spacial average intensity}}$$

A low BNR minimizes the risk of developing "hot spots" and allows the athletic trainer to deliver higher doses of ultrasound without causing pain and discomfort. The BNR must be listed by the manufacturer on all units. Ideally, the BNR would be 1; however, this is impossible, and the acceptable range is between 2 and 6. Investigate the BNR before purchasing an ultrasound unit. A unit with a low BNR will be more expensive but will allow for greater comfort and safety and maximum delivery of sound energy.

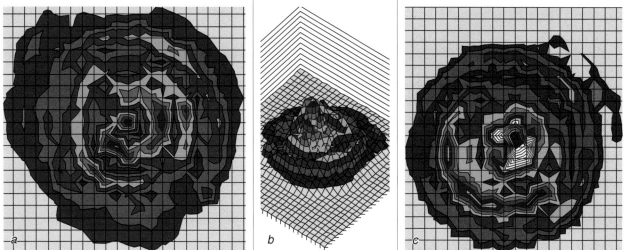

Medium crystal near field   **Near field view B**   **Medium crystal near field**

■ **Figure 9.3**   Beam scan of a crystal with a BNR of 2.32, top view *(a)* and side view *(b)*. When tested on 40 subjects, the ultrasound transducer housing this crystal produced a very comfortable treatment at 1.5 to 2.0 W/cm². Beam scan of a crystal with a BNR of 7.75 from the top view *(c)*. When this was tested on 40 subjects, the ultrasound transducer housing the crystal produced an uncomfortable treatment at 1.5 W/cm², and was not tolerated at 2.0 W/cm².

Courtesy of Brigham Young University Sports Injury Research Center.

CONDUCTING MEDIA

Air is a poor conductor of ultrasound energy. To maximize delivery of sound energy to the tissues, a conducting medium must be used. Several substances have been used to conduct ultrasound, including ultrasound gel, gel pads, mineral oil, lotions, and water. The amount of sound energy conducted varies substantially between conducting media. Commercial ultrasound gel (Draper 1996; Draper et al. 1993; Klucinec et al. 1999) and gel pads (Klucinec et al. 1999; Klucinec 1996) (figure 9.4) are superior conducting media. Water is not a good conducting medium (Draper 1996; Draper et al. 1993; Klucinec et al. 1999; Klucinec 1996; Forrest and Rosen 1989, 1992) and should not be used to administer therapeutic ultrasound. The conducting capacities of most gels and creams have not been established. However, some have been shown to be very poor conductors of sound energy (Draper 1996; Draper et al. 1993; Klucinec et al. 1999; Klucinec 1996; Forrest and Rosen 1989, 1992; Cameron and Monroe 1992). When applying ultrasound, use gels and gel pads known to be effective conductors.

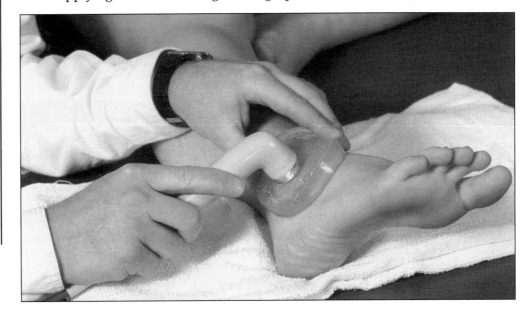

Figure 9.4 Ultrasound gel and gel pads.

PARAMETERS OF TREATMENT WITH ULTRASOUND

As with electrotherapy, you can alter the treatment parameters of ultrasound depending on the desired effect. Fortunately, the number of adjustable parameters is smaller. You can control the amplitude of the sound waves and therefore the amount of sound energy being emitted from the sound head. The sound energy emitted by the crystal is measured in watts (W). The dose of sound energy delivered is based on the amount of energy being emitted divided by the radiating area of the crystal measured in square centimeters (cm^2). Thus, ultrasound dose is measured in W/cm^2. You can also adjust the duty cycle, duration of treatment, and frequency.

As with electrotherapy, a duty cycle refers to the process of interrupting delivery of the sound wave so that periods of sound wave emission are interspersed with periods of interruption. Figure 9.5 depicts pulsed and continuous ultrasound.

Often you can select between several duty cycles. Calculate the duty cycle by dividing the time in which sound is delivered by the total time the sound head is applied. For example, if ultrasound is transmitted for 150 μs out of every second of treatment, then the duty cycle is 150/1000, or 15%. When the emission of sound energy is not interrupted, the duty cycle equals 100% and is referred to as continuous ultrasound.

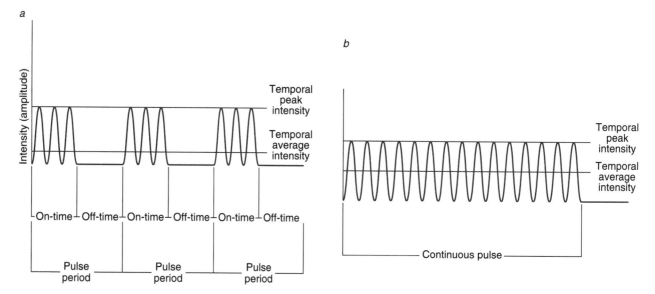

Figure 9.5 In pulsed ultrasound, energy is generated only during the on time (a). Duty cycle is determined by the ratio of on time to pulse, in this case 50%. Continuous ultrasound is shown in (b).

Much has been learned regarding the treatment duration needed to elevate tissue temperatures to beneficial levels. An interaction among the frequency, dose, and treatment duration has also been found. Findings indicate that recipes for duration and intensities of ultrasound treatments used in the past do not increase tissue temperature sufficiently.

The frequency of the sound waves affects the depth at which the greatest amount of ultrasound energy is absorbed as well as the time required to increase tissue temperature. Ultrasound units that allow for treatment with more than one frequency are relatively new, and some older units have a single fixed frequency of 1 MHz. Treatments with higher frequencies are often more appropriate for musculoskeletal injuries.

SOUND ENERGY ABSORPTION IN TISSUES

The amount of acoustic energy absorbed by tissues is influenced by many factors. The tissue characteristics, as well as the frequency, dose (W/cm²), duty cycle, and duration of treatment with ultrasound, affect the amount of acoustic energy absorbed. When continuous ultrasound is delivered, the greater the energy absorption, and the greater the tissue heating. Tissues with greater protein density have a higher rate of absorption, whereas tissues with a higher water content have lower absorption rates. Thus, tendon, ligament, and muscle tissue absorbs more sound energy than skin and adipose tissue. Superficial bones and nerves absorb the most energy.

Ultrasound at a higher frequency (3 MHz) is absorbed more rapidly than that at a lower frequency (1 MHz) (figure 9.6). Therefore, ultrasound at higher frequencies affects tissues that are more superficial, whereas at a lower frequency less energy is absorbed superficially and more is available to penetrate into deeper tissues. Thus, if treating a condition such as lateral epicondylitis with ultrasound, you should use a 3 MHz frequency. If the target tissue is deeper, for example, a hamstring muscle, use a lower frequency.

THERMAL EFFECTS OF ULTRASOUND

Many of the benefits of ultrasound have been attributed to tissue heating. This section examines the effects of parameter adjustments on the thermal response to ultrasound. Draper (1996) suggested that an increase of 1° C (mild heating) increases metabolic

Tissue penetration at 1 and 3 MHz based on actual measurement in human subjects

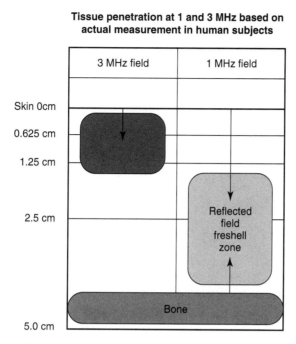

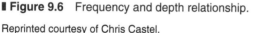
▮ Figure 9.6   Frequency and depth relationship.

Reprinted courtesy of Chris Castel.

activity; a 2 to 3° C increase reduces muscle spasm, increases blood flow, and reduces chronic inflammation; and a 4° C increase alters the viscoelastic properties of collagen.

An increase in temperature increases metabolic activity in deeper tissues. When these tissues are more active, the demand for oxygen is increased, which, in turn, increases local blood flow. Thus, one of the potential benefits of ultrasound is to increase local blood flow. Following injury, the body responds by building capillary networks around the damaged tissues. However, sometimes the body is unable to build enough capillaries to support repair and the body remains in a state of acute inflammation. The persistence of acute inflammation is labeled chronic inflammation. Ultrasound has the potential to push the body into tissue repair by increasing blood flow to the injured area. However, you must investigate whether inflammation is the result of a foreign object, an infection, or a disease. In addition, some chronic problems, such as tendinosis, may be due to decreased tissue vascularity; thus, the vasculature is insufficient to transport blood to the tissues even in response to increases in metabolic activity due to local heating.

The analgesic and antispasmotic responses to ultrasound are not as great as those following cryotherapy, superficial heating, and TENS application. The primary effects of continuous ultrasound are increases in collagen elasticity and local blood flow in response to increased tissue temperature. By properly selecting treatment parameters you can increase temperature more than 4° C in the target tissue.

Duty Cycle and Tissue Heating

Only continuous ultrasound results in therapeutically beneficial amounts of tissue heating. Pulsed ultrasound may have therapeutic benefits in certain circumstances, but these effects are nonthermal. Certainly the sound energy delivered with a pulsed ultrasound treatment is absorbed into the tissues at depths determined by the frequency of the sound wave. However, during the "off" times in the delivery of the ultrasound, heat is dissipated. Thus, very little local tissue heating occurs.

Dose and Tissue Heating

The greater the dose of sound energy, the greater the amount of energy delivered to the tissues. Thus, with continuous ultrasound, a higher dose results in greater tissue heating in less time. Many clinicians administer ultrasound at a low dose, often 1.5 W/cm², because they were instructed in school to do so. This practice may have come about because older units caused discomfort at higher doses due to the characteristics of the crystal. Although higher doses of ultrasound, greater than 2.5 to 3.0 W/cm², can damage tissue, you should not limit the dose to 1.5 W/cm².

Treatment Time and Tissue Heating

There is an interaction among frequency, dose, and the time required to increase tissue temperature. At a frequency of 3 MHz, 4 to 5 min is sufficient to achieve a 4° C increase in local tissue temperature at a dose of 1.5 W/cm². However, when a 1 MHz frequency is applied, a 10 min treatment at a dose of 2.0 W/cm² is required to achieve the same increase in tissue temperature (Draper 1996; Draper, Castel, and Castel 1995). Although no minimum dose has been established to obtain specific levels of heating, longer applications are needed when lower intensities of ultrasound are used. For example, a 1 MHz frequency continuous ultrasound treatment at 1.5 W/cm² requires 12 min to increase tissue temperature 4° C as opposed to the 10 min needed at 2.0 W/cm² (Draper 1996) .

Treatment Area, Sound Head Movement, and Tissue Heating

The parameters outlined in the previous sections to heat deeper tissues are predicated on treatment over an area no greater than three times the ERA of the crystal and a slow controlled movement of the ultrasound head (figure 9.7). When larger areas are treated, the amount of acoustic energy reaching any single area is decreased. In addition, heat buildup is allowed to dissipate from the target tissue. Thus, there is less temperature increase during treatment and therefore less change in tissue elasticity and local blood flow during and after treatment.

Treating larger areas such as the lower back has little or no effect on the tissues, although there may be a placebo effect. Thus, ultrasound should not be applied over large areas. Currently, the best recommendation for treatment technique suggests covering a treatment area less than four times the area of the ERA with the sound head covering less than 2 in./s.

Moving the sound head slowly prevents hot spots from developing in areas of peak amplitude and helps you maintain good contact with the skin or gel pad surface. With higher quality, lower BNR rating crystals, the sound head can be moved more slowly, resulting in a more uniform heating and greater patient comfort. Rapid, sloppy movement of the sound head with frequent breaks in contact between the skin or gel pad decreases the thermal response to treatment.

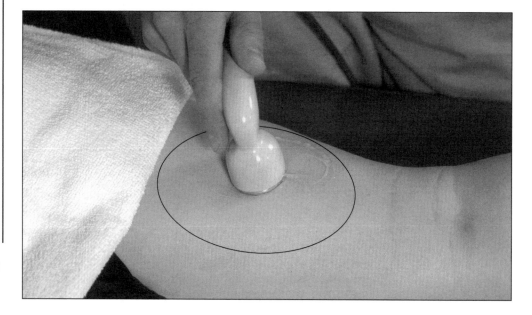

❚ **Figure 9.7** Treating an area four times the ERA.

NONTHERMAL EFFECTS OF ULTRASOUND

When ultrasound is pulsed, very little heating occurs. However, pulsed ultrasound has been shown to effect tissue healing in some circumstances and alter cellular activity in vitro (Dyson 1990). Therefore, it can be concluded that some of the responses to ultrasound cannot be attributed to a thermal response. This section discusses the nonthermal effects of ultrasound and reviews the demonstrated clinical benefits of pulsed ultrasound.

ACOUSTICAL STREAMING AND STABLE CAVITATION

The literature related to the nonthermal benefits of ultrasound attributes most of the effects to acoustical streaming and stable cavitation (figure 9.8). Acoustical streaming is the movement of fluids along cell membranes due to the mechanical pressure exerted by the sound waves. The movement occurs only in the direction of the sound wave. Acoustical streaming facilitates fluid movement and increases cell membrane permeability.

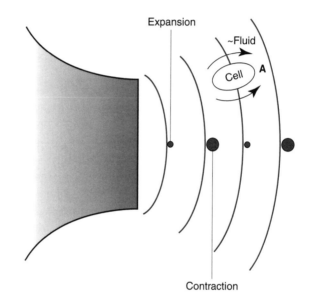

■ Figure 9.8   Acoustical streaming and stabile cavitation. Acoustical streaming is the movement of fluids around cells by sound waves. Stabile cavitation is the expansion and contraction of air bubbles due to pressure changes in surrounding fluid due to acoustic energy.

Cavitation is the formation of gas-filled bubbles. Ultrasound produces pressure changes in tissue fluids that create the bubbles and cause them to expand and contract. Stable cavitation refers to a rhythmic cycle of expansion and contraction during repeated pressure changes over many acoustic cycles. Unstable cavitation refers to a collapse of the gas bubbles. Unstable cavitation, which is most associated with low-frequency, high-intensity sound waves, is believed to damage tissues. Stable cavitation, which occurs with therapeutic ultrasound, is thought to facilitate fluid movement and membrane transport.

The increased movement of fluid and dissolved nutrients to and across cell membranes is believed to be the mechanism by which pulsed ultrasound facilitates tissue repair. Certainly acoustical streaming and stable cavitation also occur during continuous ultrasound. However, most of the benefits of continuous ultrasound are thought to be secondary to tissue heating.

ACUTE INJURY AND TISSUE HEALING

Research on the impact of ultrasound in acute injury and postoperative care has been limited to animal models. The application of pulsed ultrasound has been studied following silver nitrate–induced inflammation in animal models. Pulsed ultrasound treatments of 2 to 4 min at low doses may transiently decrease capillary leakage (Fyfe and Chahl 1980) However, greater leakage of plasma over 24 hr followed by a more rapid resolution of effusion has also been reported by the same investigators (Fyfe and Chahl 1985). The mechanism by which pulsed ultrasound affects swelling has not been fully explained, and much more study into mechanism and dose response is needed before pulsed ultrasound is routinely used following acute soft tissue injury.

In animal studies, investigators have found that following treatments with pulsed ultrasound, tissue repair is expedited (Dyson and Pond 1970) and tensile strength of healing tissues increased (Dyson and Pond 1970; Enwemeka, Rodriquez, and Mendosa 1989; Friedar 1988). These findings have not been replicated in humans. Thus, at this time the optimal treatment parameters for ultrasound following acute musculoskeletal injuries are unknown.

Further investigation of these issues is clearly warranted. Low doses of ultrasound may promote mast cell degranulation and speed the completion of acute inflammation, limit capillary leakiness, and promote collagen synthesis during the repair phase. Excessive exposure may result in tissue breakdown and prolong the acute inflammatory response. In closed wounds, sprains, strains, and fractures, the precise amount of sound energy reaching the damaged tissues is not known. However, when using pulsed ultrasound to treat acute injuries, proceed with caution. Too little is better than too much sound energy.

CHRONIC, SLOW-TO-HEAL SKIN ULCERS

The treatment of chronic, slow-to-heal, and nonhealing ulcers is frustrating and expensive. In the past 10 to 20 years, clinicians have found that low doses of sound, electrical energy, and light energy appear to speed healing in many cases. Reports on the use of pulsed ultrasound in treating human patients with chronic ulcers suggest that pulsed ultrasound has a physiological impact (Callam, Harper, and Dale 1987; Dyson and Suckling 1978; Erikson, Lundeberg, and Malm 1991). However, the subjects of these studies differ from healthy athletes in many respects, and we must use caution in generalizing these results to the treatment of musculoskeletal injuries.

PHONOPHORESIS

Phonophoresis is similar to iontophoresis in that a modality is applied to drive medications into the tissues. Phonophoresis utilizes sound energy, as opposed to electromagnetic energy, to drive the medication; thus, the medications driven into the tissues do not possess an electrical charge in solution.

Dexamethasone and hydrocortisone are the most common medication administered with phonophoresis by athletic trainers. The medication is often mixed in a cream. Unfortunately, many of the creams, gels, and ointments used to administer these medications with phonophoresis are poor conductors of ultrasound energy (Cameron and Monroe 1992). If you choose to use phonophoresis, use only commercial preparations in which hydrocortisone is mixed in a gel that is known to be a good conductor of acoustic energy.

Perhaps the greatest similarity between phonophoresis and iontophoresis is the lack of evidence concerning efficacy. Very little research evidence supports the practice of phonophoresis. The work of Griffin (1967; Griffin and Touchstone 1972) is perhaps most commonly cited as evidence of the efficacy of phonophoresis in treating musculoskeletal conditions. However, the benefits of phonophoresis observed by Griffin may have been due to placebo, because more recent studies have questioned the efficacy of phonophoresis (Cicone, Leggin, and Callamaro 1991; Oziomek, Perrin, and Harrold 1991). Of additional concern with phonophoresis is that the exact amount of medication reaching target tissues is unknown. Thus, the clinician does not know whether a pharmacologically effective dose of medication has been administered.

Of iontophoresis and phonophoresis, iontophoresis has the greatest potential to relieve pain and inflammation in cases of persistent symptoms such as tendinosis and tenosynovitis. However, much more work must be done to determine the efficacy of these treatments and establish parameter settings that optimize medication delivery to the target tissues.

EFFICACY AND CONTRAINDICATIONS TO ULTRASOUND

Although ultrasound is commonly used by certified athletic trainers and physical therapists to treat musculoskeletal conditions, there is little evidence that the treatments really relieve symptoms or speed recovery. Many treatments may have little effect due to errors in parameter selection or treatment technique. Earlier in this chapter parameters and treatment guidelines were provided to optimize the thermal response to ultrasound. You should use these guidelines until more is known about ultrasound, especially the effects of pulsed ultrasound on closed tissue injuries.

Using ultrasound to increase the temperature of deeper tissues has application in the treatment of persistent problems, including tendinosis, capsulitis, and myofascial restrictions. Ultrasound may also reduce pain and muscle spasm; however, other approaches such as cryotherapy and TENS are easier to administer and appear to be more effective. Limit the application of ultrasound to conditions where compromised vascularity may be responsible for persistent symptoms, such as occurs with tendinosis, and in circumstances where tissue heating is desired before muscle and connective tissue (fascia) are stretched.

Ultrasound is a relatively safe, easy-to-use therapeutic modality with few contraindications. Of greatest concern are the use of ultrasound in individuals with cancer and the impact of ultrasound on fetal development. Ultrasound has been reported to promote growth (Sicard-Rosenbaum et al. 1995), and perhaps metastasis, of malignant cells in laboratory animals and should not be used near tumors. The impact of therapeutic ultrasound on fetal development in humans is not fully known. Thus, theraperutic ultrasound should not be applied near the abdomen during pregnancy or to women of child-bearing age who could be pregnant. Ultrasound also should not be applied over an infection.

Despite considerable confusion in the literature over the years, ultrasound can be applied safely over metal implants such as plates and screws. Gersten (1958) and Lehman, Delateur, and Silverman (1966) concluded that it is safe to apply ultrasound over metal implants. Joint replacements contain metal and synthetics such as polyethelene and are held in place by methylmethacrolate cement. Because low-frequency ultrasound is used to loosen prostheses for removal and revision, and because the long-term impact of ultrasound on joint replacements is not fully known, it should not be used over joint replacements.

Ultrasound should not be applied over the heart or in the area of a cardiac pacemaker. Ultrasound should also not be applied over the eyes or genitalia. The use of ultrasound directly over open epiphyses should be minimized, because the impact of such exposure is not fully known and may involve accelerated closure of epiphyses. However, adolescents and children rarely experience problems for which ultrasound is indicated. Ultrasound is often used to treat back conditions. The use of ultrasound should be restricted to an area no more than four times the ERA to increase tissue temperature to therapeutic levels. Exposure of the spinal cord to ultrasound should be minimized. In patients who have had a laminectomy, do not apply ultrasound directly over the area of the cord that is no longer protected by bone. Although these precautions and contraindications should be observed, they rarely affect the selection of ultrasound as a therapeutic modality.

DIATHERMY

Diathermy is the therapeutic generation of local heating by high-frequency electromagnetic waves. Most diathermy units are classified as short-wave diathermy and generate an alternating current at 27.12 MHz. When the body is placed in an electric field, known as the capacitance technique, heating occurs due to the rapid rotation of dipoles (structures with positive and negative poles) (figure 9.9). As the current alternates between positive and negative, the dipoles rotate to align with the electric field. The mechanical friction and the movement of electrons result in local heating. Tissues with large numbers of dipoles, such as skin and muscle, have a greater capacitance to store an electrical charge. Thus, more current must be generated to cause dipole motion in these tissues. The greatest heating occurs in tissues with fewer dipoles, particularly fatty tissues. Thus, capacitance technique diathermy heats the subcutaneous fat more than the underlying muscle.

Heating of tissue in a magnetic field, also known as the inductance technique, differs in that the body is not placed in an electrical field. Instead, magnetic waves are generated by driving an electrical current through a coiled wire (figure 9.10). The magnetic field creates small currents in the tissues. The greatest heating occurs in tissue with low impedance, especially muscle. Thus, inductance technique is preferable for heating deeper tissues.

Like ultrasound, diathermy is effective for heating deeper tissues but it can heat larger areas. Unlike ultrasound, pulsed diathermy can heat the deep tissues 3 to 4° C (Draper et al. 1999). However, diathermy units are expensive and can be used on only one person at a time. In addition, diathermy carries a number of precautions and contraindications. All metal must be removed from the patient. Metal implants and cardiac pacemakers are absolute contraindications for treatment with diathermy. Diathermy must not be used near the uterus of a pregnant woman or near the abdomen or back of a woman of child-bearing age who could be pregnant. Finally, diathermy should not be used on individuals with infections; acute inflammation; moist, open wounds; malignant tumors; or large joint effusions (table 9.1).

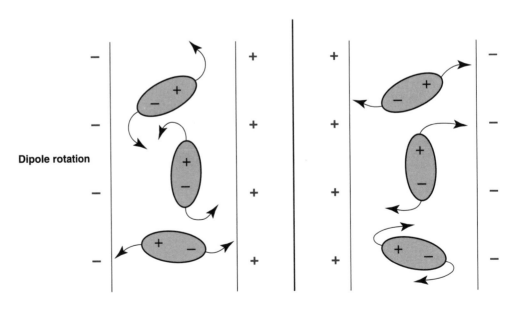

Dipole rotation

▮ Figure 9.9 The effects of oscillating, high-frequency electrical fields on the molecules and ions of the tissues. This figure shows dipole rotation.

Reprinted from Low and Reed 1994.

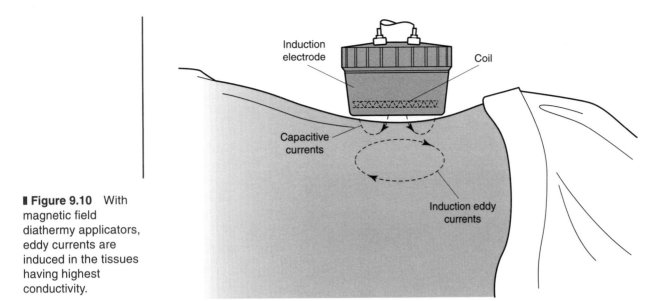

Figure 9.10 With magnetic field diathermy applicators, eddy currents are induced in the tissues having highest conductivity.

Table 9.1	Indications and Contraindications for Ultrasound and Diathermy	
	Indications	**Contraindications**
Ultrasound		
Continuous	Heat protein rich, deeper tissue. Increase blood flow in deep tissues.	Application over cardiac pacemaker, eyes, genitalia, joint replacements Pregnancy Cancer Infection Acute inflammation Minimize exposure over open epiphyses and spinal cord
Pulsed	May speed repair in slow-to-heal wounds, including nonunion fractures and tendinopathy.	Application over cardiac pacemaker, eyes, genitalia, joint replacements Pregnancy Cancer Infection Minimize exposure over open epiphyses and spinal cord
Diathermy		
Continuous and pulsed	Heat large area of deeper tissue. Increase blood flow in deep tissues. Decrease pain and muscle spasm.	Application over cardiac pacemaker, eyes, genitalia, joint replacements, and metal implants Pregnancy Open wounds Cancer Infection Acute inflammation and joint effusion

PULSED ELECTROMAGNETIC FIELDS AND DIATHERMY

Although diathermy has limited use in athletic training, the underlying technology has been used to promote tissue healing. Like ultrasound, diathermy can be pulsed to decrease the total energy transmitted to the tissues. Pulsed short-wave diathermy can be adjusted to provide a thermal response or to produce no tissue heating. When short-wave diathermy is adjusted to a low frequency (less than 600 pps) with a short phase duration (65 μs) into the nonthermal range, it is often classified as pulsed electromagnetic field (PEMF) or pulsed radio frequency energy (PRFE). This reclassification is important because diathermy implies heating, whereas the labels PEMF and PRFE imply a nonthermal therapy.

PEMF therapy has been investigated, with some studies suggesting that PEMF may speed wound healing (Brown and Baker 1987; Goldon et al. 1981; Itoh 1991) and relieve persistent pain (Foley-Nolan et al. 1990). However, not all reports agree, and the use of PEMF in treating soft-tissue injuries warrants further investigation. At present there is not enough information to recommend PEMF in the treatment of soft-tissue injuries sustained by athletes.

STIMULATION OF FRACTURE HEALING

In the past several years, the use of PEMF and pulsed ultrasound to treat nonunion and acute fractures has increased. Although more research is needed, there is evidence that these modalities can promote healing of nonunion fractures (Bassett 1984; Heckman et al. 1994; Sharrard 1990), and the use of these treatments in sports medicine has increased. You should understand the physical properties of these units and stay up to date as the technology evolves, in case a "bone stimulator" (figure 9.11) is prescribed for an athlete in your care.

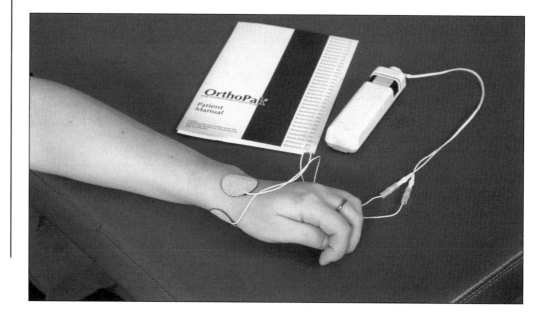

❚ Figure 9.11 Bone stimulating unit.

SUMMARY

1. *Describe how therapeutic ultrasound is generated by the treatment unit.*

   Ultrasound is generated through vibration of a crystal in an electrical circuit with alternating current. The rapid reversal of polarity creates the vibration and the emission of sound waves.

2. *Identify and describe the use of effective conducting media for ultrasound treatments.*

   Because air is a poor conductor of ultrasound energy, a conducting media must be used between the ultrasound head and the skin. Commercial ultrasound gels are designed to transmit ultrasound energy. Ultrasound gel is inexpensive and clearly the best transmitter of sound energy. Other conducting media, such as mineral oil, have been used but are substantially less efficient. A water bath has been recommended for ultrasound treatment over uneven surfaces such as the knuckles of the hand. Water, however, is also a poor conductor of high-frequency sound energy. Uneven surfaces are best treated with a gel pad, with ultrasound gel placed between the sound head and the pad, and between the pad and the skin.

3. *Define dose, duty cycle, treatment duration, and frequency as parameters of therapeutic ultrasound.*

   Ultrasound dose is measured in watts of energy over the ERA, or W/cm^2. The frequency of therapeutic ultrasound ranges from 0.8 to 3 MHz, with higher frequency (3 MHz) used to treat more superficial tissues. When pulsed ultrasound is used, the duty cycle refers to the amount of time ultrasound is transmitted in relation to total treatment time. For example, a 20 μs burst of ultrasound followed by an 80 μs interruption would create a 20% duty cycle. Treatment duration is simply the length of time an ultrasound treatment is applied. To achieve optimal increases in tissue temperature, a longer (8–10 min) treatment of continuous (no duty cycle) ultrasound is required at 1 MHz than at 3 MHz (4–5 min).

4. *Describe the thermal effects of therapeutic ultrasound.*

   When 8 to 10 min of continuous 1 MHz ultrasound is delivered, temperature increases 4° C in deeper (2.5–5 cm) tissues. A similar increase in temperature can be achieved at 1.0 to 2.5 cm with 4 to 5 min of continuous 3 MHz ultrasound.

5. *Describe the treatment parameters and physiological effects of pulsed ultrasound.*

   The primary parameter of pulsed ultrasound is duty cycle, which may vary from 10% to 90%. Pulsed ultrasound has been shown to increase the metabolic activity of fibroblasts in vitro and to speed healing of slow-to-heal skin lesions such as decubitus ulcers.

6. *Discuss the technique and efficacy of phonophoresis.*

   Phonophoresis is the use of ultrasound energy to drive medications through the skin. Although some studies have reported that medication can be driven through the skin, it is unknown whether pharmacologically effective doses can be delivered. There is little evidence that phonophoresis is clinically effective in treating musculoskeletal conditions.

7. *Identify indications, contraindications, and precautions for treatment with therapeutic ultrasound and diathermy.*

   Continuous ultrasound is indicated when the certified athletic trainer wants to heat deep tissues. Heating will increase blood flow to the tissues and make them more elastic and less viscous. Thus, ultrasound is commonly used before manual therapies and stretching. Pulsed ultrasound may be used to treat slow-to-heal skin wounds and with special devices in the treatment of nonunion fractures. Therapeuic ultrasound is contraindicated in individuals with cancer, infection, or acute inflammation and those who are pregnant. Ultrasound should not be applied over the eyes, the genitalia, joint replacements, or cardiac pacemakers. Exposure over the spinal cord and epiphyses should be minimized. Diathermay is indicated when the certified athletic trainer wants to heat a larger area of deeper tissue. In general, diathermy has the same contraindications as ultrasound. In addition, diathermy cannot be used over metal implants or open wounds.

8. *Describe the differences between therapeutic ultrasound and diathermy.*

   Diathermy heats deep tissues with electromagnetic energy as opposed to acoustic energy. Modern diathermy units are considerably more expensive than ultrasound but have similar heating effects and can heat larger areas of tissue.

CITED REFERENCES

Bassett CA: The development and application of pulsed electromagnetic fields (PEMFs) for ununited fractures and arthrodeses. *Orthop Clin North Am* 15:61-87, 1984.

Brown M, Baker RD: Effect of pulsed shortwave diathermy on skeletal muscle injury in rabbits. *Phys Ther* 67:208-214, 1987.

Callam MJ, Harper DR, Dale JJ: A controlled trial of weekly ultrasound therapy in chronic leg ulceration. *Lancet* 2:204-206, 1987.

Cameron MH, Monroe LG: Relative transmission of ultrasound by media customarily used by phonophoresis. *Phys Ther* 72:142-148, 1992.

Cicone CD, Leggin BG, Callamaro JJ: The effects of ultrasound on trolamine salicylate phonophoresis on delayed onset muscle soreness. *Phys Ther* 71:666-675, 1991.

Draper DO: Ten mistakes commonly made with ultrasound use: Current research sheds lights on myths. *Athletic Training Sports Health Care Perspectives* 2:95-107, 1996.

Draper DO, Castel JC, Castel D: Rates of temperature increase in human muscle during 1 MHz and 3 MHz continuous ultrasound. *J Orthop Sports Phys Ther* 22:142-150, 1995.

Draper DO, Knight KK, Fujiwara T, Castel JC: Temperature change in human muscle during and after pulsed short-wave diathermy. *J Orthop Sports Phys Ther* 29:13-22, 1999.

Draper DO, Sunderland S, Kirkendall DT, Richard M: A comparison of temperature rise in human calf muscles following applications of underwater and topical gel ultrasound. *J Orthop Sports Phys Ther* 23:247-251, 1993.

Dyson M: Role of ultrasound in wound healing. In Kloth LC, McCullough JM, Feeder JA (Eds), *Alternatives in Wound Healing*. Philadelphia, Davis, 1990, 259-286.

Dyson M, Pond JB: The effect of pulsed ultrasound on tissue regeneration. *Physiotherapy* 64:105-108, 1970.

Dyson M, Suckling J: Stimulation of tissue repair by ultrasound: A survey of mechanisms involved. *Physiotherapy* 64:105-108, 1978.

Enwemeka CS, Rodriquez O, Mendosa S: The effects of therapeutic ultrasound on tendon healing. *Am J Phys Med Rehabil* 6:283-287, 1989.

Erikson SV, Lundeberg T, Malm M: A placebo controlled trial of ultrasound in chronic leg ulceration. *Scand J Rehabil Med* 3:211-213, 1991.

Foley-Nolan D, Barry C, Coughlan RJ, O'Conner P, Rodeo D: Pulsed high frequency (27 MHz) electromagnetic therapy for persistent neck pain: A double blind, placebo controlled study of 20 patients. *Orthopedics* 13:445-451, 1990.

Forrest G, Rosen K: Ultrasound: Effectiveness of treatments given under water. *Arch Phys Med Rehabil* 70:28-29, 1989.

Forrest G, Rosen K: Ultrasound treatments in degassed water. *J Sport Rehabil* 1:284-289, 1992.

Friedar S: A pilot study: The therapeutic effect of ultrasound following partial rupture of Achilles tendons in rats. *J Orthop Sports Phys Ther* 10:39-45, 1988.

Fyfe MC, Chahl LA: The effect of single or repeated applications of "therapeutic" ultrasound on plasma extravasation during silver nitrate induced inflammation of the rat hindpaw ankle joint in vivo. *Ultrasound Med Biol* 11:273-283, 1985.

Fyfe MC, Chahl LA: The effect of therapeutic ultrasound on experimental oedema in rats. *Ultrasound Med Biol* 6:107-111, 1980.

Gersten J: Effect of metallic objects on temperature rises produced in tissue by ultrasound. *Am J Phys Med* 37:75-82, 1958.

Goldon JH, Broadbent NRG, Nancarrow JD, Marshall T: The effects of Diapulse on the healing of wounds: A double blind randomized controlled trial in man. *Br J Plast Surg* 34:267-270, 1981.

Griffin JE, Echternach JL, Price RE, Touchstone JC: Patients treated with ultrasonic driven cortisone and with ultrasound alone. *Phys Ther* 44:20-27, 1967.

Griffin JE, Touchstone JC: Effects of ultrasonic frequency on phonophoresis of cortisol in swine tissue. *Am J Phys Med* 51:62-78, 1972.

Heckman J, Ryaby JP, McCabe R: Acceleration of tibial fracture-healing by noninvasive low-intensity pulsed ultrasound. *J Bone Joint Surg* 76:26-34, 1994.

Itoh M, Montemayor Jr JS, Matsumoto E, Eason A, Lee MH, Folk FS: Accelerated wound healing of pressure ulcers by pulsed high peak power electromagnetic energy (Diapulse). *Decubitus* 4:24-30, 1991.

Klucinec B. The effectiveness of the aquaflex gel pad in the transmission of acoustic energy. *J Athl Train* 31:313-317, 1996.

Klucinec B, Scheidler M, Denegar C, Domholt E, Burgess S: Transmissivity of common coupling agents used to deliver ultrasound energy over irregular surfaces. Manuscript submitted for publication, 1999.

Lehmann JF, Delateur B, Silverman DR: Selective heating effects of ultrasound in human beings. *Arch Phys Med Rehabil* 47:331-338, 1966.

Oziomek RS, Perrin DH, Harrold DA, Denegar CR: Effect of ultrasound intensity and mode on serum salicylate levels following phonophoresis. *Med Sci Sports Exerc* 23:397-401, 1991.

Sharrard WJW: A double blind trial of pulsed electromagnetic fields for delayed healing of tibial fractures. *J Bone Joint Surg* 72B:347-355, 1990.

Sicard-Rosenbaum L, Lord D, Danoff JV, Thom AK, Eckhaus MA: Effects of continuous therapeutic ultrasound on growth and metastasis of subcutaneous murine tumors. *Phys Ther* 75:3-11, 1995.

ADDITIONAL SOURCES

Michlovitz SL: *Thermal Agents in Rehabilitation*, 3rd ed. Philadelphia, Davis, 1993.

Prentice WE: *Therapeutic Modalities for Allied Health Professionals*. New York, McGraw-Hill, 1998.

CHAPTER TEN

Mechanical Energy

OBJECTIVES

After reading this chapter, the student will be able to

1. discuss the potential benefits of using manual therapy techniques in rehabilitation;

2. describe massage, myofascial release, strain–counterstrain, muscle energy, and joint mobilization;

3. describe the afferent and efferent innervation of intrafusal and extrafusal muscle fibers and the relationship between the gamma and alpha motor neurons;

4. apply the "convex–concave rule" in performing joint mobilization;

5. describe the manual and mechanical traction techniques used to treat cervical spine dysfunction;

6. identify contraindications for manual therapies and mechanical traction;

7. describe the mechanical traction techniques used to treat lumbar spine dysfunction; and

8. describe the application of, and contraindications for, intermittent compression therapy.

A field hockey player is referred for care of her injured right wrist. She states that she injured the wrist 2 months ago when she fell on her outstretched hand. She was diagnosed as having a carpal sprain and her arm was placed in a cast for 3 weeks due to concerns over a possible fracture of the scaphoid. Recent x-rays did not reveal a fracture. However, she complains of pain after activities and stiffness in the wrist. Whirlpool treatments and stretching of the wrist flexors and extensors have not provided any benefits. Evaluation of the wrist reveals restrictions in wrist flexion and extension as well as decreased glide of the radial carpal and midcarpal joints. You administer ultrasound (3 MHz, continuous, 1.8 W/cm^2, 5 min) and perform joint mobilization. After three treatments over 6 days, range-of-motion of the wrist is normal and the athlete is experiencing much less pain after activity. How did the new treatment make a difference? Joint mobilization and other manual therapy techniques can speed recovery from a variety of musculoskeletal injuries. This chapter introduces manual therapies and other modality applications that deliver mechanical energy to the body.

Some therapeutic modalities, such as mechanical traction and intermittent compression, are beneficial because they exert mechanical forces on the body. However, the most common "devices" used in athletic training to impart a mechanical force on the body are the hands of the athletic trainer, which are powerful assessment and treatment tools. In past years, many certified athletic trainers abandoned manual therapy because of demands on their time and infatuation with devices such as TENS and isokinetic dynamometers. Now, manual therapy techniques, which have largely been developed in osteopathic medicine, chiropractic medicine, and physical therapy, are increasingly being practiced by certified athletic trainers.

This chapter covers the topics of mechanical traction, intermittent compression, and manual therapy. Much of the chapter is devoted to introducing several manual therapy approaches. However, this chapter is intended only to introduce manual therapy. Detailed discussion of manual therapy techniques has been reserved for the next text in the Athletic Training Education Series: *Therapeutic Exercise for Athletic Injuries*.

Much of this text is devoted to understanding how therapeutic modalities affect the nervous system and connective tissues. Although manual therapies can be thought of as procedures as opposed to applications, the certified athletic trainer's hands impact the connective tissues and alter neural input. Some clinicians shun the use of therapeutic modalities such as ultrasound and TENS for newer manual techniques, whereas others view manual therapies as a subspecialty separate from contemporary athletic training practice. A treatment that combines modalities like ultrasound or TENS and manual techniques may provide the greatest relief of symptoms. For example, when treating an individual with myofascial pain, you may find TENS, superficial heat, or occasionally cold combined with massage, strain–counterstrain, or release techniques to be effective. All alter neural activity at the spinal level and relieve pain and muscle spasm. Also, because heated tissues are more pliable, ultrasound may be useful before treatments such as joint mobilization where the goal is to stretch connective tissues and restore normal joint function.

Unlike cold therapy or TENS, manual treatment cannot be learned from a book but must be learned through laboratory instruction and hands-on practice. Students, as well as experienced athletic trainers, will continually refine their manual therapy skills and add variations and new techniques. Over the years, proprioceptive neuromuscular facilitation, joint mobilization, myofascial release, and strain–counterstrain techniques have been successfully used to treat physically active individuals. This is not to say that other modalities should be abandoned in light of the refinements in manual therapies; furthermore, no single manual therapy approach has been shown to be universally superior to another. Rather, developing skill in the manual therapy techniques offers you a greater number of options when developing a plan of care. Practice and experience will guide your development of manual therapy skills and your ability to integrate traditional therapeutic modalities with manual therapy.

In addition to providing you with more treatment options, manual therapy refines your ability to evaluate somatic dysfunction and structural lesions. A final benefit of manual therapy techniques is that they can be learned and applied in any setting; these skills require time and practice rather than a large budget and athletic training room. This chapter will provide a foundation on which to build your skills and inspire you to pursue further training in manual therapy.

MANUAL THERAPIES

Unfortunately, the scientific foundation for manual therapy has evolved more slowly than the art. There is relatively little evidence of cause-and-effect relationships between manual therapy and recovery of injured individuals. However, there is scientific support for much of the theory behind many forms of manual therapy, and the following sections include important components of the theoretical foundation for manual therapy. Before discussing individual therapies, the text will discuss one additional aspect of manual therapy that is neither anatomical nor clearly neurological: the power of touch and human interaction.

Certified athletic trainers often provide care to physically active people entering the medical system on an emergency basis, some for the first time. The high school athlete injured for the first time, the university freshman far from home, or the older individual whose work and family life have been disrupted present with more than an injured body part to be treated. These people come to the certified athletic trainer with anxiety, unanswered questions, and a sense of being lost in the health care system. Our increasingly bureaucratic and technology-driven health care system often leaves individuals wondering if anyone really cares about them. Manual therapy requires hands-on time with the individual. A caring touch and opportunity for conversation can ease anxiety and foster confidence that the individual is being cared for and will recover. A sense of being in good hands promotes compliance with a plan of care and a positive outlook, which in turn promote recovery. Some of the benefits of manual therapy are due to the psychological–affective responses to treatment rather than the anatomical–neurological responses. Some may call this a placebo response; however, improvement is improvement, and perhaps much of the failure of our medical system stems from the loss of the personal touch. Certainly, medical technology has advanced medical care, but at a price. The skilled manual therapist who provides a personal touch will help some physically active individuals whom others cannot.

MASSAGE

Massage, the rubbing or kneading of a part of the body, is one of the earliest recorded treatments of human suffering. Massage developed in many early cultures. The terminology and techniques of massage, as well as its acceptance as a therapy, have changed over time. Today, massage techniques are applied by several allied medical professionals as well as massage therapists.

Athletic trainers have used massage since the beginnings of the profession. Massage has been purported to relieve pain, increase blood flow, enhance lymphatic drainage, and stretch connective tissues. Experience and observation provide evidence of the effects of massage on pain and muscle spasm. Certainly relief of spasm may enhance lymphatic drainage, and mechanical energy can stretch connective tissues. However, blood flow to deep tissues is regulated by metabolic demand. The effect of massage on blood flow has not been extensively studied, but an understanding of circulatory regulation suggests that massage has little impact on blood flow to deeper tissues.

The primary benefits of massage in athletic training are pain relief, reduced muscle spasm, and increased tissue extensibility. But how does massage relieve pain and muscle spasm? Contact with the skin stimulates the cutaneous receptors and increases input along large-diameter afferent pathways. The gate control theory and the Level I model (figure 10.1) offer explanations for the analgesic benefits of massage techniques employing gentle stroking motions (effleurage) and kneading (petrissage) of muscle. Because muscle guarding and spasm are the result of pain, massage alleviates the trigger for muscle spasm and mobilizes the muscle and surrounding connective tissues.

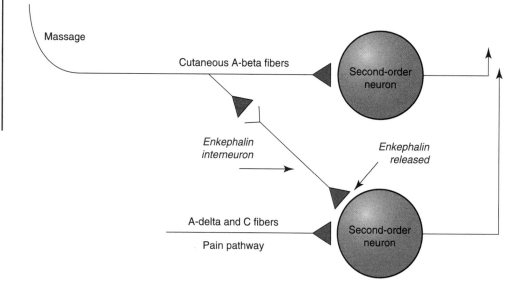

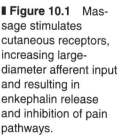
▌Figure 10.1   Massage stimulates cutaneous receptors, increasing large-diameter afferent input and resulting in enkephalin release and inhibition of pain pathways.

Deeper massage techniques over trigger points may result in a deep sensation of pain during massage yet provide extended relief. Painful stimulation activates the descending analgesic pathways described in chapter 4. Thus, the response to deep, kneading massage techniques also has a plausible explanation.

Relief of pain and muscle spasm and mobilization of connective tissues are important treatment goals. In theory, achieving these goals enhances lymphatic drainage. Certainly, pain relief and muscle relaxation promote free, active contraction of muscle, which is the primary means by which lymph is pumped through the body.

A massage is part of routine training and preparation for many endurance athletes. This is particularly true in professional cycling, and all of the European-based professional teams employ one or more *sorvoiners*, or massage therapists, to take care of their riders.

MYOFASCIAL RELEASE

Myofascial release is similar to massage in that the certified athletic trainer uses his or her hands to influence the connective tissues and neural input. Furthermore, there are multiple release techniques, and the techniques and terminology of myofascial release overlap with those of other manual therapies. However, myofascial release, as a component of manual therapies, has a much more elaborate theoretical basis, which has resulted in a greater understanding of somatic dysfunction.

Myo refers to muscle and *fascia* the system of supporting connective tissue that maintains the integrity of the human body. Injury, illness, stress, repetitive movements, poor posture, and fatigue can contribute to changes in the length–tension relationship of the fascia and muscles over time. For example, extensive swimming can strengthen and shorten the chest muscles while stretching and weakening the

Gamma Gain, Myofascial Release, and Strain–Counterstrain

Muscle is made up of two types of fibers. Extrafusal fibers are the contractile fibers that allow muscle to generate force. The extrafusal fibers are innervated by alpha motor neurons.

Interspersed within the extrafusal fibers, which make up most of the substance of muscle, are intrafusal fibers. Intrafusal fibers house muscle spindles that are specialized mechanoreceptors that send information regarding changes in muscle length, and therefore movement, to the central nervous system. Intrafusal fibers receive neural stimulation from gamma efferent neurons. The efferent input allows for continual adjustment of the length of the spindle so that it is maintained at an optimum length to detect changes within the muscle.

In some circumstances, there may be excessive activity in the gamma efferent neurons to a particular muscle or portion of a muscle, which is referred to as gamma gain. The effect of gamma gain is to maintain the spindles in a hypersensitive state resulting in normal movements causing reflexive contraction throughout a muscle via the reflex arc depicted in figure 10.2.

The increased tension, (hypertonicity) in a muscle will ultimately result in adaptive shortening in surrounding fascial tissues. The taut bands of tissues and hypersensitive trigger points associated with myofascial pain syndrome are thought to result from gamma gain.

The question of what causes gamma gain has not been fully answered. The likely trigger is pain. Acute pain results in muscle spasm and guarding. Rapid movement of muscle in spasm results in a reflexive contraction of the affected muscle suggesting that muscle spindles are in a hypersensitive state due to increased gamma efferent activity. The increase in gamma activity is the result of input from nociceptors. This explanation makes sense when applied to the response to acute injuries, but how does it relate to persistent pain problems such as MFPS?

The increased tone and resulting fascial adaptations found in MFPS are an insidious process. When fascia becomes shortened it too becomes hypersensitive to stretch. Stretch of fascial tissue is painful; free nerve endings are being stimulated. Noxious input from the fascia triggers an increase in gamma efferent activity perpetuating a cycle of spindle hypersensitivity, increased tone in muscle, fascial adaptations, and painful movement when the tight fascia is stretched. The cycle builds from mild discomfort into a pain pattern that can include referred pain and frequent headaches. Effective treatment of MFPS requires that the causes, which may include a combination of stress responses, muscle imbalance and poor posture, injury, and illness, be addressed in order to break this cycle.

Breaking the cycle described above by arresting gamma gain is the focus of two manual therapy techniques, strain–counterstrain and indirect myofascial release. These techniques place muscles and fascia in shortened positions of comfort. Such positioning decreases gamma efferent activity and interrupts the cycle that is maintaining the body in a dysfunctional state.

muscles of the upper back. The surrounding fascia adapts accordingly, setting the stage for a myofascial pain pattern.

Injuries such as whiplash can cause a pattern of guarding that in turn results in fascial adaptations. Psychological stress also results in tension and can contribute to the development of a myofascial pain pattern.

At the center of myofascial pain is gamma gain. When muscle is in spasm or protective guarding, it becomes hypersensitive to stretch due to increased input along gamma efferent nerves to the muscle spindles (figure 10.2). The cycles of pain, protective guarding, and fascial shortening gradually escalate until the athlete experiences myofascial pain.

The role of the certified athletic trainer is to break the cycle and address the physically active person's symptoms. Many modalities can be used to treat physically active individuals, and all treatment plans for myofascial pain should include active therapeutic exercises. However, these interventions do not directly address the problem of fascial restrictions and gamma gain.

Myofascial release techniques can be divided into direct and indirect techniques. In applying indirect techniques, the athletic trainer attempts to place muscle and fascia in positions that remove stress from the tissues, resulting in decreased noxious input from the fascia which, in turn, diminishes activity in gamma efferent nerves. These techniques are gentle but require practice to master. Direct techniques attempt to stretch bound fascia to decrease the stress on and afferent input from the tissue. Both techniques can be used to treat a physically active individual's myofascial pain pattern. Practice and experience will improve your manual skills as well as your ability to integrate traditional modalities, manual therapy, and exercise into a comprehensive plan of care.

Myofascial pain patterns are common in the neck, upper back, and shoulders. Poor posture, several hours spent driving or sitting in front of a computer, stress , and general fatigue slowly take a toll. Gentle release techniques often dramatically relieve pain, spasm, and accompanying headaches.

STRAIN–COUNTERSTRAIN

Strain–counterstrain, another type of manual therapy, was originated by Jones and colleagues. (1995). Like myofascial release, strain–counterstrain relieves pain and

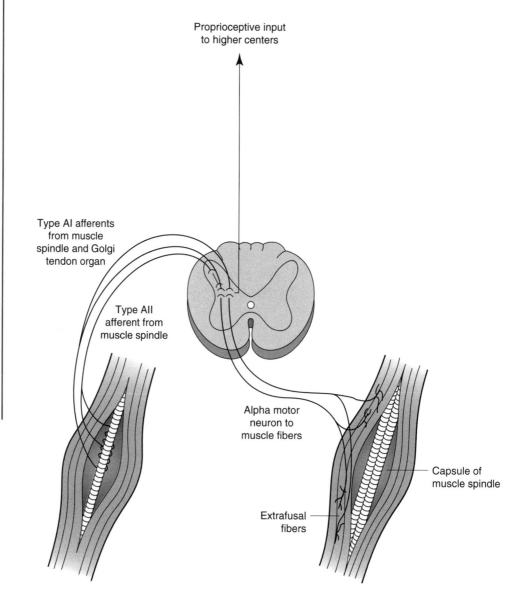

▌Figure 10.2 Sensory input from the muscle spindles and Golgi tendon organs affects motor function of the same muscle via synapses at the spinal cord level.

Adapted from Wilmore and Costill 1999.

dysfunction by altering neural activity. Strain–counterstrain is a technique where a body segment is passively moved into a position of greatest comfort thereby relieving pain by reducing or arresting inappropriate proprioceptive activity that is responsible for the dysfunction.

Jones provided a holistic view of somatic dysfunction, recognizing that injury to one structure, such as a ligament, impacts other tissues, including muscle, fascia, blood vessels, lymphatic vessels, and neural elements. Strain–counterstrain techniques are directed toward treating not the primary lesion, such as the sprained ligament, but rather the resulting dysfunctions.

Strain–counterstrain techniques can increase pain-free range of motion following musculoskeletal injury. As with myofascial release, direct and indirect techniques of strain–counterstrain are described. Direct techniques involve applying force against a restrictive barrier to improve motion, whereas indirect techniques involve moving the body away from a motion-restricting barrier to a position of comfort and relaxation.

By placing a body segment in a position of comfort, the indirect techniques inhibit the cycle of pain and increased muscle guarding due to increased gamma efferent outflow (figure 10.3). One key element of indirect techniques is to slowly move the treated body segment back to a resting position after a period (90–120 sec) of passive positioning. The slow, painless movement prevents a surge of input from spindles and reestablishment of the movement dysfunction.

Laboratory instruction and practice are necessary to become proficient at both myofascial release and strain–counterstrain techniques. Over the years athletic trainers have become increasingly interested in these manual therapies, probably because they address the notion of a pain–spasm cycle. Athletic trainers appreciate that modality applications do not repair injured tissue but are used to treat the signs and symptoms of injury, including loss of function. Strain–counterstrain techniques are most useful in short-duration pain patterns and during tissue repair and early maturation. Myofascial techniques, although similar, seem to be most effective in treating more long-standing pain patterns, especially those related to the spine.

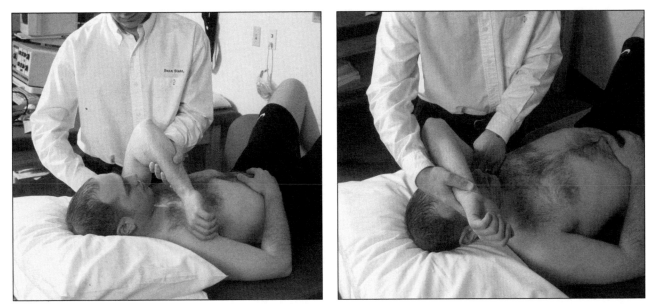

❚ **Figure 10.3** Strain–counterstrain for short *(a)* and long *(b)* heads of the biceps brachii dysfunction.

Pain results in muscle guarding and spasm, which in turn causes pain. Sometimes this cycle persists despite adequate time for tissue repair. Strain–counterstrain can be used to place a body segment in a position of comfort and break the cycle. A slow return to anatomical or resting position prevents recurrence of pain, often leading to prolonged relief.

JOINT MOBILIZATION

Muscle energy and joint mobilization are manual therapies primarily directed to restoring joint function. Joint mobilization is used to restore intrinsic joint motion or arthrokinetics. Joint mobilization also stimulates joint receptors and increases afferent input across large-diameter afferent fibers. Thus, joint mobilization may also ease pain and improve the individual's willingness to move a joint.

To appreciate the value of joint mobilization techniques, you must fully understand how joint movement occurs. Joints are formed by the articulating surfaces of bones. Muscles, through the attachments of tendons, cause bones to move upon one another at the joint. Outwardly, the articulating surface of one bone appears to pivot about a single, fixed axis, but few joint motions actually occur about a single axis.

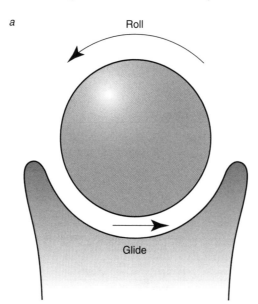

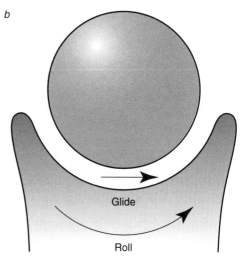

Figure 10.4 When a convex surface moves on a concave surface, roll and glide are in opposite directions *(a)*. When a concave surface moves on a convex surface, roll and glide occur in the same direction *(b)*.

During most joint movements, the articulating surfaces slide and glide upon one another while the rolling or pivoting occurs about a moving axis.

The subtle slides and glides are referred to as arthrokinematics, whereas the pivoting of one bone upon another is referred to as osteokinematics. Joint mobilization involves the assessment and treatment of arthrokinematics. The "convex–concave rule," illustrated in figure 10.4, will help you assess and treat restricted arthrokinematic movements.

When arthrokinematic movement is limited, range of motion is limited and the joint is often painful. From the perspective of modality application and pain management, joint mobilization addresses the first two priorities in an injured person's plan of care: pain relief and restoration of range of motion. In fact, when pain and loss of motion are due to arthrokinematic dysfunction, joint mobilization is the treatment of choice.

A more thorough discussion of joint mobilization and treatment techniques is included in *Therapeutic Exercise for Athletic Injuries*. However, this technique is introduced in the context of therapeutic modalities because of its application in managing joint pain and loss of motion.

A loss of range of motion is common following musculoskeletal injury such as a sprain of the lateral ankle ligaments. A loss of dorsiflexion affects the ability to walk and run. Stretching of the gastrocnemius and soleus can help restore motion but often the problem is related to a restriction of posterior glide of the talus in the mortice. In these case, joint mobilization techniques where the talus is manually moved posteriorly will be far more effective at restoring motion than stretching.

MUSCLE ENERGY

Muscle energy techniques are manual procedures in which the injured person's muscles are actively contracted against a counterforce in a specific treatment position. Muscle energy techniques may be used to stretch tight muscles and fascia, strengthen weakened muscle, or mobilize restricted joints (Woerman 1989). These techniques are often very effective in the treatment of sacroiliac (figure 10.5) and lumbar facet dysfunction.

Like joint mobilization, muscle energy can be considered a procedure rather than a modality application. However, when restricted joint movement causes pain and movement dysfunction, a therapeutic modality usually fails to improve the patient's

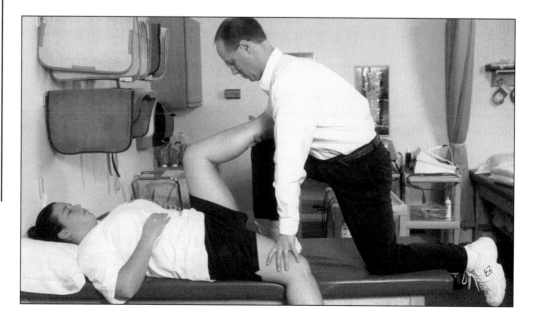

❚ Figure 10.5 Muscle energy technique for an anterior innominate rotation, a common source of sacroiliac dysfunction.

situation. Muscle energy and joint mobilization techniques address the cause of the injured person's complaints and often speed the recovery of normal movement and function. You can use TENS and moist heat with most manual techniques, including myofascial release, muscle energy, and joint mobilization; TENS and heat relieve pain and reduce muscle spasm, so the injured person becomes more relaxed and comfortable, allowing for more effective manual therapy.

Like all modalities, manual therapy techniques are contraindicated in the treatment of some injured physically active individuals. These contraindications are summarized in table 10.1. Injuries to ligaments and bone are the most common contraindications for manual therapies. However, these contraindications are not absolute and require that the certified athletic trainer make sound clinical decisions. For example, if an athlete suffers a fracture and dislocation at the ankle, this injury would contraindicate all manual therapies. However, once the tissues have healed and the leg is removed from immobilization, massage, myofascial release, and joint mobilization could be used to restore range of motion in the foot-ankle complex. It is also possible that the prolonged use of crutches could result in sacroiliac dysfunction that may respond to muscle energy techniques.

The certified athletic trainer must also be able to recognize signs and symptoms of infections and diseases in the physically active individuals they treat. Treatment of infection and organic diseases is beyond the scope of athletic training practice. If the certified athletic trainer is unsure of the nature and etiology of musculoskeletal pain, an evaluation by a physician must be conducted before any manual therapy is attempted.

In addition to the specific precautions and contraindications discussed previously and in *Therapeutic Exercise for Athletic Injuries*, there are additional contraindications for joint mobilization and muscle energy procedures, due to the greater force applied to the body during those procedures. Joint mobilization and muscle energy procedures should not be used in the presence of joint or bony instability or when degenerative changes result in a bony block to motion. Joint mobilization and muscle energy procedures also should not be used in the presence of malignancies or advanced osteoporosis; mobilization of the cervical spine should not be performed in the presence of advanced rheumatoid arthritis.

There is considerable debate as to whether dysfunction at the sacral iliac joint is a common cause of low back pain. Identification and treatment of asymmetry with muscle energy techniques do dramatically relieve pain and spasm for some individuals. Muscle energy techniques incorporated into a comprehensive plan of care can be the key to relief of weeks or months of pain and dysfunction.

TRACTION

Mechanical traction involves using a machine or apparatus to apply a traction force to the body (figure 10.6), whereas with manual traction the force is applied by the hands of the certified athletic trainer. Most traction treatments are administered to distract or separate segments of the cervical or lumbar spine. Research has demonstrated that vertebral separation occurs (Colachis and Strohan 1965, 1969). However, gravity reduces the separation as soon as the individual sits or stands. Thus, the efficacy of traction in the management of spinal dysfunction is questionable. The use of mechanical traction, in particular, has declined in all allied medical fields and has never been extensive in athletic training.

Although the use of mechanical traction by certified athletic trainers is limited, an understanding of the principles and applications of manual and mechanical traction is useful. Some cervical manual traction is necessary during joint mobilization.

Table 10.1 Indications and Contraindications for Manual Therapies, Traction, and Intermittent Compression

	Indications	Contraindications
Manual therapies		General: symptoms of organic disease or cancer must be followed up before a modality, including a manual procedure, is administered.
Massage	Pain Muscle spasm Edema	Infection Skin breakdown or disease
Myofascial release	Persistent pain with fascial restrictions; taut bands or trigger points	Acute inflammation, recent fracture, or surgery Caution with joint instability or joint prosthesis Caution if pregnant
Strain–counterstrain	Persistent pain with well-localized tender points	Increased pain during treatment Caution following fracture or if joint instability present
Muscle energy	Subluxation or malpositioning of a bony element	Recent fracture Joint instability Joint fusion Bony instability Severe osteoporosis
Joint mobilization	Loss of range-of-motion due to arthrokinematic restriction	Infection Joint instability Bone-on-bone end feel Recent fracture Bony instability Advanced osteoporosis Mobilization of cervical spine in the presence of advanced rheumatoid arthritis
Traction		
Cervical	Pain Muscle spasm Hypomobile facet Disc herniation	Positive vertebral artery test Positive alar ligament test Acute neck injury (fractures, sprains with joint instability) Advanced rheumatoid arthritis Bone cancer Increased pain or radicular symptoms with treatment Advanced osteoporosis
Lumbar	Pain Muscle spasm Disc herniation Hypomobile facet Nerve root impingement	Pregancy Claustrophobia Internal disc derangement Fractures, sprains with joint instability Bone cancer Increased pain or radicular symptoms with treatment Advanced osteoporosis Hiatal hernia
Intermittent compression	Swelling and edema	Thrombophlebitis Infection Acute fracture Pulmonary edema and congestive heart failure

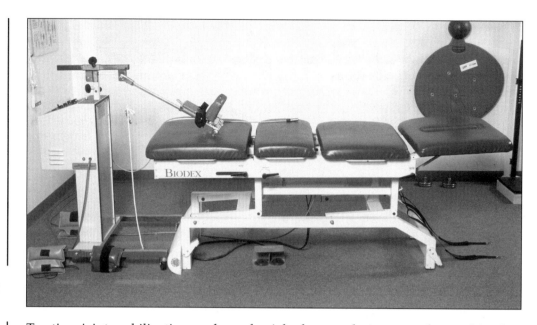

▌Figure 10.6 A split traction table.

Traction, joint mobilization, and myofascial release techniques can be combined to treat cervical facet dysfunction and myofascial pain patterns. Some individuals with acute low back pain respond well to traction, especially when placed in a position of comfort.

CERVICAL TRACTION

Distraction of the cervical spine can benefit individuals with cervical facet dysfunction or cervical disc pathology, degenerative changes that narrow the intervertebral foramen and cause myofascial pain. Manual traction should be performed before mechanical traction is considered. Manual traction allows you to carefully control force application and head position to maximize the relief of symptoms. Manual traction also allows you to combine manual techniques. If manual traction relieves pain and/or radicular symptoms, you can move to mechanical traction for longer treatments that require less of your time. Take care to reproduce the position and traction force that provided the greatest relief. You cannot precisely quantify the traction force that you apply through your hands. However, a force of 15 to 25 lb will result in a perceived elongation of the cervical spine. The best approach to adjusting the mechanical force is to gradually increase it until the individual reports relief similar to that experienced with manual traction.

Manual Traction Technique

To apply cervical traction manually, place the physically active individual in a supine position. Place your hands in a position that allows distraction of the cervical spine without causing discomfort (figure 10.7). Relax your hands as much as possible, because tension in your hands will result in tension and guarding by the individual being treated. When this occurs the traction forces are resisted by the muscles, defeating the purpose of the treatment. Massage or release techniques can be used first to minimize tension in and guarding by the paraspinal muscles.

As traction is applied, the head can be positioned for greatest comfort. In neutral position, the greatest separation occurs in the upper cervical spine. As the neck is flexed to 30°, the traction forces are directed to the lower cervical spine. You can also carefully side-bend and rotate the head and neck to find the position of greatest relief (figure 10.8). Side-bending is especially useful in relieving pressure on spinal nerves in individuals with degenerative changes that result in radicular symptoms.

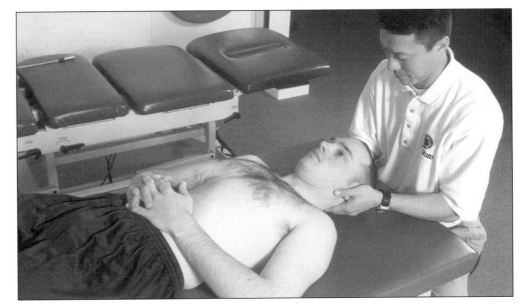

❚ Figure 10.7 Manual cervical traction.

Traction treatment does not structurally change the spine. However, the treatment can break the cycle of pain, muscle spasm, and guarded movement. Postural training and upper body reconditioning can result in long-term management of symptoms in some individuals.

Mechanical Traction Technique

In individuals who respond well to manual traction, mechanical traction is an option that requires less of your time. The physically active individual should be positioned supine, with the neck flexed and side-bent to a position of greatest comfort. A halter or Saunder's traction device (figure 10.9) can be used to transmit the traction forces. Saunder's device is easier to set up than the halter, especially for those who rarely apply cervical traction. To apply the device, position the individual's head so that the pads align with the base of the occiput, then adjust the pads securely at the base of the occiput. If the pads are too tight, the individual will complain of pain. If they are too loose, the pads will slide and pinch the ears and little traction force will be transferred to the spine.

You can select continuous or intermittent traction. Intermittent traction, where the maximum traction force is applied for a set time period (typically 30 sec) and then a reduced force is applied, is more comfortable and better tolerated in most cases. The period of reduced force, or rest period, is usually about the same duration as the length of time the maximum force is applied. The traction force during rest is usually 50% of the maximum traction force.

The amount of traction force should be gradually increased to provide a tolerable distraction. Begin with 15 lb on smaller individuals and those with more pain and 25 lb on larger individuals with more

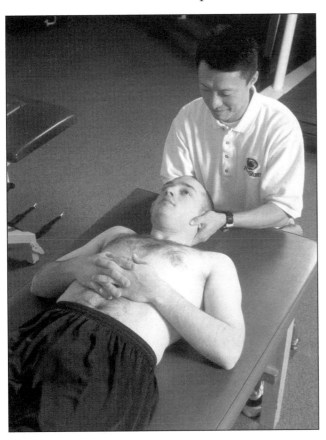

❚ Figure 10.8 Manual side-bending.

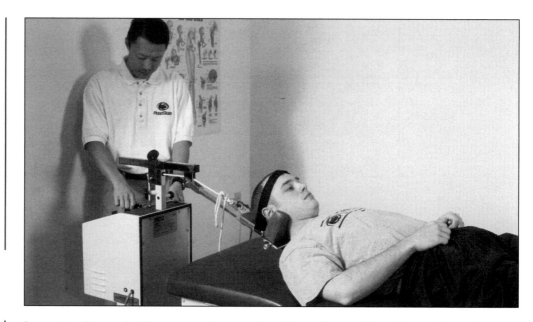

Figure 10.9 Cervical traction with Saunder's device.

long-standing pain. Treatment time can be adjusted up to 20 to 30 min depending on the individual's response. Traction can be combined with moist heat to control pain and promote muscle relaxation.

Irritation of a nerve root due to herniation of an intervertebral disc or stenosis causes pain that radiates along the course of the nerve. This pain, referred to as radicular pain, can be excruciating. Manual and mechanical traction can relieve radicular symptoms. Often relief is temporary at first; however, short-term relief offers hope. A combination of appropriate positioning, exercise, and the frequent use of cold or superficial heat at home can reduce stress on damaged and irritated tissues and result in long-term resolution.

Precautions and Contraindications

Mechanical cervical traction is not appropriate for everyone and could result in catastrophic injury when applied inappropriately. In general, mechanical and manual traction is contraindicated following acute injury to the neck, the term *acute* implying that trauma caused the symptoms. Trauma to the head and neck may damage bone, ligament, and musculotendinous structures, resulting in laxity or instability. Fracture and injury to the stabilizing soft tissues must be ruled out or allowed to heal before you use traction. If traction is applied too early, the result may be greater permanent laxity and instability or, in the worst case, subluxation and injury to the spinal cord. As a rule, use manual traction rather than mechanical traction for individuals with a history of traumatic injury to the cervical spine.

One additional consideration of extreme consequence is fracture of the dens or odontoid process of the second cervical vertebra (axis) (figure 10.10). Trauma, especially with a whiplash mechanism, can fracture the dens. Unfortunately, this fracture is not always recognized and may not be particularly painful. If traction is applied in the presence of a dens fracture, dislocation of the first or second cervical vertebra could result, an often fatal injury. The alar ligament test allows you to evaluate the integrity of the dens. The alar ligament attaches to the occiput and the dens (figure 10.11). When the head is rotated or side-bent, the pull through the alar ligament causes a palpatable rotation of C2. If the dens is fractured, the leverage to rotate C2 is lost. Thus, to assess the integrity of the dens, you can palpate the spinous process of C2 and passively side-bend or rotate the individual's head. If the spinous process does not move, the individual should be evaluated for fracture of the dens by the team or referring physician. You should perform the alar ligament test before using

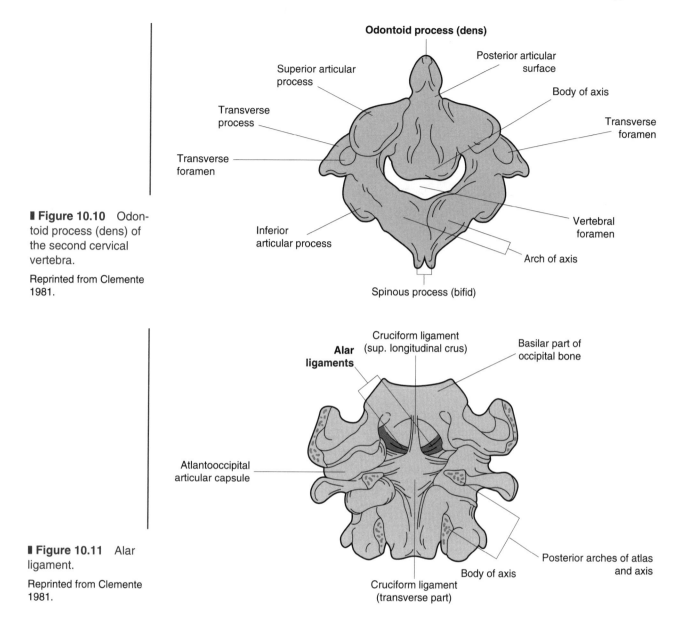

cervical traction when treating an individual with a history of traumatic injury to the neck, especially if a whiplash mechanism was involved.

Another concern related to cervical traction involves the potential to place the head in a position that compromises the vertebral arteries. The vertebral arteries pass through the foramen in the transverse processes of the fifth to second cervical vertebrae. These vessels ascend to the circle of Willis, which distributes blood supply to a large area of the brain (figure 10.12). Rotation and extension of the head will diminish blood flow through the vertebral artery on the side to which the head is rotated. Normally this does not pose a problem, because the vertebral arteries are paired and sufficient blood supply is provided through the contralateral side. However, some individuals present with a compromised vertebral artery on one side. Prolonged positioning of the head can lead to an insufficient blood supply to the brain and pose the risk of stroke. To test the integrity of the vertebral arteries, extend and rotate the head (figure 10.13). If the individual notes dizziness or blurred vision or you note nystagmus or slurred speech, the vertebral artery on the opposite side

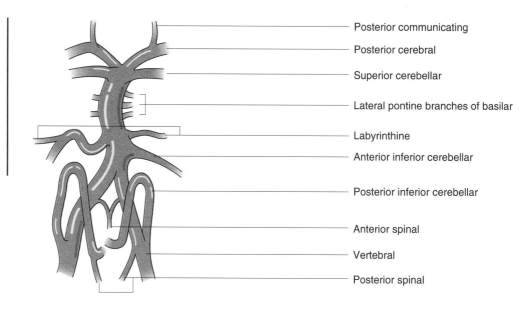

Figure 10.12 The vertebral arteries and their intracranial branches.

Reprinted from Hollinshead and Rosse 1985.

may be compromised. The situation can be quickly reversed by repositioning the head in neutral and restoring flow through the vertebral artery system. A positive vertebral test is not common, yet you should perform a vertebral test on any individual before you administer mechanical cervical traction. A positive vertebral artery test contraindicates mechanical traction where long-term positioning of the head poses a risk.

Traction is also contraindicated in some individuals with osteoporosis and rheumatoid arthritis, conditions that may render the bone or connective soft tissues of the cervical spine unable to withstand traction forces. If you have any concerns when treating individuals with these conditions, consult with the referring physician. It is much better to err on the side of caution than risk injury to the cervical region. The contraindications to cervical traction are summarized in table 10.1.

LUMBAR TRACTION

Distraction of the lumbar spine can also be accomplished with mechanical traction. The traction forces can separate or distract the facet joints and relieve pressure on spinal nerves caused by disc injury. Most facet dysfunction, or mechanical low back pain, responds better to manual techniques such as mobilization and muscle energy.

Most physically active individuals with disc pathology need help to find a resting position that alleviates symptoms. Most disc injuries involve the posterior lateral aspect of the disc. Lumbar extension is believed to encourage the nucleus to migrate anteriorly, away from the spinal nerves. Thus, lying prone with a tolerable extension of the lumbar spine often

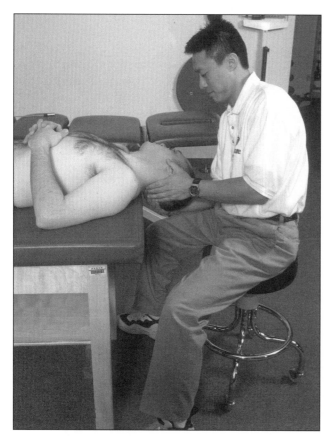

Figure 10.13 The vertebral artery test.

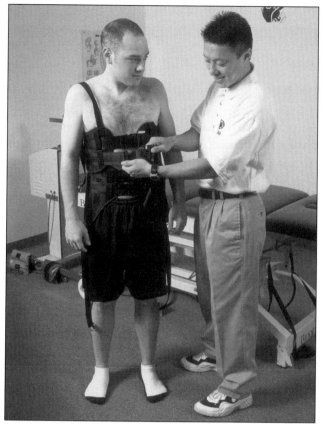

■ Figure 10.14   Placing lumbar traction harnesses.

alleviates the radicular symptoms associated with disc injury. The advantage of finding positional relief is that the individual can control symptoms at home.

Because of the nature of managed care and success in treating low back problems without mechanical lumbar traction, it is not used often. However, it may be very useful in the management of acute conditions where manual techniques and positioning fail to bring relief.

Setup

Setting a physically active person up for lumbar traction is somewhat involved. Two wide harnesses must be applied, one above the iliac crests and one over the lower ribs. The belts must be snug or the traction force will cause the belts to slide, diminishing the traction forces at the lumbar spine. The belts can be applied with the individual supine but might be much easier with the individual standing (figure 10.14). Once the belts are in place, you can position the individual on the traction table. Individuals whose symptoms are worse in sitting or improved with lying or lumbar extension should be positioned prone (figure 10.15a). If sitting is more comfortable or lying and lumbar extension more painful, position the individual supine with the hips and knees flexed (figure 10.15b).

Once the person is positioned, traction forces are administered in either a continuous or an intermittent mode. Intermittent traction (30–45 sec on, 15–30 sec rest) is better tolerated. Shorter on times (15 sec) have been suggested for treating facet dysfunction and longer on times (60 sec) for disc injury. Unfortunately, little research supports the efficacy of mechanical lumbar traction or provides well-substantiated treatment parameters.

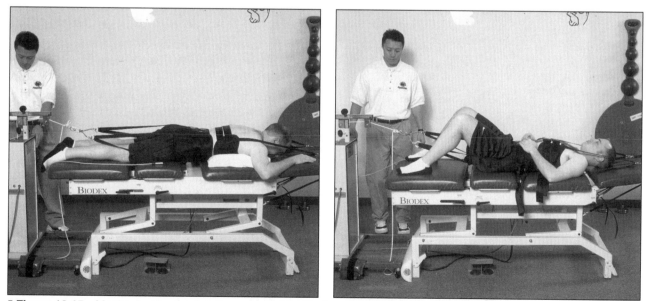

■ Figure 10.15   Mechanical lumbar traction: an individual in the prone position to extend the lumbar spine *(a)*, and an individual in the supine position with hip flexed to approximately 90° *(b)*.

An initial traction force of 25% of body weight is a reasonable starting force. If the initial force is tolerated, increase the traction force up to 50% of body weight. Treatment times usually range from 10 to 20 min, depending upon the nature of the problem and the response to treatment.

Precautions and Contraindications

There are fewer contraindications for lumbar traction (summarized in table 10.1) than for cervical traction. Pregnancy, hiatal hernia, and advanced osteoporosis are absolute contraindications. Fractures and medical conditions, such as cancer, that affect the integrity of the connective tissues also contraindicate mechanical traction. Occasionally individuals will experience a significant increase in pain during traction, in which case traction must be terminated. This is particularly common in individuals suffering from internal disc derangement.

In daily practice, practical considerations such as belt adjustment and an inability to tolerate treatment affect decisions about the application of mechanical lumbar traction more often than do absolute contraindications. The harness used to apply lumbar traction is adjustable; however, it is often difficult to fasten the belts snugly on very thin individuals, and the belts cannot be fitted on many obese individuals. Furthermore, some people experience claustrophobia when the belts are tightened to prevent sliding.

INTERMITTENT COMPRESSION

Intermittent compression involves the use of a pneumatic device that intermittently inflates a sleeve around an injured joint or limb. Intermittent compression devices are used to reduce edema and posttraumatic swelling. In athletic training, the primary cause of fluid accumulation in the tissues is trauma. Chapter 3 reviewed the mechanism for posttraumatic swelling and discussed the role of the lymphatic system in resolving swelling. Elevation of an injured extremity and intermittent compression can speed the resolution of posttraumatic swelling by increasing lymphatic drainage. However, active muscle contractions are the strongest drivers of lymphatic drainage under normal physiological conditions.

Therapeutic modalities that relieve pain and muscle spasm followed by active exercise reduce swelling more effectively than does intermittent compression. The exercise activity must be well tolerated and must not cause further tissue damage. However, simple active range of motion exercises within the limits of pain are sufficient to increase lymphatic drainage over a resting state. Thus, intermittent compression is better reserved for treating complicated problems such as persistent swelling and wounds caused by venous insufficiency.

SETUP

Intermittent compression is easy to administer. A compression stocking is applied to the limb to be

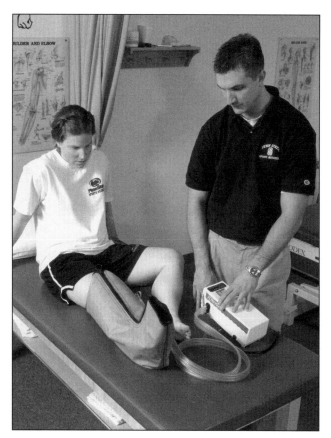

▌ Figure 10.16 Intermittent compression pump with sequential air filling.

treated (figure 10.16). Once the stocking is in place, the intermittent compression unit is adjusted for duty cycle and maximum pressure. No duty cycle has been established as the most effective. Inflation times of 30 to 40 sec are well tolerated when interspersed with 20 to 30 sec "off" or deflation periods.

There is some disagreement regarding the optimal inflation pressure. Manufacturers have developed guidelines for various conditions (Fond and Hecox 1994). The maximum pressure in treating posttraumatic edema is recommended to be 50 to 90 mm Hg (Fond and Hecox 1994; Hooker 1998). A setting just below diastolic blood pressure is well tolerated by physically active individuals and appears to reduce edema. Once the duty cycle and pressure have been set, the injured individual remains with the affected limb elevated throughout a 20 to 30 min treatment.

CONTRAINDICATIONS

There are few contraindications for intermittent compression (table 10.1). Certainly all situations in which tissue movement is restricted such as healing fractures and gross joint instability would contraindicate intermittent compression. Infection, thrombophlebitis, pulmonary edema, and congestive heart failure also contraindicate intermittent compression.

Intermittent compression is a relatively safe, passive approach to reducing posttraumatic edema. However, setup is somewhat time-consuming, and the individual is not actively engaged in the rehabilitation process. Thus, the injured individual will likely improve faster by performing pain-free active exercises to encourage lymphatic drainage during treatment in the clinic or athletic training room and three to four times daily at home as long as the swelling persists.

SUMMARY

1. *Discuss the potential benefits of using manual therapy techniques in rehabilitation.*

   Because manual therapies require hands-on treatments, they offer time for conversation and an opportunity to develop open communication and mutual understanding. Manual therapies offer additional approaches to relieving pain and muscle spasm and restoring range of motion.

2. *Describe massage, myofascial release, strain–counterstrain, joint mobilization, and muscle energy.*

   Massage is a collection of techniques that involve rubbing or kneading part of the body. Myofascial release (MFR) is similar to massage in that the certified athletic trainer uses the hands to influence the connective tissues and neural input. However, MFR is directed at specific trigger points and areas of fascial tension and restriction. Strain–counterstrain involves placing the body into a position of greatest comfort, thus relieving pain by reducing or arresting inappropriate proprioceptive activity. Joint mobilization is used to restore intrinsic joint motion or arthrokinetics. Using the convex–concave rule, you can use joint mobilization techniques to identify and treat motion restriction resulting from the loss of normal gliding between bones during rotation at a joint. Muscle energy techniques are manual procedures that involve active contraction of the individual's muscles against a counterforce in a specific treatment position. Muscle energy techniques can be used to stretch tight muscles and fascia, strengthen weakened muscle, or mobilize restricted joints.

3. *Describe the afferent and efferent innervation of intrafusal and extrafusal muscle fibers and the relationship between the gamma and alpha motor neurons.*

Muscle is made up of contractile, extrafusal fibers and sensory, intrafusal fibers called muscle spindles. The contractile fibers are innervated by alpha motor neurons. When an impulse is transmitted down an alpha motor neuron, all of the extrafusal muscle fibers it innervates contract. When many alpha motor neurons are stimulated, many extrafusal fibers contract and the muscle generates force. The length and tension of a muscle are perceived by the muscle spindles. Gamma afferent fibers send information from the spindle to the central nervous system. The length of a muscle spindle must be constantly adjusted for it to optimally sense changes in muscle length and tension. The gamma efferent motor nerves innervate the spindle to adjust the resting length.

4. *Apply the "convex–concave rule" in performing joint mobilization.*

Joint mobilization is used to restore normal joint arthrokinematics. In normal joint function, when a convex surface, such as the head of the humerus, moves on a concave surface, such as the glenoid, the convex surface will glide in the opposite direction that it rolls. For example, during abduction of the arm, the head of the humerus will roll upward but glide downward. If a concave surface, such as the tibial plateau, moves on a convex surface, such as the femoral condyles, roll and glide occur in the same direction. For example, during knee flexion, the tibia rolls and glides posteriorly.

5. *Describe the manual and mechanical traction techniques used to treat cervical spine dysfunction.*

The cervical spine can be distracted manually or using a traction device. Manual traction offers the advantage of finding the position and traction force that provide the greatest relief. Mechanical traction, with the recipient laying supine, can be accomplished with a traction harness or a Saunder's traction device.

6. *Identify contraindications for manual therapies and mechanical traction.*

Symptoms of organic diseases such as cancer must be followed up before treatment with any modality, including manual therapies. Massage is contraindicated if infection or skin breakdown or disease is present. Release techniques should not be used during acute inflammation or shortly after a fracture or surgery. Caution is advised if the recipient is pregnant or has a joint replacement or joint instability. Strain–counterstrain should be discontinued if pain increases and should be used with caution following a fracture or if a joint is unstable. Muscle energy is contraindicated in those with a recent fracture or when there is joint instability or a joint fusion. Infection, joint instability, recent fracture, and a "bone-on-bone" end feel contraindicate joint mobilization; also mobilization of the cervical spine is contraindicated in the presence of advanced rheumatoid arthritis. Both muscle energy and joint mobilization are contraindicated in the presence of bony instability and advanced osteoporosis. There are several contraindications for cervical traction including a positive vertebral artery or alar ligament test, acute neck injury, including fracture and joint instability, advanced rheumatoid arthritis, bone cancer, and advanced osteoporosis. Cervical traction should be discontinued if pain increases or radicular symptoms are exacerbated by treatment. Lumbar traction is contraindicated by pregnancy, claustrophobia, internal disc derangement, fractures and sprains with joint instability, bone cancer, advanced osteoporosis, and hiatal hernia. Lumbar traction should also be discontinued if pain is increased or radicular symptoms are exacerbated by treatment.

7. *Describe the mechanical traction techniques used to treat lumbar spine dysfunction.*

Traction to the lumbar spine can be administered with the individual in prone or supine position. If symptoms are reduced when the individual is sitting, as is often the case with foraminal or spinal stenosis, having the individual lie supine with the hip flexed is preferred. If symptoms decrease when the spine is extended, such as occurs when the individual lies prone, the individual should be treated in prone position. A traction force of one fourth to one half of body weight with intervals of traction (e.g., 40 sec) and rest (e.g., 20 sec) is generally recommended.

8. *Describe the application of, and contraindications for, intermittent compression therapy.*

Intermittent compression involves the use of a pneumatic device that intermittently inflates a sleeve around an injured joint or limb. Intermittent compression facilitates lymphatic drainage, which will reduce swelling. Intermittent compression should not be applied in the presence of thrombophlebitis, infection, or acute fractures or in cases where the individual has pulmonary edema or congestive heart failure.

CITED REFERENCES

Colachis SC, Strohan BR: Cervical traction relationship of time to varied tractive force with constant angle of pull. *Arch Phys Med Rehabil* 46:815-819, 1965.

Colachis SC, Strohan BR: Effects of intermittent traction on separation of lumbar vertebrae. *Arch Phys Med Rehabil* 50:251-258, 1969.

Fond D, Hecox B: Intermittent pneumatic compression. In Hecox B, Mehreteab TA, Weisberg J (Eds), *Physical Agents*. Norwalk, CT, Appleton & Lange, 1994, 419-428.

Hooker D: Intermittent compression devices. In Prentice WE (Ed), *Therapeutic Modalities for Allied Health Professionals*. New York, McGraw-Hill, 1998, 392-403.

Jones LH, Kusunose R, Goering E: *Jones Strain–Counterstrain*. Boise, ID, Jones Strain–Counterstrain, Inc., 1995.

Woerman AL: Evaluation and treatment of dysfunction in the lumbar-pelvic-hip complex. In Donatelli R, Wooden MJ (Eds), *Orthopaedic Physical Therapy*. New York, Churchhill Livingstone, 1989, 403-483.

ADDITIONAL SOURCES

Dvorak J, Dvorak V: *Manual Medicine: Therapy*. New York, Thieme Medical, 1988.

Dvorak J, Dvorak V: *Manual Medicine: Diagnostics*, 2nd ed. New York, Thieme Medical, 1990.

King R: *Performance Massage*. Champaign, IL, Human Kinetics, 1993.

Kuprian W: *Physical Therapy for Sports*, 2nd ed. Philadelphia, Saunders, 1995.

CHAPTER ELEVEN

Treatment Plans for Acute Musculoskeletal Injuries

OBJECTIVES

After reading this chapter, the student will be able to

1. develop rehabilitation plans of care to control the signs and symptoms of acute inflammatory response,

2. provide a rationale for the application of therapeutic modalities to treat the signs and symptoms of acute inflammation,

3. provide guidelines for progression of a rehabilitation plan of care through the repair and maturation phases of tissue healing, and

4. discuss the role of therapeutic modalities during the repair and maturation phases of tissue healing.

It is a busy Monday in the athletic training room. A baseball pitcher sustained an acromioclavicular sprain of his throwing shoulder while horseback riding over the weekend. A soccer player also sustained a shoulder injury. A wide receiver sustained a sprain of the tibial collateral ligament of his right knee, and a field hockey player sprained her left ankle. All are acute injuries, but each will require a unique rehabilitation plan of care.

To safely return these athletes to competition, you must do more than apply therapeutic modalities or instruct the athlete in therapeutic exercises. First you have to consider the injury, the healing process, and the demands placed on the body by each athlete's sport. The initial goal of treatment for each athlete will be to control pain and swelling and protect the damaged tissues, and the next goal will be to restore range of motion and neuromuscular control. Therapeutic modalities can help achieve early treatment goals. Each athlete, however, will return to sport at a different time. The soccer player will return sooner than the pitcher because of the stresses that throwing places on the shoulder. The field hockey player is found to have a mild ankle sprain and may return to play in only a week because the injured ligaments can be protected with taping and bracing. The football player has sustained a Grade II injury and will miss more time. This chapter integrates the information presented on inflammation and healing, pain, and the therapeutic modalities and establishes the framework for applying specific therapeutic exercises and procedures.

To properly manage acute musculoskeletal injuries, you must understand the inflammatory process. Although the physiological events that occur from the time of injury to the maturation of regenerated or scar tissues occur sequentially, the timing of the events varies with the extent of injury and the general health of the injured person. Neither are there absolute boundaries between the stages of the inflammatory process. However, the principal purpose of the inflammatory, repair, and maturation phases, and the symptoms experienced during each, provide a framework for a plan of care.

The acute inflammatory response initially limits the loss of red blood cells from the vascular system through clotting and vasoconstriction. The initial response, mediated through epinephrine and thromboxane, begins at the moment of tissue damage. Unless larger vascular structures are damaged or the skin is lacerated, your actions probably have little impact on this initial response. Thus, it is unlikely that you can apply a modality quickly enough to influence these early events in the inflammatory response.

Once further loss of red blood cells is prevented, the acute inflammatory response proceeds to remove damaged tissues and set the stage for repair. During this time the cardinal signs of inflammation appear. It has long been suggested that modalities, particularly cold, can be applied to limit inflammation. At this point you must ask whether the goal of treatment is to inhibit inflammation or to limit swelling and relieve the pain and loss of function associated with acute inflammation.

The cases presented at the opening of this chapter further illustrate the challenges of clinical decision making. Efforts to relieve pain, limit swelling, and preserve neuromuscular control are warranted in each case. However, in each case the damaged ligaments will heal because of the physiological process of inflammation. Often return to competition depends upon the ability of the sports medicine team to protect healing tissues. The soccer player with the injured shoulder may return to play sooner than the baseball player because a pitcher cannot throw without stressing the acromioclavicular joint. The field hockey player may return sooner than the football player because taping and bracing will adequately protect the ankle but not the knee. An individualized, goal-oriented plan of care must be developed for each injured person. Therapeutic modalities should be applied when they can help the individual achieve specific treatment goals.

Case Study

A soccer player is assisted into the athletic training room. Examination by you and later by the team physician reveals that she has suffered a Grade II sprain of the tibial collateral ligament. The physician believes that the player will be able to return to soccer in about 6 weeks. What are the short-term treatment goals for this athlete? Which modalities should be applied?

REST, ICE, COMPRESSION, ELEVATION

If the inflammatory process is not completed, tissue is not repaired. Thus, the initial treatment goals following tissue damage should be to protect the damaged tissues and control swelling, pain, and loss of function. These goals can be accomplished with a combination of rest, elevation, compression, and cryotherapy. The RICE recipe (rest, ice, compression, elevation) is well known by athletic trainers, and it makes sense. However, elevation and rest are often overlooked, because clinicians assume that ice has significant anti-inflammatory properties and is the only really important treatment intervention. In fact, elevation likely has a greater effect on swelling than does ice. External compression promotes rest of the injured tissue and can potentially limit swelling. However, most compressive dressings applied following athletic injuries do not provide sufficient counterforce to effectively limit swelling. Felt pads, donuts, and horseshoes (figure 11.1) can increase the effectiveness of external compression.

Cold relieves pain. There is evidence from an animal model that cold alone may also limit swelling (Dolan et al. 1997), although the efficacy of cryotherapy in controlling swelling following musculoskeletal injury in humans has not been substantiated. Therefore, ice application should be viewed as a component of the RICE recipe that controls pain and limits the loss of function associated with acute inflammation. You should outline an appropriate course of action for the injured individual that includes each component of the RICE recipe (figure 11.2).

MODALITIES USED IN ADDITION TO REST, ICE, COMPRESSION, ELEVATION

You are not limited to RICE in managing the acute inflammatory response. Microcurrent has been proposed as a treatment that limits the retraction of endothelial cells and minimizes increases in capillary membrane permeability. Studies involving animal models support the effects of these modalities (Bettany, Fish, and Mendel 1990). However, the effects of this intervention on the injury response over several days following tissue damage have not been fully investigated.

It is difficult to make generalizations about the effect of modalities on the inflammatory response

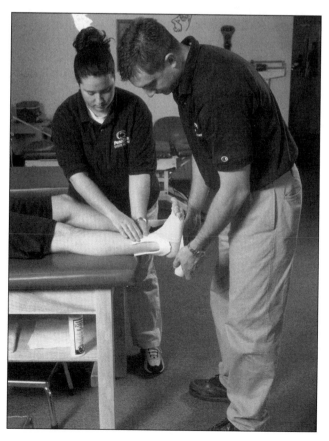

■ **Figure 11.1** A felt horseshoe-shaped pad provides an excellent compress when held in place by an elastic wrap.

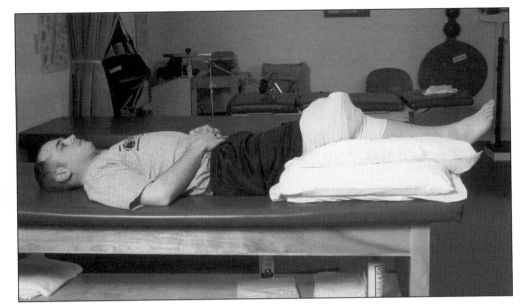

Figure 11.2 Protect damaged tissues and control swelling, pain, and loss of function with rest, ice, compression, and elevation.

following musculoskeletal injuries in humans. The increased capillary membrane permeability promotes movement of leukocytes from the circulation to phagocytize necrotic tissue. It is likely that modality intervention with cold or microcurrent might slow this response. However, the presence of necrotic tissue stimulates continuation of the acute inflammatory phase. Thus, the question remains: will minimizing increases in capillary membrane permeability limit the development of swelling, delay tissue repair, neither, or both? Further study should be completed before these modalities are used to manage acute inflammation.

TENS can be applied as an adjunct to RICE. Although it seems illogical to use a modality that relieves pain by increasing sensory input in conjunction with cryotherapy, which decreases sensory input, the combination of these modalities may be more effective in decreasing pain and muscle spasm than either used alone. This observation has not been fully explained; however, it may be that cold has a greater effect on the thinly myelinated and unmyelinated afferent fibers that transmit pain information than the heavily myelinated A-alpha and A-beta afferent fibers. Research has indicated that cryotherapy has little impact on proprioception and pressure sensation, supporting the notion that large-diameter afferent fiber impulse transmission is not slowed by cold application (Ingersoll, Knight, and Merrick 1992; West, Buckley, and Denegar 1998). Thus, TENS with conventional parameters may block pain through the Level I model while the cold slows transmission along pain-carrying fibers, decreases the sensitivity of muscle spindles, and relieves muscle spasm.

The hockey player's low back injury described previously is an example of a situation where combining cold and TENS may be much more effective than using cold alone. In fact, the use of superficial heating and TENS may also warrant consideration. If the muscle spasm was not severe, superficial heat may have a greater impact than cold and, given the depth of the lumbar facets, is unlikely to affect the temperature at the joint capsule.

Therefore, RICE is usually the treatment of choice following acute musculoskeletal injury. TENS appears to be a useful adjunct to relieve pain and reduce muscle spasm. During the acute inflammatory response, movement of the injury area is restricted. As pain subsides, the individual's rehabilitation program should be modified to address losses in range of motion and neuromuscular control. Because there is no single physiological landmark that signals the end of acute inflammation and the beginning of repair, it is difficult to know when you can initiate treatments to restore range of motion and neuromuscular control. In general, you must be certain that therapeutic activities do not compromise tissue repair, and you should let pain guide the advancement of exercise. In some situations, such as a mild to moderate lateral ankle sprain, the individual can progress toward functional exercise rapidly because the healing tissues are not stressed during weight bearing. In other cases, such as mechanical low back pain, the pain–spasm response is more disabling than the tissue damage. However, in situations such as a tibial collateral ligament sprain or a fracture, tissue repair must occur before many exercises can be initiated because weight bearing and strong muscle contractions could disrupt the repair process.

REPAIR PHASE

As the physiological events of an acute inflammatory response proceed, necrotic tissue is phagocytized and a new vascular network to support repair is established. The injured area is less hot and swollen. Pain is experienced with movement but not while the injured part is at rest.

During the repair phase, new treatment goals are established. Restoring range of motion and neuromuscular control become the focus of treatment. As range of motion and neuromuscular control improve, muscular strength and endurance emerge as the new short-term treatment priorities.

The transition from treatment directed at controlling pain and the other symptoms of acute inflammation to treatment that addresses losses of motion, neuromuscular control, endurance, and strength is no more clear-cut than the physiological events that distinguish acute inflammation from early tissue repair. However, a few simple guidelines are available.

When the injured person no longer experiences pain at rest and demonstrates a willingness to move the injured part, you can initiate efforts to restore motion and neuromuscular control provided that the therapeutic activities do not jeopardize the repair process. You may find that modality application before or during manual therapies and therapeutic exercises can help you reach treatment goals.

For example, after spraining the lateral ligaments, an individual often experiences a loss of ankle range of motion, especially dorsiflexion. Once active motion can be initiated, you can use cold water immersion (figure 11.3), contrast therapy, or superficial heat in the form of whirlpool at the beginning of treatment. These modalities reduce pain and may relieve stiffness and allow for more aggressive therapeutic exercises, in terms of active range of motion and weight bearing, as well as less muscle guarding during manual procedures such as joint mobilization.

If healing tissues can be protected, the rehabilitation program can be progressed as rapidly as tolerated. For example, if the sprain is isolated to the lateral

❚ Figure 11.3 Cold water immersion and active range motion can be used to reduce pain and stiffness and allow for more aggressive therapeutic exercises.

ligaments, activities such as balance, walking, and jogging will not significantly stress the damaged ligaments. Thus, the individual can be progressed from partial weight bearing to walking and jogging as rapidly as tolerated. In general, therapeutic exercises should not be painful; pain indicates that the acute inflammatory response has not resolved or that the stress of the exercise exceeds the capacity of the damaged tissues. Painful exercise will inhibit neuromuscular control and slow the return to sports.

One dilemma you will face is defining the limits of pain. All injuries hurt, and individuals differ in their sensitivity to and tolerance of pain. In addition, most competitive athletes train intensely with the attitude of "no pain, no gain." Therefore, follow these guidelines for therapeutic exercise: The exercise is inappropriate if the pain experienced alters proper movement mechanics and if the injured individual is unable to do tomorrow what was done today.

If we continue to use a lateral ankle sprain as an example, an individual may rapidly progress to full weight bearing and be able to walk without a limp. However, as the individual begins to jog, a limp becomes apparent. You must now choose from the following four options: (1) Continue the exercise if instructional or visual feedback (a mirror is good for this) corrects the faulty mechanics; (2) apply a modality such as cold to allow for pain-free activity; (3) limit the individual to exercises that are pain-free; or (4) terminate the exercise session. There isn't a single right answer, and clinical experience will help you make the best decision. If the mechanical flaws are minor and the athlete feels able to continue exercise, it may be possible to correct faulty mechanics. If mild pain appears to be altering the movement mechanics, the analgesic (not anesthetic) response to cryotherapy may allow progression to jogging. If pain and altered gait pattern are more substantial, the individual may need more time to master less demanding tasks or may have reached his or her limit for activity that day.

The skilled clinician will usually err on the side of caution. Overstressing the tissues will stimulate an acute inflammatory response and can slow recovery by days. The master athletic trainer progresses a program of rehabilitation at just the right rate, using pain and quality of movement as guides.

MATURATION

The point of transition from repair to maturation is no better defined than that from the acute response to the repair phase. However, several distinctions delineate repair from maturation. Clinically, the individual will experience pain after, but not during, movement. Physiologically, the quality of the collagen formed during maturation is better than that formed during the repair phase, and the alignment of the protein fibers permits for greater tensile strength. The vascular network needed to support repair retracts.

In general the tissue maturation phase is a long, gradual process during which the rate of new tissue growth is gradually matched by the rate of tissue resorption. The intensity, duration, and complexity of therapeutic exercise can be increased, and the body responds to the demands imposed upon it. Appropriate levels of activity will facilitate the maturation process, but excessive activity will result in pain and perhaps other symptoms of acute inflammation.

The goals of treatment during tissue maturation differ from those established earlier. During the maturation phase, pain control is no longer required. The individual should be well along in terms of regaining full range of motion and neuromuscular control. At this stage functional progression back to practice and competition becomes foremost in the plan of treatment. Thus, there is less need for therapeutic modalities during this period of recovery.

TISSUE RESTRICTIONS AND REST–REINJURY

Modality application during tissue maturation may be necessary, however, in selected circumstances. Occasionally an athlete may have difficulty regaining full motion and tissue pliability due to scarring and the formation of adhesions. In these cases, modalities such as ultrasound, massage, joint mobilization, and fascial stretching can be used.

Perhaps the most common example is the use of joint mobilization with postoperative scarring. For instance, after ACL reconstruction there is a tendency for loss of patellar mobility and formation of a tight, dense scar. If patellar mobilization is not addressed early in the postoperative care, loss of mobility can restrict knee range of motion and cause knee pain with functional activity.

The surgical incision cuts across tissue boundaries and the scarring process can result in adhesion between dermal and fascial layers. These adhesions can become hypersensitive and restrict normal tissue movement. Optimal treatment involves early tissue mobilization.

However, if tissue maturation is underway when the scar and capsular tissue restrictions are identified, successful treatment is possible. Heating the tissue with ultrasound or, in some cases, superficial heating modalities can increase tissue elasticity and enhance the response to manual therapies.

Modality application also may be indicated when overuse of the injured area results in postexercise pain, swelling, and stiffness. These minor exacerbations can be controlled with cold and occasionally TENS. Repeated bouts of therapeutic exercise and athletic activity that aggravate the condition should be avoided by establishing appropriate guidelines for return to unrestricted participation. Failure to follow such guidelines will ultimately slow the athlete's return to competition (see Rest–Reinjury Cycle in chapter 5).

DELAYED AND FAILED TISSUE HEALING

The human body possesses a truly amazing ability to recover from injury and repair itself. Knowledge of the processes by which the body heals is fundamental to effective athletic training. However, despite the body's innate ability to heal and an ever-increasing understanding of the physiology of tissue repair, sometimes the process fails. Over the last 15 years there has been an increase in the treatment of delayed and slowed healing responses with modalities. The failure to heal indicates a breakdown in the acute inflammatory, tissue repair, and tissue maturation processes.

Nonhealing or Slow-to-Heal Skin Wounds

The most common and costly nonhealing wounds are skin wounds. You are unlikely to encounter a nonhealing or slow-to-heal skin wound in the athletic training room; however, certified athletic trainers working in nontraditional settings may observe these wounds. Many of the new dressings available for skin lesions were developed in efforts to improve care and promote healing of slow-to-heal skin lesions.

Slow-to-heal and nonhealing skin lesions are caused by pressure (decubitus ulcers) and vascular compromise, leading to arterial and/or venous insufficiency. Medical complications, limited mobility, and poor nutrition contribute to the development and compromised healing of these wounds. At one time many of these wounds were treated with regular cleansing in a whirlpool. Unfortunately, many of the additives used to prevent infection and the action of the water actually damaged fragile granulation tissues and delayed healing. Many new dressings have been developed, and better wound management has been extensively investigated.

The application of electrical, acoustic (ultrasound), and light (laser) energy has been shown to speed wound healing through increased collagen production by fibroblasts. The wound healing literature indicates that optimal responses occur within a fairly narrow range of energy delivery. Dyson's (1990) summary of the findings of several studies from the 1970s and 1980s revealed that wounds respond to pulsed ultrasound delivered at an amplitude of $1.0 \, W/cm^2$ or less. Kloth and Feeder's (1990) summary of clinical trials with electrical energy yielded similar conclusions. Slow-to-heal wounds respond favorably to low-amplitude ($< 800 \, \mu A$) direct current as well as pulsed monophasic currents with low average current. There is some indication that wound healing responses to laser treatment are similar, in that low average energy stimulates the greatest response (figure 11.4).

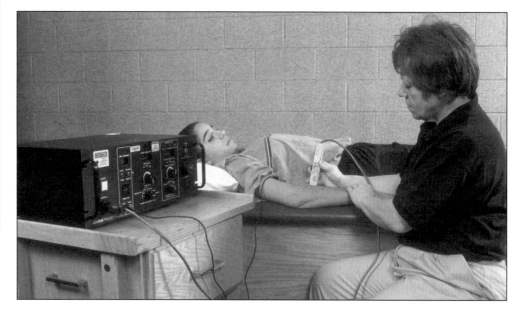

Figure 11.4 Treating a wound with a laser to speed collagen production.

Delayed Healing and Nonunion Fractures

Unlike nonhealing skin ulcers, nonunion fractures can affect otherwise healthy, physically active people. Delayed or nonunion fractures of the scaphoid, fifth metatarsal, and tibia are not uncommon in physically active people. Nonunion of scaphoid fractures is related to the vasculature surrounding the bone and the potential for disruption of blood supply to a portion of the bone following fracture. Early recognition and proper management greatly minimize the risk of nonunion following scaphoid fracture. The causes of nonunion in other areas are less well defined; infection, poor nutrition, or other medical conditions may contribute. In some cases, the cause of delayed healing or nonunion is never identified.

Small electrical currents and pulsed ultrasound have been reported to promote healing in delayed and nonunion fractures. This section briefly summarizes modalities in wound and fracture healing as well as potential implications for treatment of physically active individuals.

Researchers studying the healing of nonunion fractures following treatment regimens with pulsed ultrasound (Heckman et al. 1994; Kristiansen et al. 1997) and pulsed electromagnetic fields (Heckman et al. 1994; Holmes 1994; Marcer, Musati, and Bassett 1984) report that the optimal response requires low levels of energy. These devices are used upon physician prescription. In states where law permits, athletic trainers can apply these modalities if there is access to the devices. Exogen, Inc. (Piscataway, NJ) manufactures a pulsed ultrasound unit to stimulate fracture healing (figure 11.5).

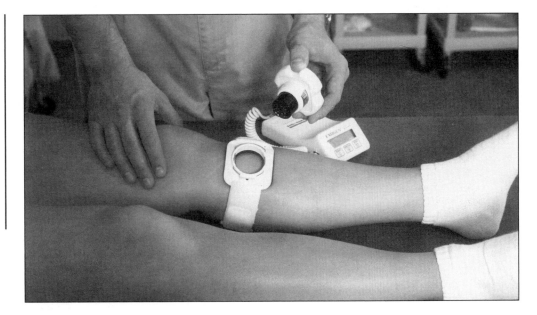

Figure 11.5 A pulsed ultrasound unit used to stimulate fracture healing.

The device delivers a low average power of 117 mW, and clinical treatment consists of one 20 min application daily. If more research is conducted and the use of these modalities increases, athletic trainers may more frequently administer them.

The study of modality application and healing is not limited to skin lesions and fractures. Researchers are also investigating the impact of electrical current introduced through indwelling electrodes on ligament and tendon repair. The vascularity of some areas of tendon is limited, which compromises healing through a normal inflammatory response. It is possible that devices similar to those used to stimulate fracture healing will be developed for use on ligaments and tendons.

The discussion in the previous three paragraphs gives rise to one important question: if modalities can speed healing of slow-to-heal skin wounds and nonunion fractures, can they speed healing of tissues damaged by athletic injury and promote an earlier return to sport? At present there is no evidence that any of the modalities discussed in this text can speed tissue repair in a healthy individual free from conditions known to compromise the repair process. However, work is in progress to answer this question more definitively.

SUMMARY

1. *Develop rehabilitation plans of care to control the signs and symptoms of acute inflammatory response.*

   Acute inflammation is associated with pain, swelling, and loss of function. Rest, ice, compression, and elevation, used in combination, will alleviate pain and minimize swelling. Early pain-free range of motion can be initiated to enhance lymphatic drainage if motion does not disrupt tissue repair.

2. *Provide a rationale for the application of therapeutic modalities to treat the signs and symptoms of acute inflammation.*

   Cold pack application and TENS can be applied following injury to relieve pain. Cold slows nerve conduction velocity, whereas TENS increases large-diameter afferent nerve input into the central nervous system. The decrease in pain message transmission may be accompanied by enkephalin release at the dorsal horn; each has an analgesic effect. Elevation decreases capillary hydrostatic pressure and compression may raise interstitial pressure. Cold causes vasoconstriction. Used in combination, ice, compression, and elevation will limit swelling. Cold also reduces metabolic activity and may protect against secondary tissue injury.

3. *Provide guidelines for progression of a rehabilitation plan of care through the repair and maturation phases of tissue healing.*

It is impossible to know exactly how much stress healing tissues can tolerate without being reinjured. Pain, however, offers the best guide for progression of a rehabilitation program. If pain is defined as a discomfort that alters normal movement mechanics, then two guidelines for progression can be established: active therapeutic exercise should be pain-free, and the injured individual should be able to do tomorrow what was done today. Pain during or following exercise is a sign that excessive stress is being applied to the healing structure and that the frequency, duration, and/or intensity of the activity should be reduced.

4. *Discuss the role of therapeutic modalities during the repair and maturation phases of tissue healing.*

During tissue repair, cold or superficial heat may be applied to reduce pain and facilitate completion of therapeutic exercises. There is no clear choice, although as time passes and pain and spasm give way to soreness and stiffness, superficial heat may be preferred. During this time, whirlpools and fluidotherapy provide an environment where cold and heat can be combined with active range-of-motion exercises. As repair gives way to maturation, pain, swelling, and limited motion no longer affect therapeutic exercises and attention turns toward functional, sport-specific exercise. During this time, modality application is no longer indicated.

CITED REFERENCES

Bettany JA, Fish DR, Mendel FC: Influence of high volt pulsed direct current on edema formation following impact injury. *Phys Ther* 70:13-18, 1990.

Dolan MG, Thornton RM, Fish DR, Mendel FC: Effects of cold water immersion on edema formation after blunt injury to the hind limbs of rats. *J Athl Train* 32:233-237, 1997.

Dyson M: Role of ultrasound in wound healing. In Kloth LC, McCullough JM, Feeder JA (Eds), *Alternatives in Wound Healing*. Philadelphia, Davis, 1990, 259-286.

Heckman J, Ryaby JP, McCabe J, Frey JJ, Kilcoyne RF: Acceleration of tibial fracture-healing by non-invasive, low-intensity pulsed ultrasound. *J Bone Joint Surg* American Volume 76:26-34, 1994.

Holmes Jr GB: Treatment of delayed unions and nonunions of the proximal fifth metatarsal with pulsed electromagnetic fields. *Foot Ankle Int* 15:552-556, 1994.

Ingersoll C, Knight KL, Merrick MA: Sensory perception of the foot and ankle following therapeutic applications of heat and cold. *J Athl Train* 27:231-234, 1992.

Kloth LC, Feeder JA: Electrical stimulation in tissue repair. In Kloth LC, McCullough JM, Feeder JA (Eds), *Alternatives in Wound Healing*. Philadelphia, Davis, 1990, 221-257.

Kristiansen T, Ryaby JP, McCabe J, Frey JJ, Roe LR: Accelerated healing of distal radius fractures with specific, low-intensity ultrasound. *J Bone Joint Surg* American Volume 79:961-973, 1997.

Marcer M, Musati G, Bassett CA: Results of pulsed electromagnetic fields (PEMFs) in ununited fractures after external skeletal fixation. *Clin Orthop & Related Res* 11(190):206-265, 1984.

West, TF, Buckley WE, Denegar CR, Newell K: The effects of a topical anesthetic and cryotherapy on the perception of rod length through exproprioception. Manuscript submitted for publication, 1998.

ADDITIONAL SOURCE

Kloth LC, McCulloch JM, Feeder JA (Eds): *Wound Healing: Alternatives in Management 2d ed.* Philadelphia, Davis, 1994.

CHAPTER TWELVE

Neuromuscular Control and Biofeedback

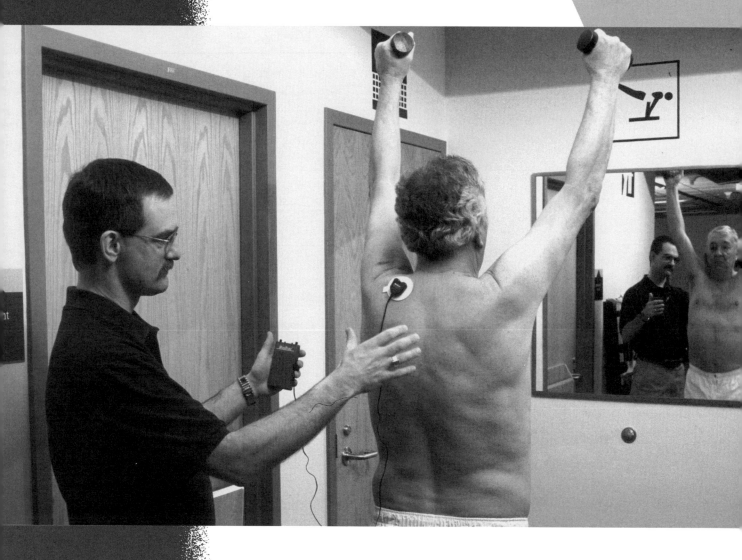

OBJECTIVES

After reading this chapter, the student will be able to

1. define biofeedback,

2. describe the application of EMG biofeedback in treating impaired neuromuscular control,

3. describe the instrumentation and signal processing related to EMG biofeedback, and

4. describe the use of biofeedback in relaxation training.

A high school cross country runner complains of anterior knee pain. She states that her family physician diagnosed her as having patellofemoral pain syndrome. She was advised to wear arch supports because of excessive pronation and to work with her coach to strengthen her quadriceps muscles. Despite the use of arch supports and strengthening exercises, her knee pain has persisted.

Evaluation by the team orthopedic surgeon confirms the diagnosis of patellofemoral pain syndrome and the runner is referred to the athletic training room for evaluation and treatment. Examination reveals a hypermobile patella, bilateral hyperpronation, and obvious inhibition of the vastus medialis muscle with active quadriceps sitting. You decide to use biofeedback to improve recruitment of the vastus medialis. First biofeedback is used during quadriceps setting and straight leg raises. As neuromuscular control improves, the therapeutic exercise program is progressed to include minisquats, step-ups, resisted balance exercises, leg extensions, and leg presses. Initially, biofeedback is used during each exercise. After a few treatments, this athlete demonstrates control over the vastus medialis in all exercises and biofeedback is discontinued. She also reports much less pain during and after running. After a few weeks of regular therapeutic exercise her knee pain resolves completely.

What was missing from the initial treatment program? Why did the knee pain improve following treatments that included biofeedback? This chapter explores impaired neuromuscular control and the use of biofeedback in treating musculoskeletal injuries.

Neuromuscular control incorporates the efferent neural output to skeletal muscles with the afferent neural input received by the central nervous system. Coordinated, purposeful movement requires precise feedback from the periphery to allow for refined control over muscle contractions and ultimately movement of the body through space.

The basic concepts of neuromuscular control, as well as the impact of pain and injury on neuromuscular control, were discussed in chapter 6. As described in chapter 1, neuromuscular control is an important component in a comprehensive rehabilitation plan. Once the pain and swelling associated with acute inflammation or persistent pain subside and active range of motion is sufficiently restored, neuromuscular control must be assessed and deficits addressed before advancing into resistance training and functional rehabilitation.

The paradigm presented in chapter 6 included three levels of neuromuscular control: volitional muscle contractions, reflex responses, and control of more complex, coordinated movement. In this chapter, general concepts of biofeedback are presented followed by a more detailed description of EMG biofeedback. EMG biofeedback can help physically active individuals regain control of volitional muscle contractions and transition to functional activities. Several examples of clinical strategies to promote control of volitional contractions and more complex movements are provided to illustrate functional progression.

Retraining reflex responses, sometimes termed proprioception, requires other treatment strategies. Reflex muscle contractions occur in response to input from peripheral sensory receptors into the spinal cord. Impaired reflex responses are due to damage to the peripheral receptors. A program of progressively greater challenges to reflex responses can improve performance. However, these responses occur very rapidly and biofeedback is not useful in retraining.

Although EMG biofeedback is used more commonly to increase tension and force production by a muscle or groups of muscles, it can also be used with other types of biofeedback to help individuals learn to control tension and stress responses. An introduction to this aspect of enhancing neuromuscular control is provided at the end of this chapter.

BIOFEEDBACK

Biofeedback is the use of instrumentation to bring physiological events to conscious awareness. EMG biofeedback permits awareness of neural recruitment of muscles by transducing the electrical activity during muscular contractions into audio or visual signals. Biofeedback devices can also measure heart rate and galvanic skin response (sweating) during relaxation training. Visual feedback during therapeutic exercise can be enhanced with mirrors. Sometimes a combination of feedback devices is used in neuromuscular reeducation following musculoskeletal injury.

WHY IS BIOFEEDBACK EFFECTIVE?

Biofeedback is really a teaching aid. Effective learning requires precise and timely information about the quality of performance. This is true in the cognitive, psychomotor, and affective domains. Feedback must be timely, so the individual can assess performance and identify areas for improvement. As a student, you know that tests returned months after you take them lose their value as a learning tool because your focus has shifted to other coursework and new information.

The feedback provided must also be as precise as possible, as illustrated by the process of learning golf. Everyone in sports medicine should attempt to learn golf, because proficiency in this game requires considerable coordination and the learning process is a study of neuromuscular education. Step up to the tee, swing the club, and see what happens. Unless you are truly gifted, your first swing will result in the ball rolling forward or slicing wickedly, or perhaps no contact at all. You're not sure what went wrong, only that the outcome was flawed. Slowly you improve through trial and error. To speed the acquisition of the basic skills, find a good golf coach and watch the improvement. Effective coaching provides far more precise information as to the reasons for poor shots. Swing speed, swing plane, head and hand position, and other factors can be quickly assessed and improved. Thus, precision of feedback is as important as timeliness.

Chapter 6 addressed the reasons for impaired neuromuscular control. At this point it is important to understand the certified athletic trainer's role in restoring volitional control during simple and more complex motor tasks. In addition, the role of biofeedback in relaxation training must be introduced. However, before proceeding to these topics, this chapter will review instrumentation, especially EMG biofeedback.

INSTRUMENTATION

If EMG biofeedback is to provide useful information, the electrical activity of the muscle must be recorded and transformed into visual and auditory signals. This process begins with the detection of electrical activity by electrodes. In clinical practice, surface electrodes are used. In some research applications, the electrodes consist of fine wires inserted into the muscle. The indwelling electrodes provide very specific information from a portion of a muscle but are not appropriate for clinical use. Surface electrodes provide less specific information, but the convenience of these electrodes and their ability to quantify activity of muscles and muscle groups make them ideal for sport rehabilitation.

There are several configurations of surface electrodes. All consist of two active leads and a ground. The self-adhesive electrode with a single three-pole attachment is illustrated in figure 12.1. These electrodes are easy to apply, stay in place, and are inexpensive.

Once the raw electrical signal is detected at the electrode, it is conducted to the electrical circuitry within the EMG biofeedback unit. Within the unit, the raw EMG signal received through the electrodes is filtered, amplified, rectified, integrated,

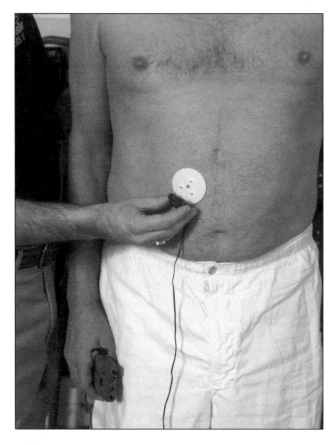

Figure 12.1 An EMG electrode.

and transduced into visual and audio output that is proportional to the amount of electrical activity in the muscle (figure 12.2). Advances in technology allow for signal processing with much smaller components, permitting greater portability of the unit and expanding the applications of EMG biofeedback in rehabilitation.

Filtering removes "noise" from high- and low-frequency sources. Electrical activity of muscles falls into the 80 to 250 Hz range. It is important that electrical activity below and above this range is filtered before the signal is processed. For example, the electrical current that runs the lights and equipment in athletic training rooms and clinics is 60 Hz, so turning on an ultrasound or a TENS unit could cause signal fluctuation without effective filtering.

Effective signal processing requires that the raw EMG signal be amplified. Actual electrical activity in muscle falls in the microvolt range, so a signal amplifier is used to amplify the signal into the millivolt range.

When a signal is rectified, all deflections from the isoelectric line are made positive or negative. Signal integration involves sampling the rectified signal and fitting a curve through the sampled points. This process essentially "smoothes" the signal, allowing for the area under the curve to be quantified (integrated). The integrated electrical signal is then used to power lights, sound, or a signal meter to provide immediate and highly specific feedback about the amount of electrical activity within the target muscle.

Other forms of biofeedback operate in a similar manner. Heart rate monitors detect the electrical activity of heart muscle contractions. Changes in the conductivity of the skin, or galvanic skin response, can provide feedback regarding the body's reaction to stress. Feedback is provided by measuring changes in conductivity of a small, imperceptible electrical current and converting the electrical signal into visual and auditory feedback.

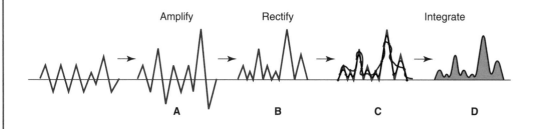

Figure 12.2 EMG signal processing. Electrical signal detected at an electrode is amplified **A** and rectified **B**. The signal is then integrated **C** by taking samples at specific time intervals (i.e., every 0.1 sec for sampling rate of 100 Hz). The sampling points are connected and the electrical activity is quantified by calculating the area under the curve **D**.

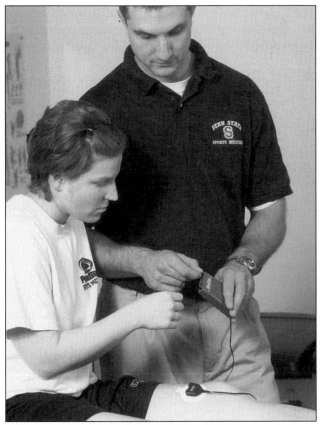

Figure 12.3 An individual performing a quadriceps set with biofeedback.

Skin temperature can also provide valuable feedback. Surface temperature monitoring does not require electrical signal processing but does require thermometers that can be attached to the skin and very sensitive temperature gauges.

CLINICAL APPLICATIONS: RESTORING CONTROL OF VOLITIONAL CONTRACTION

Restoring control over isolated, volitional muscle contraction is often an early goal of rehabilitation, especially following knee injuries and surgeries. If you examine an injured physically active person the day before arthroscopic knee surgery, you will probably find that all of the quadriceps muscles contract strongly during active quadriceps sitting and straight leg exercises. Reexamine the knee the day after surgery, and a decrease in active control of the vastus medialis is often evident with these activities. The effect is more dramatic following arthrotomy.

The affected muscles have not atrophied. Rather, the individual has lost the ability to contract the muscles fully because of neural inhibition. As in learning to play golf, precise and immediate feedback speeds neuromuscular reeducation. Electromyography provides positive feedback when the appropriate neural pathways are activated, eliminating much trial and error in this early stage of rehabilitation (figure 12.3).

Neuromuscular inhibition is not limited to postoperative applications. Many physically active people with patellofemoral pain syndrome also demonstrate inhibition of the vastus medialis. Furthermore, many individuals with shoulder pain due to glenohumeral impingement, instability, and rotator cuff lesions fail to properly stabilize their scapula or activate their rotator cuff during shoulder flexion and abduction. Shoulder pain appears to inhibit neuromuscular control in these muscles, leading to altered movement patterns, losses in motion, and greater losses of shoulder function.

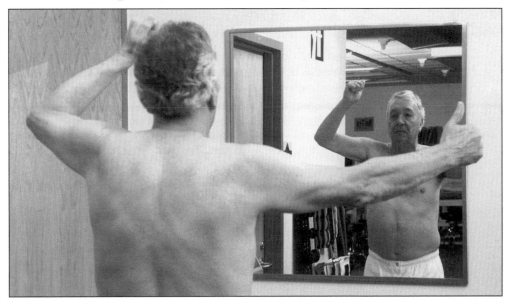

Figure 12.4 Shoulder hiking with abduction of the arm.

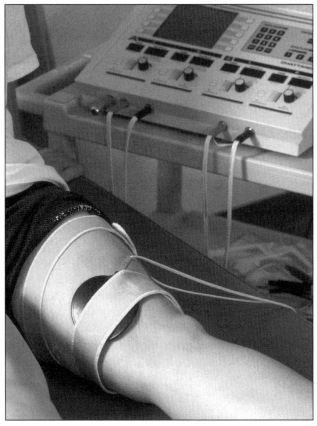

Figure 12.5 Neuromuscular stimulation of quadriceps.

EMG biofeedback, mirrors (figure 12.4), and, occasionally, shoulder taping can be used to restore neuromuscular control throughout the shoulder range of motion.

WHEN BIOFEEDBACK FAILS

Rarely, individuals are unable to generate a muscle contraction despite the use of biofeedback and their best effort. In these situations, resort to NMS to induce a muscle contraction. Using an electrical current to contract a target muscle (usually the quadriceps following knee injury or surgery; figure 12.5) generates afferent input. The object of NMS in these situations is to restart the motor efferent–proprioceptive feedback loop by inducing muscle contraction. Be aware, however, that strong electrically stimulated contractions are poorly tolerated.

Using a stimulus with the phase duration and frequency described in chapter 8, apply a 10 to 15 sec "on" time with a 4 to 5 sec ramp and a 10 to 15 sec "off" time. Longer recovery between contractions is not necessary because of the submaximal nature of the muscle contractions; in addition, longer "off" time promotes boredom. In 10 min the injured physically active person will experience 20 to 30 muscle contractions. The individual should be encouraged to contract the affected muscle volitionally during the stimulation. Some people are very timid at first and must be encouraged to adjust the amplitude of the stimulus during the treatment. Allowing the individual to control the strength of the stimulus reduces apprehension and makes the treatment more effective.

Once the injured person can contract the affected muscle volitionally, EMG biofeedback can be used to enhance neuromuscular control. You can use NMS and EMG biofeedback in a single treatment session depending on how quickly the individual responds to NMS and how much exercise he or she can tolerate.

CLINICAL APPLICATIONS: FUNCTIONAL PROGRESSION

Sports, work, and daily tasks require coordinated, complex motions rather than isolated control of a single muscle or muscle group. Performing quadriceps setting and straight leg raises has little carryover to walking, climbing stairs, running, cutting, and jumping. The rapid, coordinated recruitment of all the muscles needed to complete relatively complex motor tasks is not generated through conscious control of each individual muscle. Rather, complex motor tasks are executed from a motor pattern.

Again using the golf swing as an example, it is evident that many muscles must contract at precisely the right moment to hit the ball well. If one were to concentrate on controlling only one muscle, let alone several muscles, performance of the swing would suffer badly. Yet the accomplished golfer can consistently hit good shots. Why? The accomplished golfer can execute a complex movement generated from higher centers and continuously adjusted through afferent feedback. Injury, pain, swelling, and instability inhibit execution of the coordinated, complex movement. Thus, rehabilitation cannot end with restoration of volitional control over muscles or proprioceptive training. Once the early goals of rehabilitation are met, a functional progression of increasingly complex tasks must be introduced. Functional or sport-specific rehabilitation and work hardening are advanced stages of rehabilitation, where coordinated, complex movements are refined and the stamina and strength needed to return to sport and work are built.

As the movement patterns executed during therapeutic exercise become more rapid and complex, the value of EMG biofeedback declines. Concentration on biofeedback inhibits the automated nature of complex movements. However, biofeedback is useful in the early transition from retraining of volitional muscle control to rehearsal of more simple movements requiring contraction of multiple muscles and movement of multiple joints.

The treatment of patellofemoral pain syndrome (PFPS) provides an example of using EMG biofeedback in an exercise progression. The initial assessment of an injured person with PFPS often reveals inhibited recruitment of the vastus medialis, which is more affected by knee pain and swelling than the other quadriceps muscles. Selective inhibition of the vastus medialis worsens PFPS in some individuals because the imbalance between the forces generated by the vastus medialis and lateralis results in lateral glide of the patella. This, in turn, is believed to irritate the patellofemoral joint, resulting in more pain, swelling, and neuromuscular inhibition and perpetuating the condition.

Early treatment of PFPS should focus on relieving pain and swelling. As these treatment goals are accomplished, EMG biofeedback during open chain exercises such as quadriceps sitting and straight leg raises will restore volitional control over the vastus medialis. Although volitional control in open chain activities is an important goal, the lower extremity rarely functions in an open chain. Thus, the therapeutic exercise program must be progressed to closed chain and to work- and sport-specific activities: namely, pattern-generated movements.

Open Versus Closed Chain Exercises

open chain exercises—Exercises in which the distal segment is free to move. For example, leg extension exercises are considered open chain because the foot is free to move rather than remaining firmly in contact with the ground.

closed chain exercises—Exercises in which the distal segment is fixed in place. For example, leg press exercises are considered closed chain because the foot is firmly in contact with the exercise device.

Early restoration of neuromuscular control is most effective when activity is isolated to a particular muscle or muscle group such as the quadriceps. Open chain exercises allow individuals to isolate their effort on a single muscle group and then proceed to closed chain exercises in a progressive exercise program. Failure to establish volitional control in the open chain before beginning closed chain exercises often reinforces substitute motor patterns. Some individuals are able to perform a leg press after ACL reconstruction yet struggle to move an 8 lb plate in open chain 90° to 60° quadriceps construction, because they substitute gluteal and hamstring force generation for the quadriceps function they lack when performing a leg press. Thus, it is important to assess and retrain volitional control in an open chain before progressing to more functional, closed chain movements.

After more complex movements are initiated, EMG biofeedback provides valuable information regarding muscle recruitment. If we continue to use PFPS as an example, once the individual has gained control over the vastus medialis in the open chain, EMG biofeedback can be used during activities such as step-ups, lunges, $\frac{1}{4}$ squats, and balance exercises (figure 12.6). EMG biofeedback is also useful when you are instructing individuals to use machines for resistance exercises, including leg extensions and leg presses (figure 12.7) and for gait training. EMG biofeedback

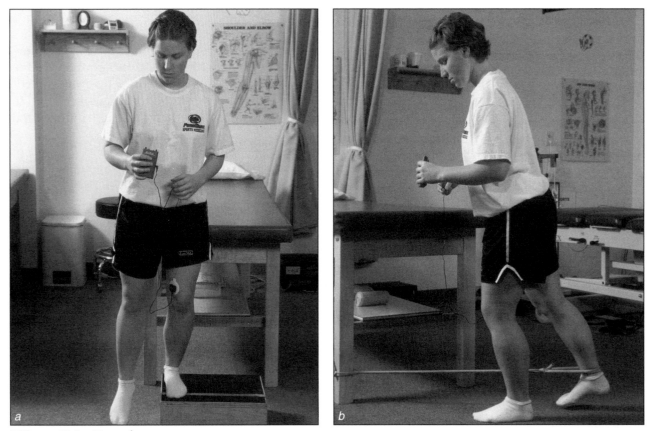

Figure 12.6 Biofeedback during step-ups *(a)* and tubing-resisted kickers *(b)*.

permits you and the injured person to monitor the quality of motor recruitment in these more advanced and functional exercises. Once the appropriate motor pattern has been established, EMG biofeedback is no longer needed. This process is very important for individuals who will complete a home-based or independent exercise program during their rehabilitation. Practicing faulty or substitute motor patterns will ingrain the pattern and slow recovery or even exacerbate the injury.

The use of EMG biofeedback is not limited to rehabilitation of the lower extremity. Biofeedback is useful for individuals with back pain who struggle to gain control over the abdominal musculature during pelvic tilts, abdominal curls, and standing pelvic tilts (figure 12.8).

EMG biofeedback is useful in treating many types of shoulder dysfunction. Impingement syndrome, rotator cuff tendinitis, and glenohumeral ligament laxity are similar in that tissues in the subacromial space become inflamed. The resulting pain appears to cause neuromuscular inhibition of the rotator cuff muscles, especially supraspinatus and to a lesser degree infraspinatus.

The use of EMG biofeedback during exercises that isolate these rotator cuff muscles such as scaption, empty can, and active external rotation (figure 12.9) speeds neuromuscular rehabilitation. Using a mirror (figure 12.10) to provide visual feedback is helpful when the injured person demonstrates a "shoulder hiking" pattern with glenohumeral abduction. This substitution pattern, which develops to avoid a painful arc during glenohumeral abduction and flexion, can be difficult to suppress without visual, and sometimes EMG, biofeedback.

The role of the scapula in shoulder dysfunction has received much attention in the past 15 years (Kibler 1991). Many physically active individuals with impingement syndrome demonstrate weakness in the scapular stabilizers, especially middle

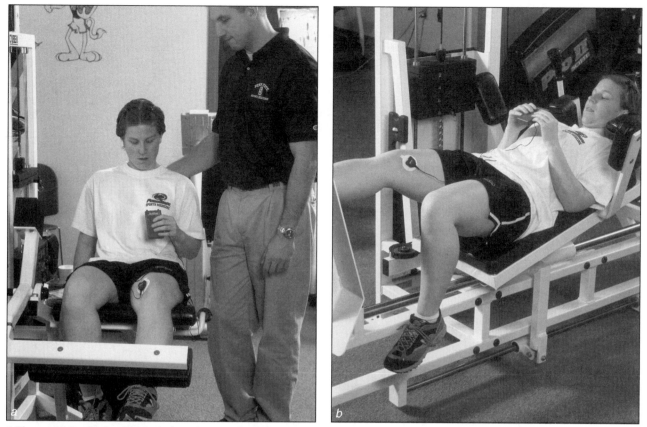

▮ Figure 12.7   Biofeedback during short arc leg extension *(a)* and leg press *(b)*.

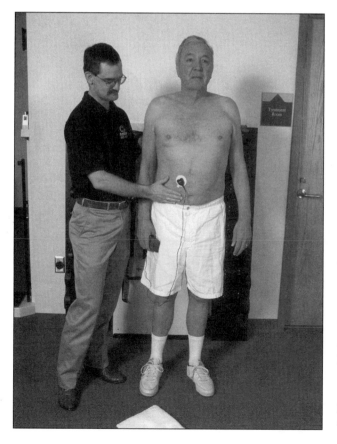

and lower trapezius and serratus anterior. Individuals with myofascial pain patterns involving the neck and upper back frequently present with similar dysfunction. Most of these individuals also have poor postural awareness. Thus, improved scapular stabilization is a common treatment goal. Once again, EMG biofeedback and visual feedback from mirrors (figure 12.11) can speed neuromuscular reeducation and recovery.

As with the treatment of knee injuries, EMG biofeedback for the shoulder can be used as the therapeutic exercise program becomes more work- and sport-specific. This is especially true when scapular stabilization is being developed. EMG biofeedback helps the individual relearn how to "set" the scapula before and during throwing and lifting (figure 12.12).

LEARNING RELAXATION

This chapter has been devoted to restoring neuromuscular control and introducing EMG biofeedback. However, increasing neuromuscular activity is only

▮ Figure 12.8   Biofeedback at the abdominal site during standing pelvic tilt.

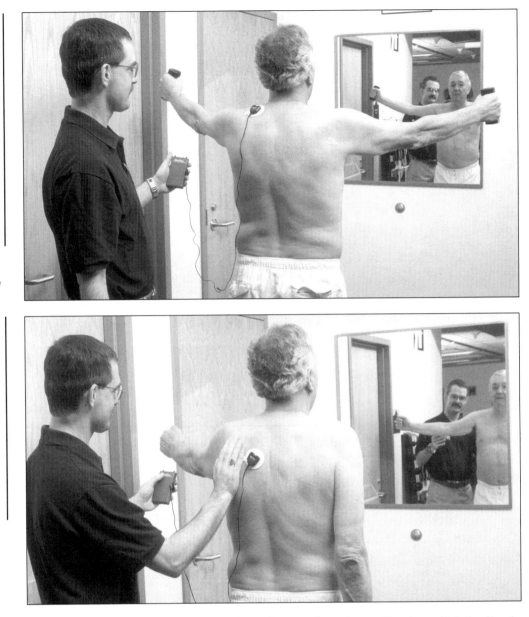

Figure 12.9 Bio-feedback during active abduction.

Figure 12.10 Bio-feedback at middle trapezius and mirrors for scapular stabilization.

one of many possible treatment goals and is not the sole application of biofeedback. Many people who suffer from myofascial pain find that their symptoms are exacerbated when they are fatigued or under stress. Unfortunately, many people are unable to relax. Biofeedback from EMG, galvanic skin response, heart rate, and skin temperature can be used in relaxation training.

Multiple forms of feedback are often used because individuals vary in their responses to stress. Some individuals experience an increase in neuromuscular activity in response to stress. Others may experience a galvanic skin response or a drop in temperature. By identifying thoughts or events that increase stress, and strategies to decrease it, physically active individuals can improve their ability to relax and break the cycle of stress, pain, and spasm.

These strategies can also be used to help individuals return to competition following injury. Psychological preparation to return to sport following injury has

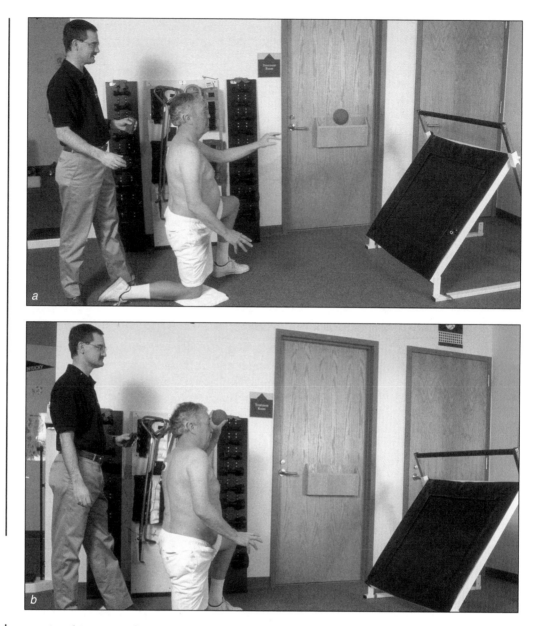

∎ **Figure 12.11**   Biofeedback at middle trapezius in throwing *(a)* catching *(b)*.

received increased attention, and it is recognized that physical rehabilitation following serious injury is not enough to enable a person to return to the environment where the injury occurred. Biofeedback can help the individual and the sports medicine team assess the stress response to returning to competition. Videotape of competition, biofeedback, and thought stopping can be very effective in managing this stress response.

Physicians, physical therapists, and certified athletic trainers typically have not devoted much attention to the psychological aspects of rehabilitation. Clinical psychologists and sports psychologists can be invaluable in the successful management of persistent pain and the individual's psychological response, respectively. The certified athletic trainer with experience in stress management and biofeedback can assist members of the health care team with this aspect of rehabilitation.

Biofeedback and Relaxation

Biofeedback Techniques

- Muscle tension
- Galvanic skin response
- Temperature
- Heart rate

Often, several forms of biofeedback are used simultaneously to identify how individuals respond to stress and to train them in relaxation.

Relaxation Techniques

- Thought stopping
- Visual imagery
- Breathing exercises
- Isolated muscle contraction and relaxation

Specialized preparation in relaxation training is needed to effectively use these techniques. Do not attempt intervention with these techniques without appropriate training or with individuals whose psychological or psychiatric dysfunction is beyond your scope of practice.

SUMMARY

1. *Define biofeedback.*

   Biofeedback is the use of instrumentation to bring physiological events to conscious awareness. EMG biofeedback permits awareness of neural recruitment of muscles by transducing the electrical activity during muscular contractions into audio or visual signals.

2. *Describe the application of EMG biofeedback in the treatment of impaired neuromuscular control.*

   An EMG biofeedback device monitors electrical activity of muscle through electrodes applied to the skin. The individual is asked to contract the targeted muscle, such as the vastus medialis. The biofeedback unit is adjusted to indicate successful recruitment of the target muscle through audio or visual feedback. As neuromuscular control improves, greater recruitment of the target muscle is required to induce positive feedback and more complex activities are added to the therapeutic exercise regimen.

3. *Describe the instrumentation and signal processing related to EMG biofeedback.*

   When a raw electrical signal is detected at the electrode, it is conducted to the electrical circuitry within the EMG biofeedback unit. Within the unit, the raw EMG signal received through the electrodes is filtered, amplified, rectified, integrated, and transduced into visual and audio output that is proportional to the amount of electrical activity in the muscle. Filtering removes "noise" from high- and low-frequency sources. Electrical activity of muscles ranges from 80 to 250 Hz. Electrical activity below and above this range is filtered before the signal is processed. Effective signal processing requires that the raw EMG signal be amplified. Actual electrical activity in muscle falls in the microvolt range. The signal is amplified into the millivolt range by a signal amplifier. When a signal is rectified, all deflections from the isoelectric line are made positive or negative. Signal integration involves sampling the rectified signal and fitting a curve through the sampled points. This process essentially "smoothes" the signal, allowing the area under the curve to be quantified (integrated). The integrated electrical signal is then used to power lights, sound, or a signal meter to provide immediate and highly specific feedback about the amount of electrical activity within the target muscle.

4. *Describe the use of biofeedback in relaxation training*.

Biofeedback can be used to teach relaxation and management of tension and stress. Biofeedback can be used to make an individual aware of muscle tension (EMG biofeedback), heart rate, sweating, galvanic skin response, and temperature, areas that reflect the stress response in most individuals. By identifying thoughts or events that increase the physiological response to psychological stress, and strategies to decrease this response, individuals can improve their ability to relax and break the cycle of stress, pain, and spasm.

CITED REFERENCES

Kibler BW: Role of the scapula in the overhead throwing motion. *Contemp Orthop* 22:525-532, 1991.

Paine RM, Voight M: The role of the scapula. *J Orthop Sports Phys Ther* 20:386-391, 1993.

ADDITIONAL SOURCE

Basmajian J: *Biofeedback: Principles and Practice for Clinicians*. Baltimore, Williams & Wilkins, 1989.

CHAPTER THIRTEEN

Clinical Management of Persistent Pain

OBJECTIVES

After reading this chapter, the student will be able to

1. identify sources of persistent pain through a medical history and physical examination, and

2. develop appropriate rehabilitation plans of care or referral to appropriate health care professionals for individuals with persistent pain due to (a) diagnostic errors, (b) faulty plans of rehabilitation, (c) rest–reinjury cycle, (d) chronic regional pain syndrome,(e) myofascial pain, and (f) depression and somatization.

The certified athletic trainer must be prepared to evaluate a broad spectrum of physically active people. Often an individual presents with a history of long-standing, or persistent, pain with no single identifiable cause. Consider the following cases and related questions.

A recreationally active financial aid officer presents to a sports medicine clinic with a history of many months of neck and shoulder pain with frequent headaches. She has no history of trauma, and a previous medical evaluation had revealed no structural problem. The individual was diagnosed with myofascial pain syndrome. What other questions should be asked in the medical history? What factors are contributing to the problem? What would you expect to find on physical examination? What are the short- and long-term treatment goals? Will the use of therapeutic modalities help her achieve treatment goals?

A freshman college track athlete with a history of "shin splints" throughout high school is evaluated in the athletic training room. She has very tight fascia in her legs and multiple tender trigger points. She states that recent x-rays and a bone scan revealed normal results. Why has her problem persisted for so long? Is there an underlying cause? How should this athlete be treated?

A freshman high school baseball pitcher presents to a sports medicine clinic complaining of 4 months of shoulder pain that has limited his ability to pitch. He states that he took 3 weeks off from pitching but the shoulder did not heal. He was concerned that he had a torn rotator cuff despite assurances to the contrary by an orthopedic surgeon. Why had this injury failed to heal?

The complaints of these physically active people are not uncommon. The questions raised in each case must be answered to develop an effective rehabilitation plan. In some cases, therapeutic modalities may help resolve the problem but in other cases they may be of little benefit. As stated in the beginning of this text, application of a therapeutic modality does not constitute a treatment but is part of a comprehensive plan of care. Developing a plan of care requires that you identify the underlying causes of symptoms. Thus, this final chapter was written to help you evaluate and treat physically active individuals with persistent pain and identify situations where therapeutic modalities may help the individual achieve treatment goals.

In a traditional high school or college athletic training room, the vast majority of individuals treated seek care for acute, sports-related, musculoskeletal injuries. The certified athletic trainer will certainly be called on to evaluate some athletes with overuse problems and, on occasion, athletes suffering from truly chronic pain. An outpatient sports medicine center is very different. Most patients referred to a sports medicine center for treatment of a musculoskeletal problem, whether they are physically active or not, have experienced pain for weeks, months, and occasionally years.

Why is the difference between settings important? Although most new jobs are in the clinical setting, and a goal of the profession is to provide health care services to a broad scope of physically active people, most athletic training students receive little clinical experience. Furthermore, students generally receive little classroom instruction from certified athletic trainers who have worked in the clinical setting. Thus, new graduates often feel unprepared to evaluate and treat physically active individuals with persistent pain.

Lack of preparation can be frustrating for newly certified athletic trainers as well as for their colleagues. Some certified athletic trainers find it difficult to adjust to practicing in a sports medicine setting. Often they enjoy working in outreach programs for high schools or other athletic organizations but dislike working with patients in the clinic. Clinical supervisors sometimes comment that certified athletic trainers are well prepared to work in high schools but perform less well in the clinic.

This is a very important issue in athletic training. The role of the athletic trainer has changed over the past 20 to 30 years. Some in the profession view these changes negatively, but others see new opportunities. The changing role of the certified athletic trainer is part of the evolution of the profession. Sports medicine clinics, practically unheard of in 1970, provide athletic training services to vast numbers of high school and amateur athletes. Today's certified athletic trainers must be prepared to work in the changing health care environment and to care for physically active people from all walks of life.

This preparation does not require lots of new skills but rather new applications of existing skills. Persistent pain is a large part of most clinical athletic trainers' practice, and most of their professional development involves refining the basic skills learned as a student athletic trainer to treat those with persistent pain.

In treating persistent pain, you must complete a thorough examination and establish a plan of care. Only then should therapeutic modalities be considered. This chapter is devoted to the clinical management of persistent pain and the appropriate use of therapeutic modalities in treating persistent pain.

TREATING PERSISTENT PAIN

The rehabilitation plan of care is developed from the medical history and physical examination. Within the plan of care, treatment goals are arranged on a hierarchy from entry into the health care system to full recovery. Therapeutic modalities are used to achieve one or more treatment goals in the plan of care.

These statements are true whether you are treating an acute injury or persistent pain; however, in the case of persistent pain the medical history and physical examination are more detailed and the data gathered is analyzed more extensively. All of this information is then combined to develop a progressive plan of care. Unfortunately, when these steps are not fully completed, multiple modalities are often administered in the hope that "something works." On rare occasions the problem resolves despite the lack of a sound plan of care; usually, however, such treatment fails.

MEDICAL HISTORY

Perhaps the single biggest problem in the clinical management of persistent pain is the failure to obtain, evaluate, and act upon a thorough medical history. Taking a medical history, which is reviewed thoroughly in *Assessment of Athletic Injuries*, appears to be simple. However, a great deal of practice and attention to detail is needed to maximize the information gleaned from a medical history taken from individuals with persistent pain. In college and high school environments, certified athletic trainers know the athletes from day-to-day contact and gain important information from the preparticipation examination. Furthermore, most of the athletes seeking treatment are suffering from acute musculoskeletal injuries, for which the time and often the mechanism of injury are easily identified. Thus, the certified athletic trainer and athletic training student often get little practice in interviewing individuals who seek treatment of persistent pain in sports medicine centers.

Contrast, for example, the medical histories required from two individuals: a 17-year-old basketball player for a team you have covered all season who sprained her ankle when she stepped on another player's foot during a practice that you attended, and a 38-year-old tennis player, computer programmer, and mother of two small children who has a 6-month history of right shoulder and neck pain of insidious onset. In the first case you know the athlete, her recent injury history, and the nature of her off-court activities, and you probably have established a rapport with her. In the second case you are establishing a plan of care for a person who is apprehensive about entering a new health care environment. During the 15 min or so allotted for the initial examination, you must find out much information. You need to know when and how the problem started, what seems to make it better and worse, and the impact of work and child care on her symptoms. You must learn what other medical evaluation has been made and what treatment has been administered (and if it helped). You must learn about the tennis player's general health and medical history. In addition, you must learn what her goals are in terms of outcome priorities. In short, you need to quickly establish communication with this individual so that you can obtain all of the information you need. This example illustrates that obtaining a medical history from someone with persistent pain, compared to an athlete you know who has an acute injury, is much more involved but far more critical to developing an effective plan of care.

At the completion of the medical history, you should have one or more working diagnoses. Developing a working diagnosis requires you to analyze information provided during the history as the interview proceeds. Thus, you must organize the interview, develop the questions, and analyze the responses while listening carefully to what is being said. Completing a thorough, informative medical history requires good clinical skills and lots of practice. A sample format for evaluating musculoskeletal injuries is included here (figure 13.1). Individual items may not be appropriate for all cases (e.g., documentation of gait following a shoulder injury).

Evaluation Document

Name: _____ Age/date of birth: _____ Sport/position: _____

Date: _____ Physician ID or medical record #: _____

Diagnosis: _____

Diagnostic tests/medications/surgical procedure: _____

Pertinent medical history: _____

Subjective report:
Ask about onset, recent improvement, or worsening of symptoms, pattern of symptoms, rating of pain and dysfunction, description of pain, report of radicular or distant pain sites, and previous experience with treatments for musculoskeletal injuries (what seemed to work or not work).

Objective findings:
Observation: General appearance, obvious guarding of movement or alteration from normal movement pattern (i.e., limping), presence of swelling, discoloration, and appearance of incisions, wound, and scars.
Range of motion: Active and passive range of motion. Circulation, motor function, and sensory function in affected limb or area.
Strength: Results of manual muscle and instrumented resistance tests.
Girth: Swelling at joint or loss of muscle mass.
Gait: Limping, appropriate use of crutches or cane, and evidence of excessive or limited pronation.
Posture: Posture, postural awareness, and postural control.
Results of special tests:
Problem list: Develop a hierarchy of problems that must be overcome to progress the rehabilitation program and return the individual to athletics.
Short-term goals and treatment plan: Develop a short list of goals to be achieved in the next few days to 2 weeks and the treatments to be used to achieve these goals.
Long term goals with criteria for progression.

∎ **Figure 13.1** A sample format for evaluating musculoskeletal injuries.

PHYSICAL EXAMINATION

The physical examination should yield information that confirms or refutes the working diagnosis established from the medical history. Conducting a physical exam without a working diagnosis is a time-consuming and usually fruitless endeavor.

The structure of the physical examination will vary based on the medical history and plausible diagnoses. Observation, range-of-motion assessment, strength assessment, and neurovascular assessment are fairly universal components. However, the order in which tests are performed and the specific tests conducted will differ depending on the nature of the problem. In a well-conducted physical examination you will complete necessary testing in an organized manner while avoiding the tendency to "test for everything" and unnecessarily increase suffering.

Some clinicians complete a physical examination in a cookbook fashion. Rather than focusing on confirming or refuting the preliminary diagnosis, they collect a quantity of data. Unfortunately, the data are not very useful because they were not collected in the context of testing the working diagnosis.

A second common flaw in a physical examination for persistent pain is the failure to examine joint, nerve, vascular, and muscle function throughout the painful region. The screening exams, described in *Assessment of Athletic Injuries*, often yield key findings that confirm the cause and therefore identify the solution to the persistent pain. You must consider and assess for the presence of radicular and referred pain patterns as well as biomechanical causes of persistent pain.

Once you have made a diagnosis and identified the causes of the persistent pain, a plan of treatment can be established. In some cases, therapeutic modalities can be used to achieve goals identified in the plan of care. In other cases, the application of therapeutic modalities may be detrimental because they promote a passive, rather than active, role of the individual in the plan of care.

In chapter 5 the causes of persistent pain were categorized (figure 13.2). The remainder of this chapter reviews treatment strategies, including effective use of therapeutic modalities, in the clinical management of these persistent pain problems.

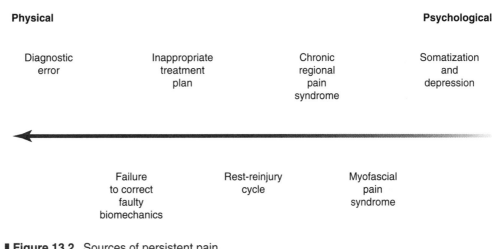

Figure 13.2 Sources of persistent pain.

Reprinted from *Athletic Therapy Today* 1997.

DIAGNOSIS AND PLAN OF CARE PROBLEMS

When pain persists, the first step in reevaluation is to confirm the medical diagnosis and review the plan of care. A sports medicine team approach to reevaluation is necessary to review the original diagnosis, the response to medications and surgery, and the response to and compliance with the rehabilitation program.

In the context of therapeutic modalities, a failure to improve can provide useful information. Transient (hours or days) relief of pain and swelling following treatment may indicate a rest–reinjury cycle or an underlying structural lesion creating a state of chronic inflammation. For example, persistent knee pain with recurrent swelling may be due to a torn meniscus or a loose body within the joint. In this case, additional imaging studies may be ordered or an arthroscopic procedure performed.

A rest–reinjury cycle can yield similar findings. For example, consider a middle-age man seeking treatment following an arthroscopic meniscectomy. He and his surgeon were concerned about a pattern of recurrent pain and swelling in the knee that was always worse following therapeutic exercises. A review of his therapy indicated that he was riding on a stationary bicycle with a very low seat and doing full-range leg extensions with a heavy weight three times per week in physical therapy. The exercise program was aggravating long-standing, mild patellofemoral pain. The treatment consisted of discontinuing physical therapy and starting a simple home exercise program. The pain and swelling were completely resolved at a 2-week follow-up appointment.

When therapeutic modalities provide little relief, there may be an organic dysfunction. Consider this example: An older golfer presented to a sports medicine clinic complaining of back pain. He was treated with TENS and received some short-term relief. His back pain, however, progressively worsened over the next 10 days. The underlying cause of the back pain, identified during this period of treatment, was cancer of the liver. Two lessons were learned: (1) pain that appears to be orthopedic in nature can be due to organic pathologies, and (2) you must know the signs and symptoms of cancer and explore this possibility in individuals with chronic pain.

Signs and Symptoms of Cancer

You should be aware of signs and symptoms of cancer so you can arrange appropriate medical follow-up. The presence of one or more signs or symptoms associated with cancer does not confirm a diagnosis. The signs and symptoms listed here should not raise alarm but rather should prompt consultation with a physician to identify the cause (Goodman and Snyder 1995).

- Change in bowel or bladder function
- Unusual bleeding or discharge
- A lump or mass in breast or elsewhere
- Obvious changes in a wart or mole or a sore that fails to heal
- Persistent cough or hoarseness
- Night pain or night sweats
- Weight loss

- Difficulty swallowing or loss of appetite
- Jaundice
- Unexplained muscular weakness or loss of coordination
- Fever
- Headaches, memory loss, poor concentration
- Fatigue, increased sleeping
- Onset of seizures

Physically active individuals suffering from somatization will also often fail to respond to treatments with therapeutic modalities. The failure to respond to a plan of treatment that may include medical and surgical interventions as well as modality applications and therapeutic exercise is important information. All too often, unsuccessful treatments are continued for too long because the sports medicine team does not thoroughly reassess the problem and question the original diagnosis.

In summary, therapeutic modalities are not beneficial in the clinical management of all cases of persistent pain. In some cases, modality application will help achieve treatment goals. Failure to respond to treatment is an important finding that should spur reevaluation.

INTERRUPTING A REST–REINJURY CYCLE

A rest–reinjury cycle develops due to excessive stress to damaged tissues during the repair and, most commonly, remodeling phases. Some individuals misinterpret the absence of pain as indicating that damaged tissues are fully healed. When the level of exercise, work, and athletic activity exceeds the capacity of the remodeling tissue, microtrauma occurs and inflammation and pain result.

Pain is a warning that the tissues are not ready to withstand the stresses being placed on them. The key to breaking the rest–reinjury cycle is education. The individual must accept the responsibility of avoiding activities that reinjure the healing tissues. However, the certified athletic trainer and other members of the sports medicine team need to provide a reasonable rationale for following a plan of care that will safely return physically active individuals to their desired level of performance.

Therapeutic modalities have a limited role in clinical management of a rest–reinjury cycle. Therapeutic modalities can alleviate pain following reinjury, but the pain relief must not be misinterpreted as indicating a full recovery.

EVALUATION AND TREATMENT OF MYOFASCIAL PAIN SYNDROME

The recognition and treatment of MFPS were presented in chapter 5. The concepts from these earlier chapters can now be applied to developing a plan of care for the individual with MFPS. MFPS is complex and the cause is usually multifactorial. Thus, the first step in developing a plan of care is to complete a thorough medical history and physical examination. Once the diagnosis of MFPS is made and causes are identified, a plan of care can be established (figure 13.3).

TREATING MYOFASCIAL PAIN

Because there is no single cause of MFPS and the condition is not completely understood, there is no single treatment approach. Each injured individual is an experiment of one. The plan of treatment needs to address the primary complaint of pain, provide a progressive plan of therapeutic exercises to improve posture and correct faulty movement mechanics, and help the individual recognize when stress and fatigue are contributing to pain. The injured individual should become an active member of the sports medicine team as the factors contributing to MFPS are identified and a plan of care evolves.

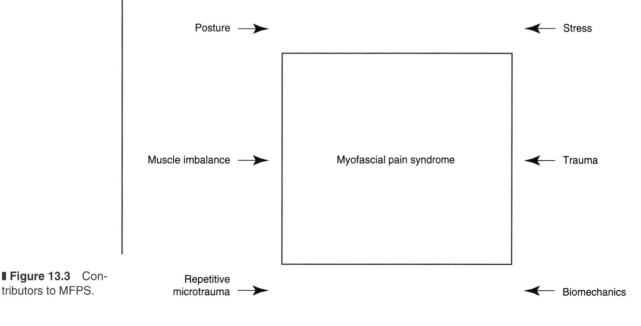

■ **Figure 13.3** Contributors to MFPS.

There are several approaches to pain control in treating MFPS. Myofascial release techniques can be used to alter neural input from painful areas and alleviate fascial restrictions. Conventional modalities including heat, cold, ultrasound, and TENS are effective adjuncts to manual therapies.

Direct stimulation of trigger points often relieves pain. Trigger point massage (acupressure) and TENS over trigger points can result in dramatic, initially transient relief of pain. Deep circular massage of a trigger point can be done with the eraser end of a pencil or an index finger. The massage will elicit a deep burning sensation that is difficult to describe. However, with experience you will be able to help injured individuals recognize the difference between pressure and the exquisite sensitivity of trigger points. Generally trigger points are massaged bilaterally for 30 to 40 sec each. The number of trigger points that are sensitive varies depending on the painful region and the individual. However, trigger point stimulation can usually be completed in less than 10 min.

TENS is an alternative to massage and may be somewhat more effective. The stimulus should be intense but tolerable. A low frequency (2–4 pulses per second) with a long phase duration (> 250 μs) or burst mode should be used. A probe-style electrode (approximately the size of a pencil eraser) such as a Neuroprobe (Physiotechnologies, Topeka, KS) is ideal. The intensity should be adjusted to produce a burning, needling sensation within individual tolerance. Each trigger point is treated for 30 to 40 sec.

Pain relief with TENS is usually rapid. Some individuals experience a dull, numbing sensation after treatment. The initial relief usually lasts for 1 to 2 h, although it can last longer. With subsequent treatments, the duration of relief increases, and complete relief can be obtained in as little as four treatments. In those whose pain continues to return, TENS with conventional parameters may also provide relief. A home TENS unit provides the individual a measure of control over pain.

Myofascial release, conventional heat and cold modalities, and trigger point therapy do not cure MFPS. However, these techniques, used individually or in combination, can break the pain cycle. If pain can be controlled, the individual generally will accept therapeutic exercise regimens and will be open to suggestions regarding stress management. Programs of pain-free exercise, improved postural awareness, correction of faulty movement mechanics, and stress management need to be combined with pain control techniques to resolve MFPS.

Although MFPS has multiple causes, there are a few basic components to an effective plan of care. The first is to correct for repetitive physical stresses that aggravate the problem. This may include modifying a workstation, providing an orthotic device, or altering how someone performs a task.

The case studies presented at the opening of this chapter illustrate the challenges of treating MFPS. The initial interview with the financial aid officer revealed that she spent much of her work day talking on a telephone while looking up account information on a computer. The risk management office of her employer evaluated her work requirements, provided a headset telephone and a new chair, and rearranged her workstation to decrease the number of repetitive movements during her work day. Without this intervention, her plan of care consisting of pain management, manual therapy, postural retraining, and conditioning of the upper back and paraspinal musculature would not have been effective.

Despite the persistence of the track athlete's "shin splints," the ultimate biomechanical source of her problem had never been identified and addressed. Examination of her foot structure and running gait revealed hyperpronation due to a hypermobile first ray and rearfoot varus. Treatments with cryotherapy and TENS decreased her pain but did not resolve the condition. Orthotic control of her hyperpronation and a very gradual (5 months) progression to unrestricted training and competition formed the foundation for an effective plan of care. Although carefully controlling her training and doing extensive cross-training was frustrating, she was able to resume her track career, setting a school record in the 100 m hurdles as a freshman.

A careful history obtained from the baseball pitcher revealed that his pain began shortly after he "learned" to throw a curveball the previous summer. He did not experience pain at rest and was asymptomatic the day he came to the clinic. Physical examination revealed tightness in the posterior rotator cuff, weak scapular stabilizers, and a few mildly tender trigger points. His throwing mechanics, which were evaluated in the parking lot, were poor, especially when he attempted to throw a curveball. Fortunately he was to attend a baseball camp at a nearby university in 10 days, and arrangements were made with the coaches to evaluate and correct his mechanical flaws. Two treatments with manual therapy, exercises to condition the scapular stabilizers and rotator cuff, and improved throwing mechanics resolved his shoulder pain.

Each case was resolved primarily because the source of the persistent pain was identified and addressed. In addition, however, each plan of care contained a program of progressive, pain-free exercise. Therapeutic and conditioning exercises are nearly universal in a plan of care for MFPS. The key to success is pain-free exercise. The neuromuscular adaptations to painful movement were addressed in earlier chapters. To break the cycle of motion, pain, and myofascial adaptation, therapeutic exercises must be pain-free; that is, pain must not alter proper movement mechanics, and activities done today must be able to be repeated tomorrow. The role of therapeutic modalities and manual therapies in the management of MFPS is to alleviate pain, desensitize trigger points, and eliminate fascial restrictions, which in turn promotes pain-free motion.

The benefits of therapeutic modalities and manual therapy in the clinical management of MFPS were demonstrated in the previous case studies. In the case of the financial aid officer, moist heat and TENS (figure 13.4) decreased tenderness of the trigger points and decreased muscle guarding. Myofascial release (figure 13.5), including suboccipital release and indirect techniques, further decreased the sensitivity and guarding. In theory, the pain–gamma gain cycle was broken (see chapter 10). The relief of pain, fascial restrictions, and muscle guarding fostered compliance with a program of postural exercises. In conjunction with her modified workstation, the plan of care resolved this physically active person's persistent pain within 4 weeks. Although 4 weeks may seem like a long time, the pain pattern had existed for several months and was gradually worsening. The certified athletic trainer and the physically active individual suffering from MFPS must have patience. Myofascial pain

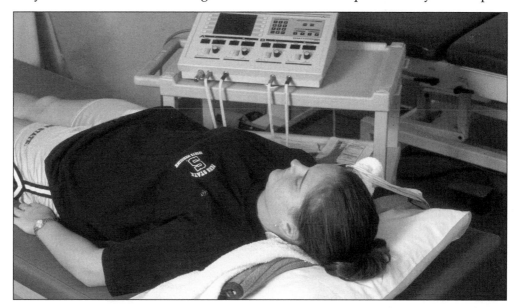

▌Figure 13.4 Moist heat and TENS in the treatment of MFPS in the upper trapezius and cervical spine.

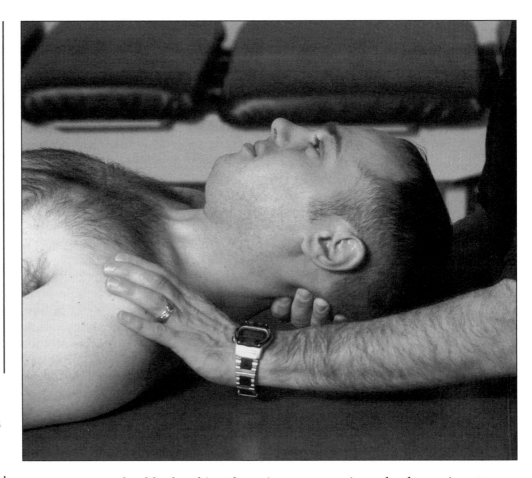

∎ Figure 13.5
Myofascial release in
the treatment of MFPS
in the upper trapezius
and cervical spine.

patterns are resolved by breaking the pain–gamma gain cycle, decreasing stresses
on affected tissues, building elasticity in tight tissues, and improving endurance and
strength in weak muscles. These changes occur over time and require continued
compliance with a plan of care following discharge from formal rehabilitation.

Trigger point therapy (figure 13.6) and soft tissue massage broke the pain pattern
in the track athlete described earlier. With repeated treatments, the trigger points became less sensitive and her pain decreased. As her pain decreased she was gradually

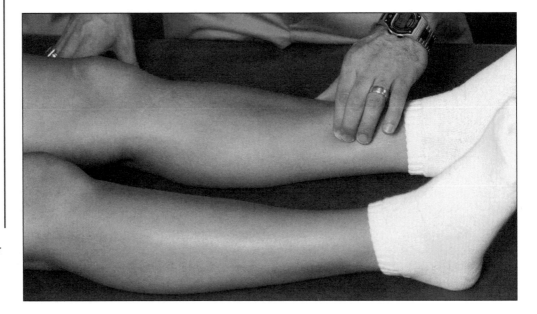

∎ Figure 13.6   Trigger
point treatments for
MFPS in the lower
extremity.

able to tolerate more intense track workouts. Cryotherapy controlled her symptoms when she trained beyond her tolerance. This athlete's coaches supported the efforts of the sports medicine team and were very helpful in developing and monitoring a carefully controlled, progressive reconditioning program. Thus, the routine use of cryotherapy to control postexercise pain was avoided, and her recovery proceeded at a steady rate with only a few minor setbacks.

In the case of the freshman baseball pitcher, myofascial adaptations were minimal. He responded well to strain–counterstrain for the posterior rotator cuff and stretching of the external rotators (figure 13.7). He did not experience muscle spasms or pain at rest. In this case, throwing mechanics and posterior shoulder weakness were the primary problems, and treatment goals were established to address these issues. Because other therapeutic modalities would not have helped achieve treatment goals, none were applied. This case reinforces the value of developing manual therapy skills, and it is a reminder that therapeutic modalities should be applied to facilitate specific treatment goals rather than as a habit.

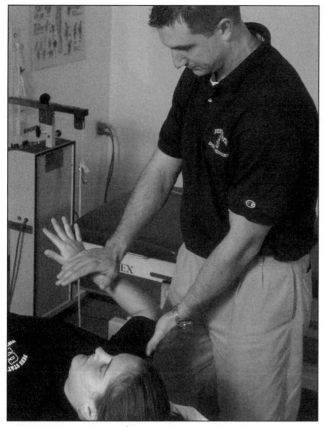

❙ Figure 13.7 Contract–relax stretch of external rotators.

TREATING COMPLEX REGIONAL PAIN SYNDROME

Successful management of CRPS requires the cooperative efforts of a team of health care professionals. As stated in chapter 5, the most important role of the certified athletic trainer in treating CRPS is recognition. Those with unrecognized CRPS can languish in programs of rehabilitation, delaying comprehensive medical management. Sympathetic blocks and medications are usually needed to prevent the progression of CRPS, alleviate pain, and resolve the condition.

A progressive program of pain-free therapeutic exercise is also needed to allow full recovery from CRPS. Thus, the certified athletic trainer and physical therapist play an important role in treating physically active individuals with CRPS. Therapeutic modalities can exacerbate or alleviate the symptoms of CRPS. In general, modalities that are uncomfortable must be avoided. Cryotherapy should not be used. Sometimes superficial heat or the weight of a hydrocollator pack causes extreme pain; thus, these treatments should be used with caution. TENS, gentle massage techniques, and pulsed ultrasound sometimes can relieve the pain of CRPS. TENS offers the advantage of an adjustable level of sensory stimulus that can be controlled by the individual. Light touch and gentle massage decrease the hypersensitivity of the tissues. In some cases, TENS and massage deliver too much sensory stimulus and increase pain. Pulsed ultrasound offers another alternative; because the cold of the sound head can increase pain, the sound head should be warmed prior to treatment. Pulsed ultrasound delivers less total energy and is better tolerated than continuous ultrasound. TENS and manual techniques are preferable in treating CRPS; however, no treatment approach has proven universally effective. In treating an individual with CRPS, communicate with the individual's physician, be certain that treatments do not exacerbate the condition, and use the resources that afford the greatest relief of pain.

DEPRESSION AND SOMATIZATION

When physical symptoms are the result of psychological or psychiatric dysfunction, one would expect therapeutic modalities to have little effect. However, bear in mind the difficulty of identifying the link between depression or somatization and complaints of musculoskeletal symptoms. When an individual fails to respond to a plan of treatment that was developed to treat a somatic lesion or dysfunction, you must reassess the problem. Once the more physical causes of persistent pain discussed earlier are ruled out, the sports medicine team must consider nonphysical causes. Thus, the failure to respond as expected may provide important information during reevaluation.

Physically active individuals suffering from depression and somatization may react negatively to changes in a plan of care that decrease or discontinue treatment by a certified athletic trainer or physical therapist. These patients commonly manipulate caregivers and demand special attention from health care professionals. Be attentive to such behavior patterns, because they provide additional information in the evaluation and treatment of individuals with depression and somatization.

SUMMARY

1. *Identify sources of persistent pain through a medical history and physical examination.*

   Careful questioning of an injured physically active person often reveals the sources of persistent pain and provides direction for the rehabilitation plan. The certified athletic trainer should obtain a history of previous injuries and surgeries as well as information regarding the onset, location, characteristics, and timing of symptoms. The results of medical testing and responses to medications and other interventions should be reviewed. Thorough questioning may lead to consideration of diagnostic error, treatment error, rest–reinjury cycle, myofascial pain, complex regional pain syndrome, or somatization as the cause of persistent pain.

2. *Develop appropriate rehabilitation plans of care or referral to appropriate health care professionals for individuals suffering persistent pain due to (a) diagnostic errors, (b) faulty plans of rehabilitation, (c) rest–reinjury cycle, (d) chronic regional pain syndrome, (e) myofascial pain, and (f) depression and somatization.*

   Diagnostic error must be considered when a physically active individual fails to respond to rehabilitation. The sports medicine team must consider the possibility of diagnostic error and should thoroughly reevaluate exam findings and request additional testing as indicated. Faulty plans of care simply require restructuring the individual's treatment regimen, which may include adding or deleting therapeutic modality application. Rest–reinjury cycles require recognition and education to reverse. The injured physically active person must understand why symptoms are recurring and follow through a complete plan of care before returning to unrestricted training and competition. Pain out of proportion to that expected following an injury or surgery is usually the first and most telling symptom of complex regional pain syndrome. Swelling, changes in skin color and temperature, and loss of motion also indicate referral to a physician. Early recognition is the key to successful treatment of CRPS. Treating myofasical pain requires identification of contributing factors, desensitization of trigger points, and release of fascial restrictions. Depression and somatization are complex problems, often requiring referral to health care professionals trained to treat psychological and psychiatric dysfunction. The certified athletic trainer should treat existing musculoskeletal dysfunction; however, comprehensive care of the individual is beyond the scope of athletic training practice.

CITED REFERENCE

Goodman CC, Snyder TEK: Overview of oncologic signs and symptoms. In Goodman CC, Snyder TEK (Eds), *Differential Diagnosis in Physical Therapy*. Philadelphia, Saunders, 1995, 387-441.

ADDITIONAL SOURCES

McCance KL, Huether SE: *Pathophysiology: The Biologic Basis for Disease in Adults and Children*, 3rd ed. St. Louis, Mosby, 1998.

Wall PD, Melzack R: *Textbook of Pain*. New York, Churchill Livingstone, 1985.

GLOSSARY

afferent—Conducting from the periphery toward the center (as in conduction of nerve impulses to the central nervous system)

alpha motor neuron—Efferent nerve innervating the myofibril

alternating current—Continuous current with positive and negative phases

ampere—A measure of electrical current (abbreviated A)

analgesia—Without pain

anesthesia—Without sensation

arthrokinematic motion—Sliding and gliding of joint surfaces during motion (e.g., during abduction at the glenohumeral joint, the head of the humerus rolls superiorly and glides inferiorly); also called accessory motion

atrophy—A wasting away or loss of muscle cell mass

beam nonuniformity ratio (BNR)—A measure of the quality of the ultrasound head

beta-endorphin—A 31-peptide chain endogenous opioid that is important in the body's pain control system

biphasic current—A pulsatile current with positive and negative phases

capacitance—Ability to store an electrical charge

chondroblasts—Cartilage-forming cells

collagen—Principal protein found in ligament, tendon, and scar tissues

complex regional pain syndrome (CRPS)—Symptom complex characterized by pain that is disproportional to the injury

coulomb—Measure of electrical charge or a quantity of electrons (abbreviated C)

cryokinetics—Use of cryotherapy to facilitate therapeutic exercise

cryotherapy—Therapeutic use of cold

depression—State of deep sadness, dejection, and gloom; distinguished from grief, which is an appropriate response to personal loss

diathermy—Heating tissue with electromagnetic energy

direct current—Continuous current without alternating positive and negative phases

disability—All limitations on performance of normal daily tasks, including those related to schoolwork, employment, family responsibilities, and sport participation, due to disease or injury

dorsal horn—Area of synapse between first- and second-order afferent nerves

duty cycle—Ratio of "on" and "off" time

effective radiating area (ERA)—Area of the ultrasound head emitting acoustic energy

efferent—conducting from the center toward the periphery (as in conduction of nerve impulses from the central nervous system)

enkephalin—A family of 5-peptide chain transmitter substances that inhibit synaptic transmission in nociceptive pathways

fibrin—A protein converted from fibrinogen to form the meshlike foundation of a clot

fibroblasts—Cells that produce collagen and elastin

free radical—A molecule containing an odd number of electrons, which can injure healthy tissues

frequency—Number of cycles or sinusoidal waves per second

functional limitations—Inability to perform physical tasks; in physically active individuals, specific examples could include sport-specific activities such as running and jumping

gamma motor neuron—Efferent nerve innervating the muscle spindle

hypertrophy—Increase in muscle cell mass

hypoxia—Lack of oxygen

impairment—Anatomical, physiological, psychological, and emotional aftereffects of disease and injury

inflammation—Series of physiological events that occur in vascularized tissue

intensity—Dose of sound energy delivered to the tissue; measured in watts per squared centimeter (W/cm^2) of area of sound head transmitting energy

interstitium—Space between the cells

iontophoresis—Use of an electrical current to drive medications into the tissues

leukocytes—White blood cells of which there are five types: neutrophils, macrophages, basophils, esinophils, and lymphocytes

mast cell—Type of cell found in connective tissue that releases several chemical mediators of inflammation

monophasic current—Pulsatile current with only positive or negative pulses

motor point—Area in which the motor nerves enter a muscle

muscle spindle—Sensory receptor of length–tension changes in muscle

myofascial pain syndrome (MFPS)—Persistent pain of soft tissue, origins characterized by taut fibrous bands and focal areas of hypersensitivity called trigger points

necrotic—Dead

neuromuscular control—Use of sensory neural input and motor output to exert volitional control of skeletal muscle

neuromuscular stimulation—Use of TENS to cause a muscle contraction

nociceptive—Pain sensing

noxious—Pain producing

ohm—A measure of resistance to the flow of electrons (abbreviated Ω)

osteoblasts—Bone-forming cells

osteokinematic—Movement of one bony segment on another; for example, glenohumeral abduction results in movement of the humerus on the glenoid

phonophoresis—Method of driving medications into tissues with sound waves

placebo effect—Improvement in a condition not related to the effect of a treatment or medication

polyphasic current—Current with multiple phases between interpulse intervals

practice act—State law regulating the practice of a profession

professional negligence—Entails (1) doing something that a similarly qualified person under like circumstances would not have done (a negligent act or act of commission) or (2) failing to do something that a similarly qualified person would have done under similar circumstances (act of omission)

pulsatile current—Noncontinuous current; the flow of current is broken by intervals between pulses

rest–reinjury cycle—Pattern of injury where physically active individuals return to activity only to aggravate a condition from which they had not fully recovered

somatization—A somatic (bodily) manifestation of psychological dysfunction

substance P—A facilitory transmitter substance in the nociceptive pathways

synapse—Junction between nerves

transcutaneous electrical nerve stimulation (TENS)—The use of a therapeutic device that stimulates peripheral nerves by passing an electrical current through the skin

transmitter substance—Chemical that influences transmission of neural impulses across a synapse; the substance may facilitate or inhibit transmission

trigger point—A hypersensitive fibrous band of tissue

tort—Private, civil legal action brought by an injured party, or the party's representative, to redress an injury brought by another person

ultrasound—High-frequency acoustic energy

volt—Measure of electromotive force (abbreviated V)

INDEX

The letters *f* and *t* after page numbers indicate figures and tables, respectively.

ABOUT THE AUTHOR

Craig Denegar, PhD, ATC, PT, is associate professor of Orthopaedics and Rehabilitation and Kinesiology at Penn State University. He has more than 20 years of experience as an athletic trainer and extensive clinical practice experience related to orthopedic persistent pain.

Dr. Denegar has contributed to a number of chapters on pain and pain control as well as numerous other publications. He is a member of the National Athletic Trainers' Association (NATA) and the American Physical Therapy Association. He serves as vice-chair for free communications on the NATA Research and Education Foundation Research Committee.

Presently serving as associate editor of the *Journal of Athletic Training* (*JAT*), he also serves on the editorial boards of *JAT*, the *Journal of Strength Training and Conditioning Research*, and the *Journal of Sport Rehabilitation*.

He received his PhD in education with a specialization in sports medicine and a master's degree in education with a specialization in athletic training from the University of Virginia. He earned a master's degree in physical therapy from the School of Physical Therapy, Slippery Rock, Pennsylvania.

In his spare time, Dr. Denegar enjoys cycling, golfing, and studying the history of the American west. He and his wife, Susan, live in State College, Pennsylvania.